ON WAR
AND POLITICS

ON WAR
AND POLITICS

The Battlefield Inside Washington's Beltway

ARNOLD L. PUNARO

WITH DAVID POYER

This book was brought to publication with the generous assistance of Marguerite and Gerry Lenfest.

Naval Institute Press
291 Wood Road
Annapolis, MD 21402

Library of Congress Cataloging-in-Publication Data
Names: Punaro, Arnold L., author. | Poyer, David, author.
Title: On war and politics : the battlefield inside Washington's beltway / Arnold L. Punaro with David Poyer.
Description: Annapolis, MD : Naval Institute Press, [2016] | Includes bibliographical references and index.
Identifiers: LCCN 2016028490| ISBN 9781612519067 (alk. paper) | ISBN 9781612519074 (epub) | ISBN 9781612519074 (ePDF)
Subjects: LCSH: Punaro, Arnold L. | Vietnam War, 1961-1975—Personal narratives, American. | United States. Marine Corps—Officers—Biography. | Veterans—United States—Biography. | United States—Military policy—Decision making.
Classification: LCC DS559.5 .P86 2016 | DDC 355/.033573—dc23 LC record available at https://lccn.loc.gov/2016028490

All photos are from the author's collection.

To be prepared for war
is one of the most effectual means
of preserving peace.

—*George Washington*

Contents

Maps

Foreword

A most distinguished group of national security experts have expressed their valuable insights about Arnold Punaro for the cover of his book *On War and Politics*. With a sense of humility, I wish to associate myself with their remarks and add to their "thrust power" to launch this well-researched book based on Arnold's career and contemporary history.

First, an amusing bit of coincidence. Roughly a half-century ago the author and I were first linked. Though we had never met, for he was halfway around the globe bravely leading an infantry combat platoon in Vietnam as a second lieutenant in the U.S. Marine Corps when the Senate confirmed me as under-secretary of the Navy and Marine Corps. Although protected by eight levels of the chain of command, I was Arnold's boss!

Fast forward a decade. In 1979, a newly elected Virginia senator "reported" to the Senate Armed Services Committee (SASC), where Sen. Sam Nunn, as a sub-committee chairman, assisted by his principal national security adviser, Arnold Punaro, are now my bosses!

Thus began two of my most valued Senate friendships—professional and personal—extending for more than twenty years, especially when Senator Nunn was a full committee chairman and I was the ranking Republican member.

The institution of the Senate has survived for well over two centuries. Its record of achievement has varied, but the generation of senators that served in the late 1970s, 1980s, and into the 1990s can rightfully take pride in their efforts to maintain a strong defense policy, as required by our Constitution. More than two-thirds of the members serving during that period had prior military service, most during World War II, others in Korea and Vietnam. Military training had hardened our values of self-confidence, ingrained in us mutual respect for each other as a basis for personal survival, and taught us how discipline and determination are essential to achieve life's missions. Yes we had robust confrontations in performing our responsibilities in the Senate, but at the end of the day, a sense of honor and duty to country prevailed. We got things done! Arnold writes in detail about this interesting historical period.

Senator Nunn advanced in seniority and became an accomplished chairman, following the SASC traditions set by his distinguished predecessors. With frequent bipartisan support from the Republican minority and a superb group of highly professional committee staff members, the SASC achieved many new initiatives. We held fast to an underlying principle that legislation intended for the specific benefit of men and women serving in uniform must stand the test of time; this goal can best be achieved if Senate records document clearly that legislation was created by bipartisan procedures and votes in the committee as well as on the floor of the Senate.

For generations, the SASC set high records for bipartisanship, and we maintained that reputation.

In 1979 the Senate and House Armed Services Committees wrote the Military Pay and Allowances Benefits Act of 1980 that was widely regarded as the most comprehensive benefits package of proposed major reforms for our military since the beginning of the all-volunteer force in 1973. Although initially many of our initiatives were opposed by the administration, a consistent bipartisan SASC pushed back and won battles on the floor, giving all senators an opportunity to debate.

When the administration proposed buying two *Nimitz*-class aircraft carriers in one fiscal budget year, there was initial opposition. Arnold led the research team in drafting unique legislative provisions that generated great cost savings for building two in tandem. Subsequent history confirms the SASC was accurate in its projections, and costs were controlled.

The sale of AWACS aircraft to Saudi Arabia was vigorously contested by many of my colleagues. President Ronald Reagan had made a bold decision and "pitched in," directing the administration to agree to key revisions that made the bill clearly bipartisan. A decade later, at the conclusion of the first Gulf War, SASC members traveling to the region of conflict learned from military operational commanders just how essential that forward-deployed AWACS system had been to the successful outcome of liberating Kuwait from Saddam Hussein in Desert Storm.

As a part of my preparation for this foreword I sought out—informally—the views and recollections of more than a dozen of our former professional committee staffers. Uniformly, they commended Arnold for strong leadership and "drive to get our work done" so that each year the SASC sent a defense bill to the floor.

During his years as staff director, Arnold, firmly, was "centerfold!"

Today he carries on as one of the most experienced, knowledgeable, and well-informed professionals in the areas of national and international defense policy, strategy, and organization. Much of his service is done pro bono.

This is a man who is always on the move, carefully balancing raising a family, holding public- and private-sector positions, and serving on numerous public commissions focusing on national security, all while serving for thirty-five years in the Marine Corps Reserve and rising through the ranks from second lieutenant to attaining two stars, as a major general.

As a young Marine in Vietnam, Arnold was seriously wounded and decorated for valor. The traits he developed in those years as a combat leader have been a pillar in his career. Totally dedicated, direct, and forceful, Arnold continues to work tirelessly to strengthen our nation's security. Currently he is a member of the DOD Defense Business Board, chairman of the Reserve Forces Policy Board, and a board member of the National Defense Industrial Association. Taking up the fight of reducing overhead within the Department of Defense, he has worked to effect changes that would improve the tooth-to-tail ratio, to get more bang for the buck out of our defense budgets. It is a formidable challenge that has been fought with little success in past years. But hope remains that the United States might eventually be able to get more actual combat capability out of the dollars taxpayers invest in our national security.

Arnold has established a commendable record: On the battlefield, in the halls of Congress, in corporate boardrooms, and especially in DOD spaces, he has always striven to help our men and women in uniform and their families.

At home, he is a warm and loving father and husband. With his wonderfully supportive wife, Jan, they have raised two sons and two daughters, all exemplary, achieving young adults. His family has been his greatest pillar of strength.

Today, Arnold's book conveys an important message at a time when our nation is being challenged from many directions. Indeed, other democracies are facing the same escalating, complex, profound period of global transformation and conflict.

But in a democracy, experienced people must never fear to speak out candidly and accurately—even knowing it will stir up controversy—in the hope others will see the need to update, reconcile, or even compromise on their views. It is essential that the military and Congress work together, sharing a basic trust, to meet our changing national security goals against the ever-evolving spectrum of new threats.

Yes, this book is partly a personal memoir, spiced with words and language intimately familiar to those of us who have served in the ranks, but the messages are, by and large, instructive. For those currently wearing the uniform, or aspiring to do so, the book provides a critical insight into how the military committees of Congress functioned in past years in following the specific mandates of the Constitution.

Even the current Congress should find the historical precedents, accurately recorded in this book, instructive! It will be of great reference value as a part of curricula in advanced educational programs and forums now being conducted by all uniformed branches. Even the nation's military industrial complex will find a pearl of wisdom to reflect upon!

Lastly, our nation is incredibly fortunate that so many young professionals want to serve in national security areas of the legislative and executive branches. Committed staff members are a bedrock upon which our system of government operates. Few outsiders appreciate the ever-increasing level of responsibility and decision making thrust upon them.

As a former chairman and ranking member of the Armed Services Committee, I freely admit that over my thirty years, there were times when deliberations between SASC members would become deadlocked—stalled—with tempers in a closed room at a high pitch. At times the hour would be late, and a presiding chairman would turn to an equally weary staff and, in a stern voice, say, "You people work out a solution, and have it on our desks by 8:30 tomorrow morning," and bang the gavel! Often staff solutions become the catalyst for the members' final decisions.

Well, here's a "field manual," a tribute to all those now serving as well as future staffers.

In closing, I'd like to express my personal appreciation to Arnold for writing this fine book. It's a playback of a period of history that I deeply revere, for our generation of members of Congress and professional staffers departed with a lasting sense of accomplishment.

This foreword is not intended as a fact check or an attempt to edit, but a grateful acknowledgment on behalf of those who have worked with Arnold. Hopefully, it will inspire new "recruits" to take up the challenges as we pass the baton, for this world is becoming ever more complex and dangerous, and volunteers like Arnold and his family are more essential than ever.

Semper Fi, my fellow Marine,
John Warner
U.S. Senator, Virginia (Ret.)

P.S. Arnold, as one of your former bosses, may I strongly suggest, as the book is released to the public, that you issue the same orders to yourself that you wisely and thoughtfully gave your men as platoon leader in the jungles and canopies of Vietnam in 1969: "Every man must now put on his flak jacket, zip it up, for the 'incoming' will soon be targeting down on us!"

Acknowledgments

This is a memoir. Events are portrayed to the best of my recollection, aided by many helpers who've both filled in gaps in my memory and done research to ensure this book is as accurate as possible. In every effort I've been involved in, I've followed the principle that collective wisdom is far superior to individual wisdom.

The first person I need to thank is my wife, Jan. As Gen. Jim Jones said at my retirement, most people refer to her as "Saint Jan." She's the most unselfish person I know, and without her I would have accomplished very little. Raising children is truly the hardest job there is. Jan chose to end a successful government career to raise our four children to be responsible, kind, and successful adults. She handled this with intelligence and grace. I do not say it nearly often enough, but I am grateful every day to have her in my life. Words do not do justice to my love and gratitude.

I am deeply indebted to Sen. John Warner, World War II sailor and Marine officer in the Korean War, director of the American Revolution Bicentennial Administration, secretary of the Navy, and chairman of the Senate Armed Services Committee, for his foreword. There is no finer example of public service at its best.

In the actual writing of the book, David Poyer, a noted author, retired Navy captain, and writing professor, was indispensable. And I was lucky enough to get a two-for-one special with his wife, Lenore Hart, an accomplished author as well.

Dr. Kim Roberts began the initial research on the Sam Nunn Papers at Emory University. Jonathan Rue, a Marine intelligence officer in the Iraq War, did additional duty researching and reviewing while serving as my business's chief of staff. Irina Plaks, another University of Georgia School of Public and International Affairs graduate, came on precisely at the right time in the final year to complete both research, writing, and editing. And thank you to the Emory University Manuscript, Archives, and Rare Book Library staff for their aid.

I could not have completed this project without the help and support of my family, who were all intimately involved. Jan and Julie were instrumental in both writing and editing (and making sure their photos were the best looking), and Joe, Meghan, and Dan made key contributions.

My company commander from Vietnam, Col. J. K. Van Riper, USMC (Ret.) was a constructive critic and, as always, got me squared away, ensuring that my military references and Vietnam recollections were accurate. Col. Keith Nightingale, USA (Ret.), a colleague from SAIC and decorated combat Ranger, shared great reminders of life as a grunt in Vietnam. Col. Mark Cancian, USMCR (Ret.), and Col. Eric Chase, USMCR (Ret.), were also eagle eyes and positive contributors.

Roland McElroy and Cathy Gwin, longtime Nunn staffers, provided clear guidance and valuable input. Roland has also authored the definitive work on Senator Nunn's winning Senate campaign. Will Goodman, an industry colleague, also provided a valuable review.

Dr. Stephanie Lindquist, herself a much published author, was an excellent reviewer. The folks at Naval Institute Press were terrific partners from start to finish. And thank you to Chris Robinson for producing the highly detailed maps. My old SAIC colleague David Tillson provided the concepts and designs for the cover art. I had good advice from friends and colleagues who themselves were published, such as George Tenet, Dr. John Nagl, and Mike and Beth Norman.

And my deepest thanks to Senator Nunn, whose standards of public and private service remain unmatched.

And to the Marines and Navy Corpsmen with whom I served in Vietnam, your examples of courage under fire are my inspiration, always.

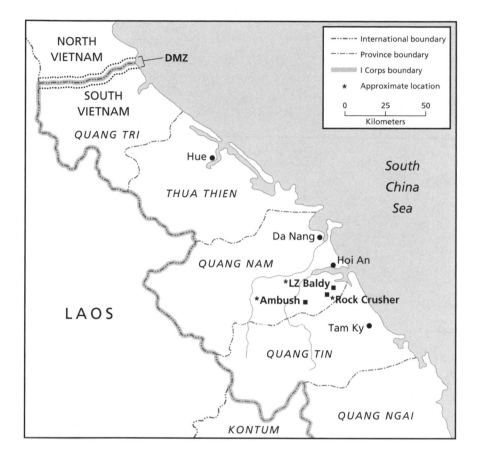

MAP 1.

Northern I Corps. USMC Area of Responsibility in Vietnam War

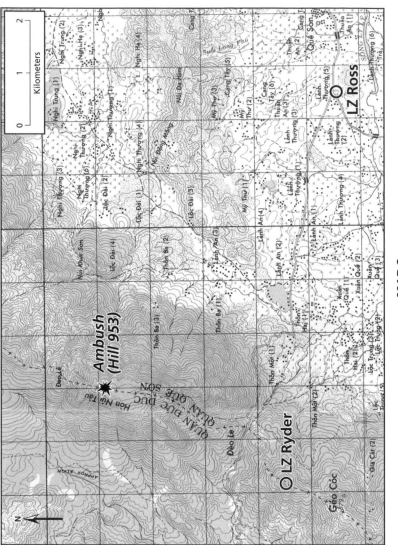

MAP 2.

Topographical Map of Que Son Mountains Tactical Operations Area

AMBUSH AT HILL 953

January 4, 1970: Que Son Mountains, Republic of Vietnam

My eyes snapped open to a sharp rap on my steel helmet. And to a miracle: above the topmost canopy of thick jungle, golden light was streaming down from the eastern sky.

"Lieutenant? Dawn."

A light sleeper, I always woke quickly, even after checking my defensive positions every two hours all night long. I also never got lost, even in the dense, overgrown gorges of the rugged Que Son Mountains. This meant battalion always made my platoon point.

It also meant we'd lead today's assault.

The heavy vinyl poncho dumped water as I slid it off. My flak jacket and tattered jungle utilities were sodden with the bone-chilling rain that had fallen that night. My muddy foxhole was dug in among enormous trees with twisted, hungry vines that hung dripping. The flash of golden light had vanished; from the look of the low, leaden clouds, it would rain again all day. I stood shivering, alert now as one can only be in war, checking my rifle first, then reaching for a canteen. The water, from the nearby Song Ly Ly, was icy cold. The purification tablets made it taste like chlorinated piss.

Subdued snaps, clanks, and murmurs rose around me. The twenty-five men of 1st Platoon, Lima Company, 3rd Battalion, 7th Regiment, 1st Marine Division were waking to another day as riflemen in combat.[1]

Yeah, Arnold, I thought. *You really put it over on Mrs. Beazley at the draft board hearing, didn't you?*

This was my fifth month in country. I'd spent all but the first two days in the bush. First Platoon's job was to clear villages, set up night ambushes, find the enemy. Then destroy him. We dug in every night, got up every dawn, and moved out. Patrolling reduced the enemy's movement and denied him access to Da Nang, the lowlands, and the fire support bases at Landing Zones Ross and Baldy.[2]

At least that was the theory. All I knew was that this was a free fire zone. To the north, beyond the mountains, lay North Vietnam. To the west, through more jungle, Laos. The Que Sons were infested with enemy tunnels and fortified positions. We endured continual harassing fire, sapper attacks, mines, and booby traps.

The previous afternoon, as we'd climbed laboriously from the valley up a hill so steep my Marines had to grab the bushes to keep from sliding back down, an outpost had opened up on us. I'd sent two fire teams to flank it and capture a DShK-38, a large-caliber Soviet-made machine gun. The enemy had died in greenish-khaki shirts and trousers, boonie hats and French-style sun helmets, their sandaled feet smeared with red mountain mud.[3] One had a pistol in a canvas holster, an officer. An observation post like that meant an enemy concentration lay nearby, probably the NVA 2nd Regiment, according to intel.[4]

The sky grew lighter. Heavy drops pattered down, swaying the corrugated leaves of the elephant ears. Bad weather meant no air support. I drank C-rat coffee from a hissing-hot canteen cup heated with a pinch of C-4, skirting the root-clogged foxholes and nighttime firing positions on a mud and leaf slurry slick as black ice. Around me Marines pissed and smoked and spooned congealed beans out of cans, or dribbled water over bearded, filthy cheeks. Our poplin four-color utilities were worn thin, bleached out.[5] Rashes and bites spotted necks and wrists. Kruithoff, my radioman, who humped the weightiest load in the platoon—the twenty-three-and-a-half-pound PRC-25 radio that was the platoon's lifeline, plus spare batteries, plus the other gear we all carried—massaged jungle-rotted feet before plunging them back into wet boots. Doc, the corpsman, was kneeling before each man, handing out malaria pills like communion wafers.

A corporal reloaded his magazines obsessively, tapping each against his helmet to seat the rounds and prevent jams. A street kid, from Detroit. One of McNamara's 100,000, the defense secretary's experiment at drafting those who otherwise were not considered qualified.[6] As if overhearing my thoughts, he glanced up, blinking. "Shoot first and shoot often, L-T."

"Roger that, McNew."

I joshed with each man, trying not to show nervousness. A Marine was opening his ham and mothers with his bayonet. Supply never had any C-rat openers, just like there were never any heat tabs or dry socks.[7] Another guy broke a cigarette in half, lit both butts, and handed one to a buddy. The stream trickled from rock to rock. The cold air felt heavy as ice.

The Corps had been here intermittently since 1965.[8] In 1967 they turned this jungle over to the Army's American Division, who patrolled from the air and deemed it pacified. But when the Marines got the territory back in 1969, we found bunkers, caves, heavy guns. We forced the North Vietnamese Army (NVA) back into the mountains, denying passage across the heavily populated coastal plains. And paying a heavy price in casualties and those killed in actions (KIA).

Now Nixon was Vietnamizing the war. One division had already been withdrawn. Scuttlebutt said the 7th Regiment would go next and the area would be turned over to the South Vietnamese. Yet December had seen significantly more sapper and mortar attacks, assassinations, kidnappings, and civilian abductions.[9] Higher-ups feared a major attack during Tet, the Vietnamese New Year. There'd been major offensives then in each of the previous two years.

We'd heard about the antiwar marches back home. But the "real world" was far away, and anyway we didn't fight for them. We fought for each other.

Division suspected it had a major element cornered here on Hill 953. Regiment wanted us to move to contact. The hill—actually a small mountain—rose above the canopy, out of sight from where 1st Platoon crouched, strapping on frag grenades, entrenching tools, grenade launchers, claymores, and the other gear that added up to an average of sixty-eight pounds per man.[10]

I checked my map and compass, then my watch. "Let's move," I told the corporal. The squad leaders signaled. Fire team leaders rose from behind trees and foxholes like the resurrected dead. Draped with belts for the "Pig"—the M60 machine gun—they shuffled into a staggered column with two meters between each man.

I tightened my sodden flak jacket, buckled my helmet, and picked up my M16. I had ten magazines on my cartridge belt, each with seventeen 5.56 rounds. In the jungle, what counted was firepower. My pack felt leaden even as I hoisted it; by nightfall it would feel like the rock of Sisyphus. On my H-harness, I hooked eight hand grenades and stuffed two white phosphorus rounds—the heavy ones—into my pack. I stuffed my pockets with M79 rounds. You couldn't depend on resupply in a firefight. I had two canteens, six C-rat meals, a beefed-up first aid kit, binoculars, and a compass. There were no signposts or roads in this jungle, and the trails were booby-trapped. Our lives depended on my dead reckoning and 1:50,000 map.

As the first fire team trudged up, I nodded to the Marine on point and fell in behind him. The growth was too thick to follow the school solution and lead from the middle of the platoon. I needed to lead from the front. Kruithoff trailed me, his whip antenna snapping at leaves and low-hanging vines like a scythe.[11]

~

An hour later a crackle like distant static filtered through the green. The jungle played tricks with noise, but it seemed to be coming from the east. I took a knee and punched the air. As they passed the "halt" signal back the Marines crouched in succession. I shot a bearing to where I guessed the crest was, though I couldn't see anything except eternal gloom. The crackle rose, wavered, and fell away into individual shots.

I rose and signaled the advance again, now conscious of our own noise. Every Marine had his gear secured, but there was no way to get through bush this heavy in silence. The gurgle of the stream would cover us to some extent, but we were going up a huge ravine, a draw, with high walls on either side. A first grader could see this was ambush country. Even when everything was quiet, the enemy and we could smell each other. The NVA stank of a fermented sauce called nuoc mam. We'd tried it when we killed a "rice humper" on the Ho Chi Minh Trail. We hadn't been resupplied in days and were starving, but even so it tasted like rotten fish cooked in turpentine. Our own smell was hardly sweet; heavy with stale cigarette smoke, old sweat, and the meaty stink of C-rations.

A nudge at my elbow. "Radio, sir. Lima Six."

That would be Captain Van Riper. We knelt again as I took the handset, so I was partly concealed by underbrush. NVA snipers targeted radiomen, officers, and corpsmen. "Lima One Actual," I murmured.

The handset beeped as the encryption synced. "Lima One Actual. Lima Three Actual is whisky india alpha. Over."

Wounded in action. Damn. "Bad news, Skipper. Status? Over."

"We'll get him medevaced. Take over his platoon and assess the situation, but continue 1.5 klicks right and 3 up from Thrust Point Christmas." Where we'd bivouacked for a night during that holiday a couple weeks ago.

"Lima Six, this is bad terrain. We're moving up a draw. Alpha bravo territory. Over." I knew the skipper, on his second tour, was thinking ambush too.

"I know where you are, Lima One. Grim Reaper Six says move out."[12]

I passed the handset back, scoping the rising ground. The fire team leader on point was watching me, head cocked like an inquisitive border collie. I murmured, "Spread out. I want six meters separation. Pass the word."

It wouldn't have gotten past the tactics instructors at the Basic School in Quantico. But the NVA knew how to use mortars. If we were targeted in this draw there'd be no escape; every man would be cut to shreds.

I got the 3rd Platoon radioman on the line and passed Lima Six's order. Then took point for a few hundred yards, eyes honed for the dull green glint of a trip wire, for tree grenades, for the scuffled leaves and packed soil that meant *booby trap*. Out there, so far up my men were lost to view behind me in the pattering leafy green, I sank to a knee again. Quickly crossed myself. The words we'd worn thin at the seminary didn't seem abstract now.

O my God, I am heartily sorry for having offended you, forgive me all my sins[13] *. . . and protect my Marines. . . .* I rose and glanced behind me. Lifted an outstretched arm, grubby palm facing the sky, and said, "Move out."

⮑

The two platoons, now fifty-some strong, linked up. The 3rd fell in behind 1st and we climbed for hours, boots slipping in a gumbo of mud and crushed vegetation as the slope steepened. It began to drizzle again around midmorning, a slow, colorless pelting that tasted like Angostura bitters and deepened my unease. The air was so cold I could see my breath, yet sweat shellacked the exhaustion-etched faces around me. I shook a canteen. Empty. *Damn. Forgot to fill up. Too late now.*

At that moment, I slipped in the mud and went down. It oozed icy through my clutching fingers. I lay for longer than I had to as cold rain drenched the back of my neck under the helmet, wishing I didn't have to get up again.

No. No, I don't wish that, I thought, then flinched at a distant clunk. Only an empty canteen against some tree trunk, but I'd taken it for an 82 firing. *God, I hate being mortared. Even DShKs, but please don't let it be mortars.*

I was pushing up when a shot cracked. The men crouched, seeking cover. As if at a signal, five or six AKs or SKSs opened up on the far side of the draw, the rapid, flat cracks building to a metallic roar as a hail of bullets came in from the right flank and ahead. M16s opened up in reply. A thin scream pierced the cacophony, the relentless patter of rain. "I'm hit. I'm hit!"

"Corpsman up! Corpsman up!" The familiar cry of shit hitting the fan.

"Take cover! Take cover!" I yelled. This was the ambush I'd dreaded. I rolled, braced the rifle butt against the rope ridge on my flak vest, and triggered off half a magazine toward the incoming fire. Looking downhill, I glimpsed a body between two bushes, legs sprawled in a stream.

Fire team two leapt up and rushed in short dashes, then dropped to set up a defensive position on the flank. Bullets whipped through the brush and cracked into trees, showering bark and white, pulpy wood. The fire team leader collapsed next to me. "It's Doc, L-T. They got Doc."

Goddamn. I measured the distance to the motionless medic, around whom impacts were gouting up mud and water. "Sixty mikes: Get fire on top of that ridgeline."

"Here, L-T." Kruithoff held the handset out.

"Put arty on the top of the hill. Cover me," I yelled, and burst from behind a tree.

Projectiles whined past as I dodged down the bank. The wounded man lay prone in the middle of the stream. The M60s began hammering away at the ridgeline on the flank. Bullets were geysering around Doc, mimicking the smaller impacts of the raindrops.

When I reached him, the corpsman was hacking and coughing, face smeared with mud. I turned him over. His chest was torn open. Air bubbled deep in the pulpy red mass. Blood ran from his mouth. He tried to say something, but I couldn't make it out. He needed the chest wall sealed, quick.

A bullet smacked into the creek, spraying us with cold water. *That wasn't an AK round. A sniper.* Hunching my shoulders to stay low, I pressed a gauzed

rubber pad over the gaping wound. Heeling that with my left, I wound the bandage around his torso, half-lifting him to pass the roll beneath his shoulder. As
soon as the bandage was tied off, I started pulling him out of the line of fire.

At that moment it felt like a bulldozer hit my back, knocking me down into
the stream, tearing my helmet off. My M16 cartwheeled away through the rain. I
lay stunned, gazing after it. *I'll be doing a lot of paperwork for losing that.*

When I realized I could still move, my daze sharpened into an urgent need to
scramble for cover. Bullets were whacking all around. My back felt as if someone
had whaled at it with a sledgehammer. Blood was dripping from my utilities. Yet
my brain seemed to be functioning with perfect cold clarity. We'd been returning
fire to the east. But I'd been hit in the back. *A V-shaped ambush.*

"L-T!" Kruithoff, calling from up the hill.

I yelled back, "Tell Lima Six the enemy's to the north, on the other ridgeline."
I shouted out new coordinates from the laminated map, now smeared with my
blood. "Fire everything we've got. And gunships." Doc was still upstream, not
having moved when the bullet's impact had separated us. "Grab Doc too!"

I took a deep breath and let it out, listening for the suck and wheeze that
meant my lung was pierced, but didn't hear it. Still, blood was pouring out, dyeing
the clear water scarlet. *So cold.* Had to find cover. But I didn't feel like moving.
Why not just close my eyes, and rest . . .

Boots pounded, coming my way. Through the rattle and crack of incoming
fire, someone was thundering down the slope. The pounding grew louder. Then
he cannoned into me, like a runner sliding for home, tumbling over me in the
streambed.

Someone had come after me. Incredibly brave. Incredibly risky. I grabbed his
flak jacket and yelled, "Let's go! Let's go!"

No answer. My hand came back covered with blood. An unfamiliar pale, long
face fell back. I didn't know him. "I can't move!" I yelled, but he didn't respond.
Just lay there, on top of me, jerking as the bullets hammered his flak jacket.

"We've got to get the fuck out of here." I grabbed his H-harness, pulled him
off, and began to crawl through mud and roots and rocks toward the stream bank
as bullets peppered the water around us. Doc might be dying—I'd realized this by
now—but maybe I could save this Marine.

It seemed to take hours to crawl, dragging the limp, heavy body by the arms
to the bank and up a slight rise into dense foliage. Once into cover, I checked him
out. He'd been hit. Wasn't breathing. I pressed my mouth to his, and began CPR.
His lips were slack and cold, and tasted of blood. Finally I sat back on my heels.
This Marine was gone, the pallid, stubbled cheeks slack.

*Why come after me? Corps discipline didn't demand it. He wasn't even in my
platoon.*

"L-T! You okay?" Kruithoff, smeared in red mud from head to toe. He crouched next to me, reloading with shaking hands. The barrel steamed, raindrops bubbling as they ran down it. "We're pinned down. And we got a bunch wounded. Lima Six wants a sitrep."

I blinked hard, jerking my mind back. The steady rattle of small arms. The shattering roar of artillery working the top of the ridge, louder than I'd ever heard it. We'd stumbled on at least a regiment. I had to call in more firepower and medevacs.

"You're hit, sir. Bleeding bad."

I fumbled at the first aid kit and stuffed what was left of the gauze into the hole in my own back. When I looked down at his body again, his gray-blue eyes were open. And seemed to be following me. "You know this Marine?" I asked Kruithoff.

"That's Hammonds, L-T. Third platoon. Tough break; he only had a couple weeks to go. Better call in a chopper. Get yourself taken care of."

I looked around at the dead and wounded sprawled beside the stream, along the ravine. A leaf swayed in the pattering rain. It seemed to be speaking, but in a language I'd forgotten. Why had the kid done it? Sacrificed himself for a stranger, when his own return home had been so near? But just then a wounded man began screaming. A salvo came in, 155s by the quaking concussions, and detonated along the crest, shaking rain from the trees. Smoke drifted like bitter incense.

But there was something else too. Something important. Then I remembered, in a rush, like a wave tearing in and breaking over me.

Move to contact. Grim Reaper Six says move out.

I forced myself to my knees, then feet, swaying, weak, dizzy. But my legs held, and after a moment I could lift a hand. The dead Marine was still looking up at me, wide-eyed, as if he'd asked a question and was still waiting for my answer.

Kruithoff slapped the handset into my palm like an OR nurse presenting a scalpel. "We falling back, L-T?"

I took a deep breath, shuddered, and tore my gaze from that unblinking one. Couldn't puzzle things out now. Think about it later.

"No, Corporal," I said. "Help me get this tourniquet on. Have 3rd Platoon consolidate the dead and wounded, and follow in trace. We're going to take this hill so we can get everyone out."

No Marine gets left behind.

〜

I dug in and consolidated our position behind a wall of steel from our mortars, machine guns, automatic rifles, and grenade launchers. After I radioed our situation to Lima Six, I ordered the squad leaders to maintain a tactical perimeter, return fire, and ready the seriously wounded for medevac. I didn't tell him I'd been hit.

Unfortunately, there was nowhere for helicopters to land in this broken, heavily wooded terrain. They'd have to drop what we called a "Niel Robertson" or "jungle" sling. You bundled a wounded Marine into it, then he was hoisted through the canopy.

But as the first casualty rose through rustling branches, a shattering boom sounded overhead. Shredded aluminum rained down. It must have been an RPG. The line snapped, so the Marines grabbed the wounded man off the sling. The chopper strained to remain airborne, but slowly staggered down a few hundred yards away, impacting with an earth-shaking thud.

It was clear we couldn't medevac our wounded from this ravine. We'd have to fight our way to the top of the mountain to get a secure zone for the birds to land. The trek wouldn't be quick either; it would likely be a daylong battle against both withering enemy fire and inhospitable terrain. Dodging bullets and climbing a steep, mud-slick hillside covered with vines and other obstacles was nothing like the O-course and combat confidence course we'd trained on back in Quantico. Back there we hadn't been carrying our wounded and dead.

Meanwhile, I was still losing blood. My trousers were soaked below the gaping exit wound the sniper's bullet had left in my right thigh, where it had completed the trip it had begun in my lower back. But *never leave a fellow Marine behind* had been drilled into us. We kept our dead and wounded within our formation. Though to call my ragtag bunch of survivors a formation now might have been generous. One squad was on point, responsible for clearing the ground in front of us. The two remaining squads were deployed left and right, back about twenty-five meters, protecting our flanks. I was in the middle with the rest of the wounded and dead, trying to maintain communications, calling in air strikes and artillery to keep the NVA's heads down so they couldn't fire on us. I had no choice but to request strikes very close to our position. Saying "danger close" over the radio would alert the pilots or artillerymen to be extra careful. But sometimes they wouldn't fire "danger close" missions, and since we'd all be dead if they didn't, I didn't bother with the warning.

It took the better part of the day to carry the dead and wounded along in the final punishing climb while fighting to the top. It was dusk before we reached the mountaintop. By then I'd almost forgotten I was wounded, applying tourniquet and bandages hours earlier. Van Riper had now heard and ordered me out. The men also tried to persuade me to leave. But I couldn't go, not before all my Marines were safe.

When we got to the crest, it was burning. Artillery and bombs had left a smoking wasteland of toppled trees, smoldering jungle, ripped-up earth, and grotesquely shredded enemy corpses. It smelled like the Devil's pit barbecue. The firing had slackened at least; the NVA were either killed or retreating down the reverse slope, melting back into the jungle.

At that point, the choppers were able to come in. Our wounded went "emergency medevac," which meant getting the seriously hurt out as quickly as possible, even under fire. Next came the less seriously wounded. Last, the "permanent routine," radio shorthand for a Marine killed in action.

I went out on the last chopper. My dead rescuer and I lay next to each other on the slaughterhouse floor of that noisy, smelly angel-machine. By then blood loss had caught up with me. I was barely breathing, in serious pain, but still clearheaded. Until this fateful day, he and I had never met. I didn't know what had caused Cpl. Roy Lee Hammonds, twenty-one, of Waxahachie, Texas, to come to my rescue. He'd been in country since February 25, 1969, and was within weeks of going home.

As I lay there beside him, I began to wish he hadn't come after me. In a few days Marines in dress blues would be knocking on his family's front door. They wouldn't know what he'd done for me. They wouldn't even be told how he'd died. But as the turbines rose to a deafening roar and the rotors whooped, the thick, blasted jungle fell away. In the last fading golden light, I looked out over the rolling hills of the battle-scarred country we were leaving and laid a protective arm over Roy's body.

Two Marines. We'd never spoken to each other, never shaken hands, even at the end. But now we were bound in spirit forever.

2

THE EARLY YEARS

1946–68: Macon and Augusta, Georgia

The house at 854 Orange Terrace is a lovely white antebellum two-story, roofed with gray slate. Inside, lofty ceilings arch above fireplaces with exquisitely carved mantels. In back, a boxwood garden offers a great place for kids to play. Doric columns frame the front porch, and the huge beveled-glass door has a big letter B etched in the middle.

My mother's father, Aristide Aurelio Benedetto, bought it in 1923 for $6,000 after succeeding in the laundry business. When I was growing up, it had neither central heating nor air conditioning, and I shivered in my upstairs room in the winter and sweated every summer.

I must have been five when Grandmother Gertrude Benedetto died. In the tradition of those days, she was laid out in the big front room with the rounded windows. We knelt around her to say the rosary together the night before the funeral.

The next morning, the undertakers arrived to take the casket to the church. The turnout was huge since the Benedettos were one of the anchor families of St. Joseph's. As the family was leaving, though, I suddenly realized I was being left behind, at home. I displayed a trait that would follow me through my early days: a quick, hot temper. I pitched a fit, demanding to go too. When my mother said no, I flung my yo-yo, which hit her in the head. I still got left behind, locked in my room.

My reputation as a brat was reinforced when I slammed that beautiful beveled glass door on my older brother at age ten. But a curtain caught most of the shattering glass, and my parents were so relieved no one was hurt that my dad's usual hands-on punishment was delayed for an hour . . . but not forgotten!

Angelo Joseph Punaro was the son of immigrants who'd processed through Ellis Island, like so many others, in the early 1900s. His father, Antonio, and his mother, Rosa Zacchara, both came from Sotto il Monte ("beneath the mountain"), an impoverished village south of Naples.

My grandfather opened a small grocery store in Augusta, the Vesuvius Fruit Market. But times were tough, and the family returned to Italy after Angelo was born. They were so poor in that mountain town that many days he had only a glass of goat's milk and a piece of bread to eat. Eventually they moved back to Augusta, reopened the store, and lived above it. Over time, the business grew, and they finally bought a small house on 329 Ellis Street.

An Italian suppertime is a production, with many courses and always spaghetti. Grandmother Rosa made a special dessert called *zippoli*. She never learned English; she communicated with hand gestures and peremptory Italian. She was a real disciplinarian; my father called her "top sergeant."

In genealogy-conscious, proudly Confederate Georgia, Italians were second-class citizens, never accepted in the larger community. The only ways we could excel were in school, in the Catholic Church, or via artistic achievement. My mother's family chose the Church; her two older brothers became Jesuit priests, and two of her sisters became nuns.

My father chose academics. His grades at Richmond Academy were so outstanding he was accepted to MIT. But since my grandparents couldn't afford to send him there, he went to a closer, yet still prestigious, school: he won a scholarship to The Citadel. Excelling in academics and leadership, he rose to battalion adjutant, graduating in 1938.

After commissioning, my dad was stationed at Camp Wheeler, in Macon, where he met my mother, Annina, who worked at the hospital as an Army dietitian. They married in Macon. Then my father went off to war in late 1942.

Like most veterans of that era, my father never talked a lot about his service. But after he died at age ninety-three, we found some of his records, along with a history of his combat unit. The 399th Infantry Regiment was awarded twenty-one Distinguished Service Crosses and five Legions of Merit. The 100th "Century" Division was part of Patton's dash across France to Germany.[1] Angelo was a major by then and did detailed planning for operations. His awards included the Bronze Star with Oak Leaf Cluster, but he was proudest of earning the highly coveted combat infantryman's badge.

Dad was a perfectionist in everything he did, and this became both an advantage and disadvantage when he began to build custom homes after the war. Even when the owners were satisfied, if my father wasn't happy with how a cabinet looked, he'd tear it out and start over, at his own expense. Other builders considered him the best estimator on construction jobs; he could estimate so precisely that at the end of a job only a few bricks, nails, or boards would be left. He made sure each angle was precise and each surface was level, and his draftsmanship, especially the way he printed every word, was exquisite.

My mother worked full-time teaching nutrition in both the Catholic and public schools. She always told us that breakfast was the most important meal of the day.

My primary education was at St. Joseph's Grammar School, four blocks from my house. I walked there every day from first grade through eighth. The Catholic community in Macon was so insular that most of the girls and boys I started with at St. Joseph's in the first grade in 1951 were still in my graduating class at Mount De Sales High School in 1964. During my first year there, St. Joseph's was building a new grammar school, with Dad in charge of construction. When I went back for my fifty-year reunion, the steel-silled windows and diamond-hard ceramic floor tiles looked unworn, making good on his comment to me that he'd picked those because they'd last forever.

When we were in the eighth grade, I started a club called "The Over-the-Wall Gang." To become a member, you had to grab a kid in one of the lower grades—say, second or third—and throw him over the nine-foot brick wall that divided the upper playground from the lower. Ratted out by a first grader, we were punished. My father's favorite weapons were "switches" he cut from our rose bushes. The thorns left welts on my legs and bottom. Since my classmates nailed me as the ringleader, my desk was moved up front in the classroom, right next to Sister Mary Edward, the principal, so she could whack me good with a long ruler at a whim. I actually considered it a badge of honor to be up there, and didn't realize until later it wasn't a prestigious location.

Growing up in that small town, I palled around with Edgar Hatcher, Andy McKenna, Andy Duffy, and Fred Howe, my classmates since first grade. A couple years younger were Tommy Cassidy and Benjy Smith. All were tied to our church and parochial school; their parents had grown up with my mother, and everybody was either related to or at least knew everybody else.

But even though my friends were athletic, I became more of an organizer, or coordinator. While I was a nominal member of the various football, basketball, and baseball teams, my main job was keeping the statistics: batting averages, field goal percentage, and catches made. It taught me early the power of numbers. In the Senate, we became experts at using the Pentagon's own statistics against them. Later, in charge of business development for a $10 billion company, it was critical to our earnings calls and investor relations to have precise, reliable numbers.

I was in both the Cub and Boy Scouts. By eighth grade I was an Eagle Scout. I was also more or less forced to be an altar boy, which entailed memorizing lengthy responses in letter-perfect Latin. Since our house was so close to St. Joseph's, I was often called in. For funerals, altar boys got out of school, and if it was a wedding, we got paid the princely sum of two dollars each. As one of the most dependable acolytes, who'd mastered the intricate movements required by the High Mass, I also got to serve the long liturgies of Lent and *wear a red cape.*

As I mentioned, my uncles and aunts were Jesuits and nuns. Also, because I'd enjoyed helping my great aunt Bernadette ("queen bee" of the Mount De Sales

Convent) deliver aid baskets to the poor, I was attracted to helping others. As I was graduating from eighth grade, the diocese of Savannah was starting a minor seminary. I decided to attend.

A calling is hard to explain, but I felt attracted to the role. A Catholic priest is looked up to. He conducts services. He speaks to large groups, helps others, and is respected. Also, he takes care of people in need. Several of my gang and scouting friends—Nick Minden, Ron Perchance, and Tommy Cassidy—also decided to go.

⌇

St. John Vianney was named after the patron saint of parish priests. It stood on the grounds of Camp Villa Maria, on the Isle of Hope, outside Savannah. The diocese had built dormitories and everything else needed for a full-time minor seminary. But as I rode in on the Greyhound bus, I realized how far from home it really was. In those days, a five-hour bus trip seemed like a week.

Each day at the seminary started at 6 a.m. with Mass. Meals were taken in silence, listening to readings about what it meant to be a priest. The uniform was coats and ties with starched white shirts. Classes went most of the day. In the afternoons, we had athletics, then study hall before and after dinner. Lights out was no later than ten, and we did a half-day of class on Saturdays. We sometimes got Saturday afternoon off and could take the bus into town, but we had to be back for supper. Sunday was Mass, prayer, study halls, and athletics.

We also had chores. I drew "mess duty," food preparation and cleanup. The head cook was Mrs. Vasta, an Italian lady. We got along great; I'd been well-trained by my grandmother to cook in large amounts, with lots of pasta, tomato sauce, garlic, onions, and meats. Mrs. Vasta also drove our school's bus. In the bus we nicknamed her "Fasta" Vasta, as she had a heavy foot on the accelerator, and in the kitchen we called her "Pasta" Vasta, as there was always some variety of pasta noon and evening.

Priests did all the instruction. I took Latin and German from Father Cuddy, who would later become my parish priest at St. Joseph's. He was warm and friendly, unlike the rector, Father William Coleman, who was strict and inflexible.

In the summers, I worked at the naval ordnance plant, which made parts for Navy gravity bombs. This was a legacy of two powerful members of Congress from Georgia: Carl Vinson, the longtime chairman of the House Armed Services Committee, and Richard Russell, longtime chair of the Senate Armed Services Committee. Later, when I worked for Sen. Sam Nunn, Vinson's great-grand nephew, we would joke that we followed the Russell/Vinson model of treating everyone evenly: 50 percent for Georgia and 50 percent for the rest of the nation.

Production at the bomb plant was on dirty, noisy milling machines and metal lathes. Each worker had to produce a certain number of parts each day. I didn't get the word and would complete my quota by noon. As they were always telling us to slow down on our output, I didn't leave with a positive impression of government workers.

While I enjoyed the seminary, two factors made me rethink becoming a priest. One was Savannah's famous St. Patrick's Day parade. We were warned that when the high school bands, with the cheerleaders, came by, we were to lower our eyes and look at the pavement. I must've forgotten, because I clearly recall the girls' bare, flashing legs and broad smiles.

The second doubt came when I was asked to come back during my junior summer to work at Camp Villa Marie. One of the other counselors was an attractive, outgoing college student. While she and I did nothing more sinful than chat, it convinced me I was missing something.

I finally went to see Father Cuddy in his office—I was too chicken to face Father Coleman—and confessed I wasn't returning next year. He nodded and said he respected my decision. This didn't surprise my Jesuit uncles. Frank and Arnold had never been in favor of my going to a minor seminary. They'd told my mother I was too young to know what I wanted. Uncle Frank headed the Physics Department at Loyola University and was a noted expert in the nuclear field. My uncle Arnold taught philosophy at Spring Hill. So I was able to cite them in support when I told my parents I'd be doing my senior year at Mount De Sales.

∽

Mount De Sales Catholic High, one of Macon's elite prep schools, was two blocks from my house. I could get up at eight and be in homeroom at 8:15, a positive change from 6:00 a.m. reveille at St. John Vianney. De Sales had previously been an all-girls boarding school. My mother and her sisters had gone there (as had my future mother-in-law), but it went coed in 1959. It was also the first school in middle Georgia to integrate, in 1963.[2] The Sisters of Mercy had decided to close the boarding school, so there were just four senior girl boarders left. Since my best friends, Edgar Hatcher and Fred Howe, were dating two of them, they told me I should fill the void with one of the ones left.

Renée Johnson was a cheerleader and the student body president, a vivacious blonde. We hit it off and dated most of our senior year. When I got my first peck on the cheek as I dropped her off at the convent, I knew switching from the priesthood had been the right call. Holding hands and kissing was more fun even than holding the bishop's miter.

My pals and I picked up in my senior year with the pranks we'd played at St. Joseph's. Our principal, Sister Mary Sarto, didn't know a lot about our area.

Just as in grammar school, I'd become the statistician for our baseball team. One afternoon we had an away game in an industrial area about ten minutes from our school. I went to her office. "Sister, the team has a game in Payne City and we want to make sure we don't have to speed to get there." She said, "Well, you better get started now." It wasn't even noon, but she let me get on the PA system to announce that the team should get their gear and meet in the parking lot for our trip to Payne City. We mustered, went the two blocks to my house, and broke into my dad's liquor cabinet. I remember the coach commenting how "loose" the team was that day. The school never caught us, but I'd forgotten that bourbon does smell. When I got home that evening, my mother knew.

I also got involved in drama at Mount de Sales. In *Charlie's Aunt*, a comedy, I had the lead as a man dressed as a woman. I enjoyed it, so when Sr. Sarto's brother brought a play from Mobile called *The Fantasticks*, I helped with the production.

Acting taught me how to express myself. It also taught me how to stage events, which has been very helpful. But when I think back to my school years, the course that's been the most useful was typing. Being able to put words on paper fast has helped me in college, in government, and in the business world. I got interested in journalism working for the school paper, the *Sales Sheet*. It was straightforward reporting, but learning to write was another skill that would help me immensely.

In the summer of my senior year, I reconnected with my friend Tommy Cassidy's cousins. Jan and Fran Fitzwilliam were identical twins, and every summer they came to Macon to visit their grandmother, Mrs. William Cassidy. Anita Fitzwilliam, Mrs. Cassidy's daughter, and my mother had grown up together. One of Tommy's jobs was to get dates for his cousins. Otherwise, he couldn't go out, so he asked me to escort Jan. But we never had any serious feelings for each other at that time.

JAN'S PERSPECTIVE

The air was thick and humid in Macon that summer. I was twelve, visiting my grandmother, Momee, who lived in the same town as Arnold's family. My mother was from a large family (one sister and four brothers) as was Arnold's (three sisters and three brothers). The two families lived within walking distance of each other and attended the same church, schools, and parties.

Friendships didn't stop with that generation, though. Arnold and Tommy, my cousin, were inseparable. One day during my visit, Tommy came over to mow the grass for Momee and brought Arnold as his assistant. I can still picture these two, Tom and Huck, sipping sweet tea on the porch, taking lots of breaks. Afterward, they joined us for supper at a table laden with fried chicken, grits, rutabagas, and biscuits with butter and gravy. For dessert, Momee served vanilla bean ice cream topped with sliced Georgia peaches. Also at the table that day were my aunt Cile, her daughter, Cecile, who lived with Momee after my uncle was killed during World War II, my great-great-aunt Julia, whom I was named after and who also lived with Momee, as well as my parents and my five sisters.

Growing up with five sisters, especially in a military family, welded us close. We moved to unfamiliar places, but we were never lonely. Monet was the oldest. Fran, my identical twin, and I were born fifteen months later. Then came Elizabeth, Mary, and Ellen. People used to say to my father, "Albert, you're a saint for raising six girls." Even our boxer, Jezebelle, was female. Dad was the lone male, but he loved having a houseful of daughters, though we weren't the greatest company for watching football, his favorite sport.

Albert Fitzwilliam grew up in New Orleans, went to Loyola University on a football scholarship, then to Loyola Law School, where he coached football. World War II began shortly after he finished law school, so he joined the Navy and never looked back. He loved Navy life and decided to make it a career.

My mother, Anita Cassidy, also joined the Navy after Pearl Harbor. She earned her RN at a three-year nursing school at the Macon Hospital. During one summer of nursing school she took science courses at Louisiana State University (LSU) in New Orleans upon the urging of her Uncle Ed, a Jesuit priest teaching at Loyola University. He found her a room to rent in the house of a nice couple, Thomas and Frances Fitzwilliam. At the time, he had no idea that Albert, a handsome, eligible young man, was also living there. My mother said that if Uncle Ed could have found a nice convent for her to live in, he would have preferred that.

When Anita moved in, Albert was a bachelor. During the day, he worked at his father's printing shop, T. Fitzwilliam & Co., and at night went out on the town. Anita, as she told the story, stayed in and studied most nights. The two became friends while she lived there and went out to lunch and dinner on occasion. So, although they met briefly during this time, it wasn't until Albert was serving in North Africa during World War II that he realized she was the one. His mother must have realized it too. She sent him a clipping from the local paper about Anita joining the Navy. The article included a beautiful picture of her in uniform. This clipping, plus the dangers and stress of the war, made him realize there was more to life than having fun with his buddies. He showed them the picture and announced, "That's the girl I'm going to marry." The wedding took place shortly after the war ended, and they were together for more than fifty years.

After the brief meeting at Momee's, I didn't see Arnold again for several years. My dad was ordered to the Panama Canal Zone, and we went with him.

ARNOLD'S PERSPECTIVE

After graduating high school, I'd hoped to attend the University of Georgia, where most of my friends were going. But my mother worried that I might party too much at UGA and wanted me to go to a Catholic college. My namesake, Uncle Arnold, taught at the Jesuit College, Spring Hill, in Mobile, Alabama. Since my brother Anthony was at Loyola, where my other uncle taught, I would be going to Spring Hill. I'd get a tuition break, and my parents were strapped after putting seven children through Catholic grammar and high schools.

I got off to a strong start and was elected class president. I signed up for premed because I wanted to help people and be part of a respected profession. Spring Hill had an excellent biology department, led by Father Yancy, noted for his ability to get students into med school.

I'd meant to be one of the leaders, but I soon strayed. Baldwin was a dry county, except on the Spring Hill campus, where they served draft beer at my fraternity parties.[3] After I missed a few curfews and my midsemester grades were not that great, I got called into the Dean's office. Unfortunately, Father Rivet knew my parents and uncles and felt he had to tell them I was off to a poor start. I was restricted to campus and had to go to mandatory study hall.

A premed student has to take biology, chemistry, botany, math—lots of tough courses. English majors, instead, do a lot of reading and writing. At the end of my freshman year, I switched. My overall average was such that medical school was no longer an option and I decided I'd had enough science.

JAN

On my family's return from the Canal Zone, we once again visited Momee and our Macon relatives, en route to our new home in the Washington area. The night we arrived, my cousin Tommy was on his way to a party with his girlfriend, Anne. His mom, Clifford, a formidable woman, stated, "Tommy, you should fix up Arnold with one of the Fitzwilliam girls." Clifford's suggestions were more like orders, and I was the one Tommy drafted. Now, to hear Arnold tell the story, the prospect of this command performance was not very thrilling, but to the surprise of us both, we really enjoyed the evening. I remember thinking that night, *I'd like to get to know him better.*

This was not to be, for quite a while. After that short visit I headed back to Washington, DC, for my junior year of high school.

ARNOLD

A number of my classmates were in the Reserve Officers' Training Corps. About half were there to have a better chance of not going to war, while the others wanted to go. Me? I wasn't interested. Playing soldier, drills, and buzzcut hair looked silly.

But the draft was hanging over our heads. Through '66, '67, and '68 more and more numbers were being called. We all had friends who'd dropped out and were immediately conscripted, or who'd gone directly from high school. We felt we too would probably be called up after graduation, so we needed to make sure we had a good time first.

Early in my senior year, when I was home over Christmas break 1967, I went by my local draft board to see about a deferment for grad school. Mrs. Beazley had been in charge there for decades and had a reputation for turning down requests for deferments. But when we talked, she seemed acquiescent . . . until she learned my name.

"Are you related to *Anthony* Punaro?"

"Yes," I said, "He's my older brother."

She shot back, "Your brother asked for a deferment and did not get one and he wrote me a nasty note. If we don't get you in June, we'll get you in July."[4]

Her threat reverberated in my ears. *"If we don't get you in June, we'll get you in July."* I thought, *Maybe I shouldn't have been so hard on those ROTC folks.*

When I told my dad, his advice was, "You don't want to get drafted. You'll go to Asia as an infantryman, and there's nothing grand and glorious about war."

After the Christmas holiday, I started talking to the recruiters (except the Army one, since that was a ticket straight to 'Nam). The Navy and Air Force were only interested in guys who wanted to be pilots. Even if you were accepted, after a hard exam, you had to serve six years, which seemed far too long.

One day I walked past a fellow in blue trousers with a red stripe, wearing a white hat. He looked sharp. I admit it, I was attracted to the uniform. He introduced himself as Maj. Jim Way. I asked if the Marines were looking for anyone other than pilots. He said, "Absolutely, we have openings for a prestigious position as infantry platoon commander." I knew nothing about the Corps's fierce fighting tradition, and he made the "commander" position sound good. And when I asked him how long I had to sign up for, he said "Only two years. And I can give you the test tomorrow and let you know if you're accepted with no wait!"

I told some of my friends, and we went out to have a few beers at the Dew Drop Inn to mull it over. A few turned into a lot, as usual, but I stumbled in to the test the next morning. Way graded it on the spot and said, "My God! You have one of the highest scores we've ever seen. You're in! Sign right here."

I was relieved. I thought, *Mrs. Beazley, I've beaten you.* I had a contract with the U.S. Marine Corps. I would be a second lieutenant, would not be drafted, and I'd get to wear that snappy uniform. I told my buddies what a good deal it was, and five more classmates joined.

After graduating in May, I went back to Macon to work for Dad's firm, building a bank. I didn't have to report until November, and his job was done in

August, so I decided to go back to Mobile and train with my friend Harold Long, then head to Quantico together. Harold, a super athlete, had played football at Alabama until getting hurt and coming to Spring Hill. We ran the golf courses at the Mobile Country Club, then took advantage of the incurious waiters and ordered ample quantities of our favorite foods and beverages. We did a lot of elbow strengthening in the evenings, raising beer mugs. Neither of us was a member, but we figured we'd be long gone before a bill showed up. We'd buy rounds for everyone, and shout, "Courtesy of J. W. Pate, Montgomery, Alabama." I guess we'll never know if there really was a J. W. Pate, and, if so, how he felt when he got the bill.

Harold and I headed north at last, in the car I was able to buy while working for my Dad: a used '65 Chevy Malibu. As we hit Interstate 95 through the Carolinas, closing in on Virginia, we thought we were fit, ready, and well-prepared to become Marines.

Oh, how little we knew.

3

UNITED STATES MARINE CORPS

1968–69: Quantico, Virginia

s Harold and I turned off at the Triangle-Quantico exit on a dreary, cold November day, we passed a statue commemorating the flag-raising at Iwo Jima. We would learn in the coming weeks how more Marines had died in that battle than any other in the Corps's history: nearly 6,000, with another 20,000 wounded while fighting their way through the hundreds of death traps and ambushes the Japanese had concealed on that barren, hot, cave-honeycombed, volcanic cinder of an island.[1]

Our already-tense spines straightened at the gate, where an armed sentry shouted, "Orders!" We showed our papers and tried to ask where to go for Officer Candidates School (OCS). The sentry jerked his head at a red sign with gold letters—*OCS Check-in*—and an arrow. We followed similar signs along the winding road flanked by the Medal of Honor Golf Course, through "main side," past the airfield. Inside rolled-open hangar doors, olive drab and white-top fuselages lurked like morays; this was the home of HMX-1, the Presidential Helicopter Unit. We bumped across rusty rails and into a parking lot adjacent to a metal-walled warehouse.

The sign *OCS Check-in Here* was hardly necessary. A line of apprehensive-looking young guys in civvies with papers in their hands was headed into a large door. As we followed them through what we would shortly learn was *not* a door, but a "hatch," Marines in impeccably starched khaki shirts and trousers, wearing the famous drill instructor Smokey the Bear hats, were shouting instructions nonstop. An amplified voice boomed over the babble, "All privates A through M on this side. All privates N through Z on the far side."

Clear enough; but *we* weren't privates. I strolled over to one of the sergeants and drawled, "Hey there, sir, where do us second lieutenants go?"

In a voice more formidable than God to Moses in Cecil B. DeMille's *The Ten Commandments*, the sergeant yelled, spraying flecks of spit into my face, "I am not a *sir*. I am a *sergeant* and there are no *second lieutenants* here. And you, *private*, will NEVER be a second lieutenant, because you are *too stupid*. Now, what is it you don't understand, *private*? All privates A through N on this side. All privates N through Z on that side! Now *get in line*!"

I suddenly realized my recruiter had conned me. If I didn't make it through this, I would be heading to Parris Island for boot camp and two years' service as an enlisted grunt. In those days, recruiters were motivated solely by hitting their quotas, so they recruited kids they knew wouldn't be able to pass OCS.[2]

After being shouted into a haphazard queue, I began my introduction to three eternal truths in the military: hurry up and wait, endless paperwork, and constant changes to the "word." Drill sergeants stalked the line, screaming at us to do this and then that. They broke us into groups of ten and sat us at tables to fill out forms, fast, under such instructions as, "For those of you who can read and write, print your name in block one. Then, in block two, print the name of your mother so we can notify her when you drown in Chopawamsic Creek or get lost on the hill trail and eaten by raccoons."

After several hours of paperwork, we were reorganized. Fifty of us became 1st Platoon, Alpha Company, 53rd Officer Candidate Company. Our new drill instructor, Staff Sergeant Arnold (unfortunately no relation), a short, muscular, ugly-mean, and extremely loud DI, headed 1st Platoon over to supply to draw uniforms, boots, underwear, and socks so that we would all look identical. Dragging heavy, olive-drab sea bags of new gear, we then lined up at the barbershop. There was less wasted motion here than among the robots in a car factory. My barber sheared me to a skinhead in less than a minute. "Chrome dome" was the nickname given to all candidates, a term I liked better than private.

From the warehouse and barbershop Arnold marched us (actually, shambled or herded might have been more accurate) to four-story brick barracks on the banks of the wide, green Potomac. 1st Platoon's large, open second-floor room sported two rows of metal racks on a bare concrete floor, a dozen on each side, with green-painted plywood footlockers and a battered gray steel upright locker beside each rack. Our names were already on them; I had a top rack in the middle of the room. Staff Sergeant Arnold, flanked by two assistant drill instructors, told us to fold all our civilian clothes, stuff them in a bag, and turn them in to the staff. Then put on our utilities and boots. Nonstop yelling echoed off the concrete. "Hurry up!" "Assholes and elbows, that's all I want to see!" "You all are a sad and sorry sight." We mustered that evening on the concrete sidewalks on the river side of the barracks, platoons ranked side by side. This became familiar, as we both began and ended every day in formation on that same windy, cold riverbank.

Our first meal in the chow hall. We marched in single file and picked up metal trays. Their raised dividers meant nothing, as the mess men just slapped food on with large metal spoons. The beverage selection was milk, water, or bug juice (Kool-Aid). When your tray was full, you went straight to a table and ate at rigid attention while being constantly berated and quizzed. Five minutes after sitting down, we were done and being screamed back outside into formation again.

That evening we were ordered to compose letters to our mothers. We loved the Marine Corps, we were being well cared for, and we weren't going to have time to write ever again. One candidate raised a hand. We regarded him with mingled awe and schadenfreude.

"What is it, maggot?" the DI snapped.

"I don't live with my mother. Who should I write to?"

The drill sergeant made several unprintable comments about his mother's lifestyle, then added, "I know rocks that are smarter. Quit now. You will never make it in my Corps. You are too stupid and too ugly."

That particular candidate had graduated from Yale, but his degree obviously hadn't been in common sense.

The next morning we rolled out at 0530 in the freezing cold. After predawn PT and chow, we were judged ready for the inventory physical fitness test. The Corps wanted to know what shape each candidate arrived in. This was a crucial breakpoint; if we failed, we'd be recycled into the "fat boy" platoon for additional training, and after that we'd have to start OCS all over again. The inventory had five elements: sit-ups, dead-hang pull-ups, squat thrusts, broad jump, and a three-mile run in boots.[3]

I was never a PT stud, and I was nervous about this test. But thanks to my summer conditioning, I managed the minimum number of pull-ups, a presentable number of sit-ups, and a slow (and barely adequate) three-mile time. As it would turn out, it was smarter to have a passing but low score initially, as they actually wanted to see you improve over time.

"Keep your mouth shut and lay low," the ECPs—Enlisted Commissioning Program guys who'd earned a four-year degree before or during their active duty and who were now transitioning to commissioned status—told me. "Don't make yourself a target for the DIs. They're looking for problem children and assholes with attitudes." This sounded like good advice, and I resolved to follow it.

We would be graded in three major areas. Our days were a combination of academics, physical training, and military skills and leadership. The academics were classroom instruction, from Marine Corps history and rank structure to etiquette, field sanitation, weapons, tactics, and formations. We were tested on this, but the exams were multiple-choice. If you were good at memorizing, it wasn't that stressful.

Physical training was. This included the obstacle course, short and long forced marches with heavy packs on what was called the "Hill Trail" with forty-five-degree inclines, and much longer runs in gym gear. Military skills and leadership included close-order drill (on which the DIs were fanatics).

I actually enjoyed close-order marching. I liked the sense of many moving as one, the precision, the discipline. When it came my turn to call cadence, or maneuver the group, I liked snapping out commands and having everyone obey. We also did confidence courses, a sequence of suspended obstacles we had to negotiate, and a number of other courses to test our reactions under stress and in various leadership positions. These courses were particularly frustrating. For example, one candidate would be put in charge of three others and told to get the entire team from one balance beam to another using nothing but rope and some planks. But neither the rope nor the wood was ever the right length and so navigating the obstacle was almost always impossible to accomplish within the time limit. Part of the leadership grade was based on peer evaluations; the other candidates in our platoon would rank us from one to fifty.

I don't know how OCS was in peacetime, but during a war, from day one, the DIs told us, "You're headed for combat. Your life, and the lives of your Marines, will depend on you. There's no room for nonhackers or fuckups." There was no slack or do-overs. I was a natural organizer, so I fared well on peer evaluations. Also a problem solver, I excelled in drilling others and overcoming adverse tactical situations. I wasn't in as good shape physically as I'd thought, though. I spent my spare time on the obstacle course, learning which techniques got me through each obstacle fastest and with the least effort. I had no trouble on the forced marches. Where I continued to struggle was on the runs. A couple of times, on the longer platoon runs, I was tail-end Charlie and had to vomit as I ran. But I kept going. I didn't realize at the time that my instructors considered this a plus, since many candidates would just quit when they fell so far behind.

Graduation day was a formal parade, then a commissioning ceremony in Little Hall main side. None of my family was able to attend this and so friends pinned on my gold second lieutenant bars. We were commissioned on a Friday and did not have to report to the Basic School until Sunday afternoon. So we had a blissful Saturday off.

Unlike the other services, the Marine Corps requires all its officers to go through TBS.[4] The very name, the Basic School, is a giveaway: it's all about the basic blocking and tackling. This grounds all officers in the essentials of leadership and training before they go to their specialty schools—artillery or tanks or flight or logistics. In the other services, you're identified by your branch: signal, armor, artillery, supply, etc. In the Army you would say, "I'm a signal officer." In the Corps it's simple: "I'm a Marine."

TBS in the peak years of Vietnam was a twenty-one-week school, and a good bit of that was field training to be a small unit combat commander.[5] The instructors didn't have to remind us that we'd need to remember everything they were teaching to have any hope of coming back alive.

At TBS, we were graded on the same areas as at OCS—academics, physical training, leadership, and military skills—but there was substantially more fieldwork in terms of platoon and company tactics. This included learning how to set up and run an ambush, set up a defensive perimeter, calling in supporting fires from artillery, fighters, gunships, and naval gunfire, and learning how to shoot every weapon the United States and the enemy owned. There was a common phrase called the "school solution" that meant that whatever the tactical situation or problem they would throw our way, there was a right way to do it according to doctrine.

Again I was solid on the academics and also fared well in the leadership and peer reviews. I was also slowly getting better on the various physical tests. As Basic wrapped up, my staff platoon commander, 1st Lt. Bill Zimmerman, recommended me for an infantry military occupational specialty (MOS 0301) and a platoon command in Vietnam. At the time, this was considered the highest possible aspiration for a second lieutenant, so I felt I was at the top of my game.

I'd joined the Marines thinking Vietnam was the last place I wanted to go. But by the end of ten weeks of OCS and twenty-one weeks of TBS, I was as full of napalm and testosterone as any of my peers. Leading men in war was the test of manhood and of being a Marine.

I got that dream job: orders to the 1st Marine Division in Vietnam. My reporting-in date was August 1969. I was to go via Travis Air Force Base, which was one of the West Coast out-shipping points.

Though I'd never been west of the Mississippi, I'd heard a lot about San Francisco. The city was ground zero for the counterculture that would spread over the country during the '70s—the antiwar movement, LSD, smoking pot, and so forth. It had all started there, at the intersection of Haight and Ashbury streets.[6] I had to see what this was all about. And, not to put too fine a point on it, a couple of us also wanted to beat up some of these hippies.

So, once in the city, we took a taxi over to the District. It was . . . horrible. Long-haired, strung-out-looking men and women with piercings . . . antiwar slogans and marijuana leaves on T-shirts . . . antiwar posters on storefronts . . . the sweet scent of grass smoked on the street. None of this was what I'd been used to in Georgia or Quantico. We strode along, shouting insults, oblivious to the fact that wearing our uniforms into the heart of the antiwar movement was lacking in both judgment and discretion.

Strolling down a side street, some of us ran into a large group of individuals sitting and smoking on large motorcycles. Their uniform was new to me: short black leather jackets with threatening patches bearing the legend Hell's Angels. Some purple-hair types were mixed in. As we came abreast of them, a big, beefy dude with bare shoulders under his black leather vest got off his hog and growled, "Who the fuck are you and what the fuck are you doing on our turf?"

Having been trained with pugil sticks and in hand-to-hand combat, we had no fear of this lad, of course. We would show these hippies and dippies what the USMC was all about. I boldly informed him and all others in the alley, "We're U.S. Marines on our way to war. We came to the zoo to see the animals and low-lifers working against our country."

We had neither our issue KA-BAR nor any protective gear, however, and belatedly realized we were hopelessly outnumbered, *and* surrounded, *and* facing superior weaponry . . . to wit, the steel chains and brass knuckles all the Angels quickly pulled from their jackets and came at us with. If we hadn't run so quickly, we might've gotten more prominent bruises or even some broken bones, but they did pretty much beat the hell out of us as we dodged through their gauntlet back to the main street. It was a good lesson. Going into combat, you want superior numbers, better tactics, and better equipment than your enemy. Only a fool fights fair.

I was fortunate the next morning when I reported in that the flight commander was a junior first lieutenant. We told him we'd beat up some hippies and that they looked a lot worse than we did. He shrugged. He just wanted all our bodies on board, and didn't care what we looked like.

The engines of the 707 screamed, lifting us skyward. Around me the poker games had started. Other men looked out the windows, searching for a last glimpse of home as the coast fell away. Then we were over the blue Pacific, heading, at last, for my war.

4

ARRIVAL IN VIETNAM

1969: Da Nang, Republic of Vietnam

With a squeal of tires and a wail of engines, the World Airways 707 charter landed at Da Nang not long after dawn. Close to two hundred Marines had crossed the Pacific squeezed into this cattle car. In seat 23C, I, like all my brothers, was stiff and groggy from breathing a toxic compound of cigarette smoke and sweat and more than ready to get out and start my tour.

In 1968 Richard Nixon had swept into office on a pledge of an "honorable end to the War in Vietnam."[1] The First Tet Offensive, early that year, had been a nasty shock to both America and the military leaders on the ground and had seriously called into question the credibility of our strategy.

1968 had been our "watershed" year, with the highest number of troops, 537,000.[2] Everyone knew there was still much fighting—and dying—to be done, on both sides, even as U.S. troops were being withdrawn under the Vietnamization program.

In 1969, 11,780 U.S. troops had been killed in action, 2,694 of whom were Marines. Fifty-one of those Marines were lieutenants. Based on the statistics military briefers love, an average of thirty-two soldiers and Marines had died every day.[3]

The age of the average Marine KIA was twenty-one years and six months, barely old enough to buy a beer, but fully old enough to die for his country. None of us would come back the same. Some wouldn't come back at all, especially from my area of operation, which held the dubious distinction of having the most casualties of any in the combat zone.[4]

I emerged from the aircraft to a blast of heat like an industrial-strength paint dryer. The sun was blindingly bright. The acrid stink of burnt smokeless gunpowder and fermenting garbage, mixed with JP4 fumes, hung in the air. I groped my way down the boarding ladder. Around the airfield glinted a tangle of triple concertina wire studded with heavily sandbagged machine-gun positions. The runway edge was walled with mountains of stacked pallets, one of which held silver metal coffins, stacked four high and four across. Dollies rolled past, crammed with green-painted bombs. Helicopter gunships clattered overhead, and the roar of Marine F-4 Phantoms with screaming General Electric J-79 engines stabbed at my eardrums. Even the guys refueling our 707 from a tanker truck wore holstered pistols or shoulder-slung M16s.[5]

Not even in war, though, can you skip the paperwork. My first task in country, after lugging my sea bag from the flight line, was to check in. The 1st Marine Division G-1 personnel clerk stamped my orders REPORTED at a small table. He told me to "di-di" right over to the helipad. I was being assigned to the 7th Regiment, headquartered at Landing Zone Baldy, somewhere south of Da Nang. I was both apprehensive and excited. I was a Marine trained for combat and headed to the 7th Marine Regiment, 1st Marine Division (Reinforced) Vietnam.

"Where do I pick up my weapon?" I felt naked without one. Even this soft-looking clerk had a rifle stowed under the desk.

He rolled his eyes. "All your shit'll come from the 7th. Fall in with those guys over there. Next!"

Joining a twisting green centipede of other Marines, I hauled my sea bag and other gear toward the CH-46 twin-rotor Sea Knight helicopter, or as we liked to call it, the "phrog." Within minutes, the chopper was crammed with scared-looking grunts and crates of supplies and ammo. It would airlift us to Baldy, about a half-hour's flight.

But first, we headed east over the South China Sea, apparently to avoid flying over land. They'd told us at OCS that helicopters were vulnerable to rocket-propelled grenades or even small-caliber rounds.

The flight was noisy, the interior baking hot. Judging from the worn paint and the taped-over bullet holes, this aircraft had seen a lot of service, but I couldn't decide if that was a good sign or a bad one. The compartment was splashed with a scarlet liquid I hoped was hydraulic fluid, plus a yellowish fuel or some kind of lubricant.

We banked sharply, and the green carpet of jungle unrolled below as we headed inland. Two gunners manned .50-caliber machine guns on both sides of the CH-46. The barrels swiveled constantly as they searched for trouble. I shifted on the canvas webbing that was supposed to be a seat, imagining all too clearly how a bullet would feel as it punched through the vibrating aluminum floor, aimed straight for me.

We slammed down hard. The rear ramp dropped with a thud, raising reddish dust. An aircrewman yelled, "Move out, Marines. Smartly, we ain't got long on the ground." As soon as our gear was offloaded, the chopper dusted off, rising as quickly as it had dropped from the sky.

～

Landing Zone Baldy was aptly named. It was officially a fire support base, but not like its robust brothers, the fire support bases of LZ Ross and LZ Ryder and more than twenty others that dotted the high ground of the Central I Corps. Baldy was on flat, open, low ground along Highway 535, an east-west red line that pierced the ever-heightening hills that defined the eastern Que Son Valley. It was thirty-three kilometers south-southeast of Da Nang and sixteen kilometers east of FSB Ross, where I would head next. Baldy was flat, with no distinguishing features other than sandbagged watchtowers and foxholes, tents, hooches, and machine-guns positions with thick overhead protection. Everyone outside the beam- and sandbag-reinforced bunkers wore a helmet and flak jacket.

Off the helipad, I was handed to the paperwork gurus again, this time to the regimental S-1 personnel clerk. He told me I was being further assigned to the 1st Platoon, Lima Company, 3rd Battalion, 7th Marines, at FSB Ross, just southeast of Highway 535 and 534 in the Que Son Valley, which served to command the region.

I would not be choppering there just yet, however. An "in call" with the regimental commander was obligatory, so I'd be staying overnight. I asked, "Where am I supposed to spend the night?" The clerk grunted, "You can bunk down on the floor in the supply hut. Grab chow in the mess hall, or else eat C-rations." C-rats, as we called them, were precooked "wet meals" that came in olive drab cans. They ranged from disgusting to inedible.

I did make sure I knew where the bunkers were in case of incoming mortars. That was one TBS lesson that had stuck with me; you can't outrun mortars, so be ready to make like a mole at short notice.

I visited the head, a plywood outhouse aptly nicknamed the "shitter," where the smell was god-awful, made worse in the heat by buzzing flies. I then headed for the mess tent, a sandbagged wooden hut with sand-filled weapon discharge barrels at the doors. Each man cleared his rifle or pistol and dry-fired it into the barrel as he came in. (I, of course, walked by, still having no weapon.) The messmen slopped chow onto metal trays, just as at OCS. And, just as at OCS, I bolted the mystery meat, green stuff, and white stuff down in less than five minutes.

I would have taken more time to savor the cuisine if I'd known this would be the last hot meal I'd get for months.

The supply hut was a jungle of junk. I found a small clear area on the planks near a massive stack of boxes and passed out. I was jerked awake again by the rattle of small arms fire and the flickering glare of flares lighting the night. I'd been in country for all of eighteen hours but still didn't have a weapon. By the flare light, I spotted some loose KA-BAR knives in an open box. I figured they wouldn't miss one, and I strapped it to a cartridge belt, which I also appropriated.

I was scheduled to see the regimental commander, Col. Gildo S. Codispoti, at 0700 for my official in call. I hadn't been around any brass during training, so I was nervous. But my little green book and my Skilcraft ballpoint were in my cargo pocket, ready to take copious notes on the commander's guidance he was sure to provide.

I'd expected something a little less spartan for the 7th Marines Combat Operations Center. It was totally underground, entered through a sandbagged tunnel guarded by a young Marine. As I seemed to be the only new officer that day, I rapped on the plywood hatch frame, entered, and came to the most rigid attention I could muster. "Sir, Second Lieutenant Punaro, reporting as ordered."

Colonel Codispoti could have been from central casting for a bird colonel—totally squared away, clean uniform, gleaming eagles—sitting at a desk of planks and ammo boxes. A captured Chicom SKS rifle hung from nails. A terrain map of the whole I Corps area was tacked on the plywood bulkhead, from the demilitarized zone in the north to the Kontum and Binh Dinh provinces in the south, the blue sea on the east, and Laos and the Ho Chi Minh Trail to the west. Codispoti had a green field telephone tucked under his chin as he scribbled busily on a message pad. He barely glanced up. "Lieutenant. Dry socks."

He didn't speak again. After a moment I repeated uncertainly, "Sir . . . dry socks?"

He snapped loudly, "Lieutenant, make sure your men wear dry socks at all times! That is all."

That was clearly my cue to snap to attention again, about-face, and exit. Which I did. My commander's guidance and official inbriefing had lasted less than thirty seconds and had consisted basically of two words. About footwear.

Mulling this over . . . could he perhaps have meant something more? Was "dry socks" a metaphor for being prepared? Caring for my men? Still mystified, I grabbed my sea bag once more and headed to the helipad for transport to Fire Support Base Ross. The flight was in yesterday's chopper's twin: noisy, smelly, with oil and fuel and spent cartridges covering the scarred metal floor, and Marines manning .50-cals. They never took their eyes off the landscape below, as this flight was all overland, "down the red line" following a road.

As soon as we landed, I could tell this was even closer to the action than Baldy, and it made me nervous. Tall guard towers overlooked ranks of artillery pieces, 105s and even 155s, and stacks of shells. Scores of Marines were beavering away, in full battle gear and helmets. The perimeter was densely concertinaed, with subdivisions wired off as well. The bunkers here were even deeper and more thickly sandbagged than at Baldy. The dry brown ground was studded with trenches, foxholes, and hooches. Smoke rose here and there from trash fires and human shit burning in fifty-five-gallon drums.

I was directed immediately to the supply area. A frazzled-looking supply officer snapped, "Punaro? 1st Platoon, Lima Company, 3rd Battalion. Your company's heading into the field in an hour. Grab your 782 gear and go meet up with your platoon. Helmets over there. Flak jacket. Want a rifle, or a forty-five?"

This seemed to be my chance to stock up, at last. I picked a helmet and a flak jacket out of a jumbled pile, trying to find one without too many holes or bloodstains. The supply officer offered me what he called a "dog-handler's pack." It looked like it would hold lots of gear, so I grabbed extra boxes of ammo, hand grenades, flares, maps, canteens, Halazone tablets to purify water, and an extra-large first aid kit with plenty of dressings. I also threw in six boxes of C-rat meals, three days' worth at two 1,200-calorie meals a day.

I asked for a rifle, not a .45. NVA snipers targeted anyone with pistols, figuring them for officers. We'd trained on the M14 in basic, but now the Marines were issuing the much lighter M16A1s. What we weren't told was that the M16 wasn't designed for the mud and rain and grit of Vietnam. Let a speck of sand get in the mechanism and it would jam. The enemy's AK-47 was more dependable. I grabbed magazines and snapped them full of shiny brass rounds with tiny, wickedly pointed tips. I was also issued a pair of the coveted "Officer's" binoculars, which I had to sign a chit for, as I did for my rifle.

While I was looting the supply bunker and wondering how heavy all this crap was going to be on the march, a tall, skinny, bald captain with USMC-issue plastic-framed glasses strolled in. He introduced himself as J. K. Van Riper, the company commander. Later I'd learn he was one of the identical twins who, even at company-grade rank, were known around the Corps for superb leadership and being squared away. This was his second tour in Vietnam.

Van Riper got out his tactical map and, at last, my real briefing and read-in began. Checking it against my own map, he showed me where the company was headed that afternoon and where my platoon would dig in for the night. I had a laminated 1:50,000 map sheet for Hiep Duc, southwest of LZ Baldy and encompassing the dense jungle terrain of the Que Son Mountains. The more precise map sheet was 6640 III, Series L7014. Conscious that screwing this up could cost many lives, including my own, I used my grease pencil to very carefully mark the eight-digit grid coordinates of my own and his nighttime positions. This was long before GPS existed. We navigated by compass and the Military Grid Reference System, an alphanumeric code for finding any point on the globe. Pilots used traditional latitude/longitude; grunts used MGRS. We were leaving LZ Ross, 49P BT 025-343.[6]

As the skipper was getting ready to take me over to my platoon, I button-holed the supply guy again. "Hey, where are the socks? I need to make sure all my guys always have dry socks."

He guffawed. "Lieutenant? We haven't had any socks since I've been here. For over six months. There are no fucking *socks*. And no heat tabs for the C-rats, either."

"Damn," I muttered. I'd forgotten heat tabs were issued separately from the meal itself, and C-rats sucked enough without having to eat them cold. There were four cigarettes and some toilet paper in each box, but no heat tabs.

But how was I going to make my guys wear dry socks when there weren't any? One thing they'd made plain in training, and that Colonel Codispoti must surely have been referring to, however indirectly, was that it was my job to take care of my men's needs before my own.

"Don't forget to buckle the chin strap on your helmet and zip up your flak jacket." Van Riper led me through the camp. On the way, he explained that 1st Platoon had gone through a new lieutenant about once a month. Their most recent commander had been a sergeant, who'd just rotated out. Since I was the "boot lieutenant," he wouldn't make me point for the company or ask me to protect the command post for a while. But he did expect me to take hold from the get-go. "These Marines need leadership, and they need the benefit of your tactical training." While I'd had twenty-one weeks of TBS, they'd had less than ten of boot camp before going to war.

About two dozen raggedy-looking men were sitting or lying on the ground, most of them smoking, weapons handy, five yards from a slit trench that bordered the helipad. Van Riper said, very calm and matter-of-factly, "First platoon, listen up. This is your new commander. Second Lieutenant Arnold Punaro, from Georgia. Lieutenant, we're moving out in ten minutes. You'll be following the company CP, protecting the rear. Lieutenant, take over." With that, he moved off and left me with them.

This was my platoon. They looked at me intently, as a pack of wolves might when assessing likely prey. My introduction was brief. "Marines, my name is Second Lieutenant Punaro and I've been assigned to lead this platoon. Our first mission is to block the NVA supply lines and to clear the enemy from our area of operations. I want to get each of you home alive so we need to take care of each other. Make sure your rifles are loaded and ready at all times, keep your extra ammunition handy, and never get complacent. It doesn't matter what people are saying back home about this war. This is about your brother Marines and taking care of each other. That's what matters most and that's what we will do. Grab your gear and get ready to move out."

Since this was my first real look at real combat Marines, I took a moment to assess their appearance. This put flesh to the nightly TV news and the war stories from the corridors at Quantico.

While they were young, in fact mostly teenagers and early twenty-somethings, they had aged, worn eyes. Whatever youthful animation they once had had obviously been lost with their experiences here. Most had small, wispy mustaches or attempts at them, as if to attest to their now-mature station in life. Most had rolled up their sleeves, this being the dry season, exposing caked mud and sweat rivulets. All had on muddy, but closed flak jackets, a concession to one of the few real life-saving tools they possessed. The last item in this category, their helmets, were decorated to reflect their personalities. Names of girls, short timer's calendars, or irreverent mottos were scrawled across the covers. Some had elastic bands at the base that stored a variety of items ranging from the C-rat cigarette boxes to LSA (lubricant, small arms) to mosquito repellent. The M60 gunner had his extraction tool. The medics both had wound packets on both sides of their helmets, like floats on a raft. The boots were dirt-caked and worn. All had a single dog tag tied to the bottommost lace, just like me.

There was a machine-gun team. I'd already picked up some of the slang. The Pig, the Ripper, the Chopper, the Gun. The gunners were vying to win the Pancho Villa lookalike contest, with wrapped ammo belts crossing their chests and one fifty-round belt draped across the gun. Their A-gunners (assistants) each had a double belt across his chest and a single belt around the waist. Each A-gunner also had a spare barrel bag tied to the back of his web gear. The M60 could fire six hundred rounds per minute, but its barrel had to be changed or it would melt.

Several Marines carried the M203 grenade launcher, the Thumper. This was a black metal tube under the standard M16 barrel. Next to one of the 203 guys was a Marine with an M79 grenade launcher slung across his back. The older weapon was still loved by many for its ease of handling and versatility. It was a favorite of the point team, with its canister cartridge for short-range close encounters, and was called the Bee Hive round, named because of the hum the fléchettes made in flight. They wore ammo vests over their flak jackets, loosely draped and unclosed. I could see the gold heads of HE rounds, as well as the black tops for canisters. This group could bring some heat in a hurry.

We had two corpsmen, unusual for an infantry platoon. They were actually Navy but looked like Marines. Each carried a large combat aid kit attached to a ruck frame. They both carried M16s—and knew how to use them—and one holstered a .45 pistol.

I noted blacks and a couple of Hispanics and Asians. The rest were white. Each had the same worn, sweaty, dirty face. Most were smoking with filthy fingers and well-worn black-edged nails. Each Marine had multiple ammo pouches, full up. The rest of the web belt held a tightly packed array of smoke grenades, aid kits, and canteens. Claymore bags, tightly tied to the web belt, were obviously full. My radio operator had the PRC-25 inside his ruck, its long whip antenna sticking through the flap. He also carried an M16. He passed me several laminated three-by-five cards. These were the call signs and frequencies. A second set he kept inside an ammo pouch, but he had them all memorized. Around his neck hung other cards containing code words for secure transmission. I would soon learn that Kruithoff was both dependable and discerning, which, along with being strong, was probably why he was the radioman.

It didn't seem like I had time to meet and greet the guys. "Who's the platoon sergeant?" I asked.

A Corporal Maurone rogered up. Apparently, he was the senior enlisted man in a severely undermanned platoon of about twenty-five. This included the machine-gun section, with a gunner, tripod carrier, and ammo humpers. We had a sixty-millimeter mortar section, with one tube and a base plate and the T&E (traversing and elevating) mechanism.

Every man had to carry a mortar round, and the lieutenant got last dibs, so I ended up with the two heaviest—Willie Pete, white phosphorus, weighing four pounds each, and dangerous as hell—unceremoniously dumped in my pack. I was copying the frequencies from Kruithoff as Corporal Maurone said, "Lieutenant, we're movin'."

Just like that, the men stood, picked up rifles, shuffled into a loosely staggered file, and headed out. Past the concertina, away from the towers and bunkers, into the blasted-looking, muddy rice paddies that surrounded it. No intelligence briefing, no description of our operational plan, no five-paragraph order, or anything else the tactics section at TBS had insisted was vital before a unit went out on operations.

It was now 1400, about an hour and a half after I had hit the dirt at LZ Ross. Arnold Punaro was headed to his first firefight, less than twenty-four hours after touchdown at Da Nang. This was nothing like my training and I couldn't believe I was in the movement-to-contact phase without getting to know each of my Marines better, to hear how long they'd been in the bush, or time to remember all my troop-leading steps. I did remember to remove my shiny gold second lieutenant bars, as their glint could ID an officer a klick away. I would never wear my rank again in Vietnam, as the Marines did not issue the subdued insignia common in the Army.

As we straggled out the front gate—which wasn't a *gate* of any kind, just a gap in the wire covered by two bored-looking troops lounging behind machine guns—I couldn't help but notice the bustle outside. Marines were leaning back in folding chairs, getting haircuts in an open-air barbershop. Giggling girls sold soft drinks and beer from ice choked galvanized tubs. "Number one cold Coca Cola," they shouted as we trudged by. Snot-nosed kids barely past the toddling stage, some without pants, tagged along, begging for candy. No one had covered a scene like a village market in platoon tactics. Was this really the movement-to-contact phase? And if so, was everything else they'd taught me wrong too?

For about an hour the company tramped slowly, in a staggered file, with three meters between each Marine, down the "red line"—the hard-packed dirt road. Maurone muttered, "This was swept by engineers earlier in the day." Kruithoff trudged behind me, bent under the platoon's only link back to the firebase, the PRC-25. We headed directly south, or azimuth 180 on the olive drab, tritium-lit lensatic compass, MIL-C-10436. That, along with my M16A1, would become my best friend. For a platoon commander, his rifle, his compass, his binoculars, his map, and his radio were the essentials. Everything else was secondary.

Finally, at Maurone's murmured prompting, I aimed us off the road into the rice paddies that had flanked us as we marched. TBS training had mentioned this terrain feature, but I was unprepared for how deep the water was, with the slippery and boot-sucking muck at the bottom. The heat grew suffocating, the going harder. I began to regret loading my dog-handler's bag so liberally. We lugged gear and weapons, chow and baseplates up and then down steep, muddy, crumbling dikes. We slogged through fetid water, trampling rice shoots. At TBS, I'd been told to walk along the higher dikes, which marked off the growing areas and helped funnel the water where it was needed. But these ran north to south, and we were headed west, across them, toward low green mountains.

Not only that, Maurone muttered, the VC was known to mine the dikes that served as paths. We were actually safer slogging randomly across the paddies.

⌐

Several long hours later, at the foot of a valley that led up into those mountains, I halted us for the night. Now we had to dig in, ring our bivouac with foxholes and machine-gun positions. I had to call in my outer-ring fires and final protective fires (those I was to call in on top of us if we were being overrun). I had to set up listening posts outside the perimeter, and make sure claymore mines covered any approach to our position.

It was still suffocatingly hot, even as the sun dropped behind the mountains. We were all dripping wet with sweat, and our boots and trousers were soggy from wading through, and occasionally falling in, the paddies. I gave those who wanted it one short smoke break. We were all setting to again, digging foxholes and wiring, when the radio hissed to life.

"Lima One Actual, this is Lima Six Actual. Over."

Lima Six was the company commander, and indeed, I recognized Van Riper's soft voice on the radio. Lima One was the 1st Platoon commander . . . me. The "actual" meant the officer himself, not his radioman. I rogered up, realizing I was about to get my first tactical order.

Speaking slowly, the skipper gave me the grid coordinates for a nighttime ambush position. This was a surprise; I hadn't expected to have to set up an ambush on my first night out, or with such a small platoon.

All our TBS training had assumed a full fifty-man platoon, with three squads with three fire teams each. Typically, one squad of twelve would go out on an ambush, leaving two squads with the extra weapons section (the machine gun and the mortar) to set up the defensive position. But if I sent out ten Marines, the fewest I could reasonably get away with, this would leave only fifteen to secure the platoon perimeter.

I dreaded the idea. My Marines would be moving through unfamiliar terrain in the dark—they had no night vision equipment—to where I would direct the setup of the ambush. That position had to be extremely defensible, secure, or it could expose them to counterattack or counterambush.

I checked first squad's gear to make sure they had flak jackets zipped and helmets buckled, with the strap tight under their chins. The guys preferred soft covers in the bush, which were more comfortable but provided zero protection. They also liked to leave their jackets open, due to the heat, but this exposed chest and stomach to bullets or fragments. There would be no "John Waynes" in my platoon. The Marines had not been used to this type of discipline, as their enlisted acting platoon commander had been "one of them." I suspected they were thinking, *What does this boot lieutenant know?*

Kruithoff and I coordinated our radio signals with the ambush squad. There would be only one report—in hushed tones—when they got to the ambush location. During the night, we'd do radio checks every hour. "First squad, radio check." Their only response would be to squeeze the transmit button twice. The double click would tell me all was okay.

After they left, it was 1900: time to set the first watch. With a full platoon, you wanted four men to each fighting hole. One would be awake as the other three slept. Each Marine had a two-and-a-half-hour watch. Everyone woke just before dawn, at 0500 hours. But with only two men per hole, we each had to stay up for five hours. I was dead tired, but I still expected to walk the lines at least once a night. I'd forgotten to eat one of the C-rat meals that you were supposed to consume twice a day. This was another item for discipline, as resupply provided meals for three days (six total), which weighed about twelve pounds, and so most of the troops would "eat up" the first day and be short on chow later. The next morning I had the premier breakfast meal, ham and mothers (lima beans). They were so terrible I never ate them again.

That first night, I didn't sleep a wink. I checked the lines five or six times and found what would be a recurring problem: Marines sleeping when they had the watch. I was uncertain how to handle this. Scold them? Put them on report?

Shoot them? I felt I had to make an example so when the ambush patrol returned the next morning I gathered the entire platoon, called out the Marines who had slept, and said if it happened again there would be severe consequences.

I asked my radioman—who would copilot our two-man fighting hole—how to keep my socks dry. Kruithoff snorted softly and spat. "We never have fucking *dry socks*, L-T."

"My feet are wringing wet," I whispered. Since it was dark, there was no talking out loud and no fires or use of flashlights, which could be seen from a long distance. "We can't march like this. We'll all get trench foot."

"Only way's to take 'em off at night and lay 'em on your chest. Then your body heat dries 'em out. But then you gotta take off your boots. And what if there's trouble during the night? You're fucked, stumbling around in your bare fucking feet." He shook his head in the near dark. "No, L-T, we don't dry out our fucking socks. And supply never has any extra pairs, so we can't alternate." Within the next weeks, I also learned that the jungle boots designed for the rice paddies did not drain water out through the "weep holes" that were perpetually clogged. So I cut holes in the top front of my boots and had my Marines do the same so water would not stay inside, adding more jungle rot.[7]

The other surprise that first night was that it got cold when the sun went down. Very cold. And sleeping bags were far too heavy to carry, along with all our other gear. I shivered in my wet uniform, damp boots, and soaking socks, leaning against the side of the hole, staring into the dark. The stars were out, but they were no comfort. Somewhere far off, I could hear muffled explosions. Closer by, Marines snoring, the cries of the night in a jungle with no artificial light or moon. I worried about what to do if something happened; how would I use my map if I had to maintain light discipline?

Was my platoon a crackerjack outfit? Or a hodge-podge of McNamara's 100,000? How would I get them to respect a boot lieutenant? Gradually I went from nervous to terrified.

I couldn't wait for morning. For all this to be ancient history.

5

FREE FIRE ZONE

1969: Quang Nam Province, Republic of Vietnam

As wise men have said, "All combat is small unit."[1] That's how it was in Vietnam. Though more than half a million American soldiers, sailors, airmen, and Marines were deployed, only a few troops actually faced the enemy man to man, rifle to rifle, on equal terms. Victory, or defeat, resulted from how these units located, closed with, and destroyed the enemy.

The Marine patrol was the core element of this combat truth. We weren't just the pointy end of the spear. We were the thin, glittering, razor-honed edge of the blade. And it would change those who survived for the rest of our lives.

⌒

After a sleepless night, and with one ambush under my belt, I was uncertain how good my platoon was and how much I could depend on them. I'm sure the feeling was mutual. Over the course of the next few weeks, as the realities of combat unfolded, both they and I would learn about each other.

That first morning in the field, I was determined to get started according to the manual, with the five-paragraph order. In the Corps and in the Army, that consists of Situation (the enemy and the friendlies), Mission (the objective), Execution (concept of operations), Logistics (beans, bullets, and batteries), and Command and Signal.

The typical procedure would be for the platoon commander (me) to call in my squad leaders and the platoon sergeant and give guidance for the day. They, in turn, would pass this to the fire team leaders and the rest of the platoon. But with only nominal squads and fire teams, it made sense to just have the whole platoon circle in and give the broad-brush picture all at once.

I'd done my map recon before calling them in. When I seemed to have everyone's attention, though some stares seemed blank or even hostile, I asked, "Any of this platoon been in this area before?"

I got more blank looks, shrugs, and head shakes.

"Okay. We'll be climbing up from the valley into those mountains." I pointed at the green foothills, but no one looked in that direction. "The NVA is moving supplies and men through there, to the southward. Our mission is to interdict their supply trails from the DMZ and look for concentrations. We'll be operating in a free fire zone. As you know, that means anything that moves is fair game. If we encounter anyone, they're hostiles and we'll treat them as such. Any questions?"

There were none. Next, I had each squad leader check his troops' gear. I wanted each man's helmet buckled, his flak jacket buttoned, and seven fully loaded magazines at hand, with another in the rifle. I wanted their M16s on semiautomatic, except for the point man's. In a major firefight, against a superior force, we would have to conserve ammunition. I told them to make sure we had two cans of machine-gun ammo (two hundred rounds per can, weighing about thirteen pounds), the right number of mortar rounds, grenades, and ammo for the M79 grenade launcher, plastic explosives, firing caps, full canteens, and entrenching tools (e-tools)[2] and that the corpsmen had all their medical supplies. And of course, I wanted their field packs properly organized.

Yes, someone should have checked all this before we left Ross. But we could theoretically put in for any supplies we needed on the admin network, and they'd be helo'd out to us on the march. What I didn't know but would learn, however, was that resupply often never came, and even when it did, one never got 100 percent of what had been asked for. I soon learned that a daily gear check on my part was unnecessary. My Marines were as keen on being "full combat rounds" as I was.

⌒

The Que Son range center of mass was about thirty-three kilometers due south of Da Nang and fifteen klicks west-southwest from LZ Baldy. They towered astride the Quang Nam and Quang Tin province borders, some of the steepest, roughest terrain in Vietnam, along with some of its densest virgin jungle. Due to both their location and their forbidding geography, the mountains provided significant cover for the NVA and Chinese, infiltrating troops, weapons, food, and ammunition down to the insurgency in the coastal plain. The Que Son Valley, which unfolded from the mountains to run down into the rice paddies and lowlands and eventually the South China Sea, was a fertile source of food and recruitment for the enemy and a strategic jumping-off point into the northern provinces.[3]

This was the home of at least two regiments and the famed Second Division of the North Vietnamese Army. Circa 1965, when the Marines had first gone in to reinforce the South Vietnamese government units in this area, the Que Sons had seen some of the bloodiest battles of the war.[4] The valley encompassed Route 14E, which ran between the southern A Shau Valley and its various interconnected paths that composed the Ho Chi Minh trail, in reality a major road complex stretching from the middle of North Vietnam through Laos and Cambodia into South Vietnam. In 1967, the Marines had turned this area over to the Army. Over the past few years, taking advantage of the Americal Division's lax patrolling, the NVA had built huge supply dumps, bunker complexes, field hospitals, and transshipment points in these mountains. Now the Marines had to take this territory back.[5]

To the casual eye, Que Son might look like a charming valley, climbing steadily toward the blue-green hill masses to the west. It was in fact a rugged transition zone between lowland grasses and scrub to higher and denser vegetation, and it held a multitude of challenges. In the beginning of the climb west, we wound through sunlight-exposed slashes of low brush, then denser shades of scrub and small trees taller than a man. Small open areas were dotted with large boulders and short grasses. It was ideal ambush country, as it was impossible to see more than ten meters in some areas and even less in others. We alternately wound through daylight and darkness. Regardless of shade, the sunlight and humidity soon reduced us to quiet, autonomous objects sweating in silence except for the occasional grunt or exhalation. It was just tough infantry slogging.

As we snaked forward, following the upward tilt of the land, we soon left the road and began to pick our way along trails. Visual references were soon lost in the heavy growth, which slowly began to isolate us not only in terms of sight but sound too. Soon we could only hear the tramping and labored breathing of the men within a few feet of us. Overhead, a constant escort of slowly circling hawks rode the thermal currents far above. I wished I could see what they saw. As we wound farther along the steepening grade, we became immersed in heavier and thicker green until we were consumed by the dominating and intimidating jungle.

It was easy to see that this green inferno had been fought over many times before. Every piece of high ground had the bald scrapings of an old LZ, the grave-like holes of an old firebase, even the shattered, ghostly remnants of a reinforced concrete French or Japanese observation post. When I called a halt and squatted to consult my map, it showed seven major hill masses and fourteen named firebases, all long abandoned. Along with the decaying fortifications, we skirted huge craters rippling with bright green jungle grass.

During some of the all-out battles during Tet '68, U.S. forces had called in B-52s from Guam and fire support from seaward. This had included the massive guns of the battleship USS *New Jersey*, whose sixteen-inch shells had been as heavy as Volkswagens.[6] Elements of other Marine and Army units had been repeatedly ambushed, trapped, and bled on this ground. That's how this silent jungle had earned its Marine name: Death Valley.

In August 1969, we, the 7th Marines, were once again being sent to sweep Death Valley clean. No one—not the French or U.S. forces before—had ever completely succeeded in clearing the enemy out of this redoubt. But those were our orders.

I didn't know any of this history then, nor did I fully understand the overall strategy that was sending us to write a new chapter in it. All I knew was what Van Riper had told me. My platoon's mission was to "close with and destroy" the enemy wherever we found them. And we'd be doing it the Marine way, on foot, with only what the individual rifleman could carry on his back and in his hands. We would clear these mountains with fire and maneuver. If we met a force larger than we could handle, I was to call in air or artillery support. I asked my guys as I finished my initial brief, "Who's our most experienced Marine?"

"Sir, it's Martinez. He's been in the bush two months."

He had to be a survivor. "I want him up front as point. Saddle up and move out."

Right behind point came the first fire team leader and his three-man fire team. Then me, followed by Kruithoff, with his whip antenna tied down and hidden from view. Any sniper seeing that ten-foot, long-range whip bobbling above the scrub would know there had to be an officer within a hand's reach of it.

As we continued to climb, the cover grew heavier. There were no trails or signposts now, and we had to move as covertly as possible. It wasn't long before we got out our machetes and started hacking. Not long after that, I had to keep my compass open in my left hand, constantly taking bearings, since the sky vanished as soon as we submerged under the canopy. There were no terrain features to navigate by, just my azimuth and sense of distance. I had to trust them and a compass to get us to our eight-digit overnight coordinates before dark.

I soon realized that I couldn't even stay back behind the first fire team. I had to be up front. This wasn't doctrine, but I had to make sure the point was heading in the right direction. And I'd never gotten lost in my infantry training. I'd aced all the land navigation tests. I halted the column and moved to where I could see the point man and keep him on course.

We hacked and chopped for a couple hours before stumbling out onto a barely passable trail. It seemed to be dead on the azimuth, so I kept us on it, though I hoped Martinez knew to watch for mines or trip wires. The now-dank rainforest soil was so wet and soft the vine-choked trees sagged in every direction as if drunk, unable to keep their footing. Our boots, too, slid in the slick mud, especially the boots of those who brought up the rear of the file, negotiating a trampled trail. We staggered under our loads, barely able to fight our way upward.

But we continued to climb, and eventually we broke into the clear on what I realized was the finger of a ridgeline, a steep ridge with a dizzying drop-off on either side, letting me look down onto the canopy from above. It was blazing hot in the open, and I found myself wishing for the monsoon rains I'd heard so much about.

The going was hard, so I let the men take frequent breaks. When we fell out, we got off the trail and into a defilade position on the sides, but I kept my point and rear always on watch. During one break, about midday, one of the guys spotted an abandoned cooking fire and discarded rice bags. Someone had bivouacked here before us. We spread that word via the hand signals that were our means of communication in the jungle. Through our torpor, we took on an added alertness.

Not long after the signal for halt, the clatter of a single M16 on full auto was followed by a torrent of fire as other Marines opened up to our rear and on our right flank. The rest of the platoon hit the dirt. I crawled back to the source of the initial contact. The rear guard had closed with and killed three NVA who'd been trying to bury themselves deep in the brush as we straggled by. They lay sprawled; men in tan uniforms with rubber-soled thong-type footgear. I collected their heavily greased AKs and threw their ammo downhill. I sent men out and back along our trail to ensure there were no more out there. We took the identification and documents off the bodies, and I called in the contact. I had no idea what they did in the rear with this information. We would turn in the captured papers and weapons at our next resupply.

Then we moved on. The entire episode took no more than ten minutes, but we had an objective to reach in time to dig in for the night. Also, now that our presence had been revealed, I wanted to move off this ridge quickly. I had no idea what the enemy did when a patrol didn't show up, whether they shrugged and wrote them off, or sent a battalion after those who'd vanished. We left the NVA dead where they fell.

Eventually, much later and after a far tougher climb than I'd expected, we reached a saddle between two higher terrain features. Our skipper had given us a night position where we could observe the high ground but not be on it. As we had the night before in the lowlands, we dug our fighting holes, chopping deep through the root-infested, greasy mud and leafy overlay. I called in the coordinates for our preplanned fires and positioned our claymores. This evening, though, I decided I'd go out with the nighttime ambush to see how my Marines did it.

In an ambush you absolutely have to stay awake all night, since you want to be the ambusher and not the ambushee. We were supposed to get a radio check from the rest of the platoon once an hour, but it never came. I wasn't going to break silence to demand it. I assumed whoever was supposed to be on the radio at the platoon command post had fallen asleep. Kruithoff had the first watch, then Maurone, then Bennington. There would be hell to pay when I got to the CP in the morning. Assuming, of course, I survived.

It was cold, boring, and nerve-racking all at the same time. I felt totally cut off from everything. Exposed and alone. There was no talking and no contact with the Marines on my left and right. Very quickly, darkness descended under the canopy. An eerie silence shrouded us. Occasionally, we saw phosphorescent flashes in the dark, probably insects and the eyes of small animals. Had the moon been full and overhead, it is doubtful its light could have penetrated.

At about 0300, I saw a flicker or gleam heading in our direction. Too dark to determine context, but I assumed it was an enemy patrol. As soon as the flicker was midway into our kill zone, we opened fire.

We caught them by surprise, as there was no return fire. After a brief period with no additional activity or movement, we reported in to higher HQ. I moved the ambush to another location, since we'd compromised our position. We weren't supposed to return to the kill zone until light.

As dawn broke, we went back. I walked out into the open trail where we'd caught the enemy patrol. Instead of NVA troops, four ragged, unarmed civilians—a man, a woman, and two children—lay in the trail, surrounded by their blood-soaked belongings. We'd killed a Vietnamese family. True, they'd been walking a forbidden trail, at night, in a free fire zone known to be a supply route. But this didn't make me feel better. I was so upset I could barely make myself understood on the radio. My hands shook.

Van Riper sounded sad, but it seemed as if he'd dealt with situations like this before. He said to secure the area. I gave a full report on how it had unfolded: the previous contact with hostiles, the gleams we'd taken for combat flashlights. Van Riper said, as I crouched in the whispering jungle, "This is Lima Six. This is unfortunate. But it wasn't your fault. The local government will take it from here. Go back to your platoon and continue on your objectives for the new day."

When we got back to the platoon, I called everyone in. I told them exactly what had happened, that the skipper had said it was unavoidable, that we'd done everything right and now just needed to concentrate on today's tactical objectives. There was no time or room for second-guessing. I couldn't let this affect either my Marines or my leadership, but I knew I would never forget it. In war, innocent civilians die alongside the combatants. But you never get over the sadness that your bullets killed them.

∽

By day three in the field, I was getting to know some of my men. The platoon CP, such as it was, consisted of myself, Kruithoff, and Docs Weiser and Langley, our corpsmen. Our platoon sergeant was actually a senior corporal.

The docs were total professionals. Langley was nicknamed "Red Angel" as he had a shock of far-longer-than-regulation scarlet hair. One of the most outgoing members of the platoon, he looked nothing like a squared-away Marine, but he knew his stuff. Weiser was quieter, but firm and effective both under fire and on the march. My troops liked and trusted both of them. For me, it began a lifelong respect and admiration for the Navy medical personnel who support and fight alongside Marines.

Lance Corporal Kruithoff was a knowledgeable radio operator, but no poster Marine. A tall, skinny New Jerseyan, he was always cracking jokes. Jimmy Buffett would have loved his pencil-thin mustache. As a reluctant draftee, he had no real interest in being in the service or in Vietnam. His major goal, other than ensuring that we could depend on our tactical communications, was going home in one piece, a goal none of us could disagree with.

An officer and his radio operator develop a close relationship. Kruithoff and I shared the same fighting hole. When it was hot, we sweated together. When it was cold, we huddled for warmth. I would share my letters, as he didn't get much mail. I was sad to see that the people at home seemed to blame our Marines for the war. Many of my men never got any mail or packages. Those who were more fortunate shared with the rest of our field family.

～

Another day, another patrol. Another ring of fighting holes and defensive positions. Settling in for another night, another ambush. And, once again, I walked the lines to find my men asleep when it was their watch. The first couple of times, I pushed the sleepers over the side of the hill. They woke to find themselves rolling down a steep incline. Some screamed, which wasn't good, considering we were trying to creep through the mountains unnoticed, but they got the message.

One of our defensive measures each night was to put out listening posts, LPs, in front of the perimeter, equipped with antipersonnel mines, on any avenues enemy scouts or sappers might use to sneak in on us. The M18A1 Claymore fired around seven hundred steel ball bearings, almost like a shotgun. It was essential to have this directional mine pointed the right way. Luckily, the green plastic cover of the convex mine read FRONT TOWARD ENEMY. This didn't help the Vietnamese Popular Forces we sometimes worked with, though, so we had to supervise them when they emplaced each mine. No one liked to be out on the LP, as he would be well out in front of our lines and even more exposed than the rest of the platoon. When I strode out to an LP and heard snoring, I knew I had to take decisive action.

The next evening, I took aside the Marine who'd been asleep during his watch. "You're flying solo on tonight's LP," I told him. Then I handed him a frag grenade, with the pin pulled.

"What the fuck, L-T?" he said, staring down at his hand. Needless to say, he had his fingers carefully curled around it to keep the spoon from flying off and the fuse from starting to burn.

"If you fall asleep this time, you'll wake up dead," I told him.

I didn't tell him or the rest of his buddies, but I did tip off Kruithoff and the docs that I'd unscrewed the weapon, taken out the cap, and put it back together without the primer. If he *did* fall asleep and loosen his grip, all that would happen would be the loud *clack* of the spring-loaded spoon separating from the grenade body. And we'd know it, since the spoon would be gone in the darkness and there was no way he could put it together again.

He came back in the morning and held out the grenade wordlessly. The spoon was still on it.

I had absolutely no trouble with lookouts falling asleep from then on.

After a couple of weeks in the field, though, I began to understand why I was facing this problem. I'd never been so tired. I felt dopey all the time. At night, it grew harder and harder to get up every two hours to check the lines. If we'd ever had our full complement of fifty in the platoon, it wouldn't have been as bad. But we never got anywhere near that number, even with replacements. Nor did any other platoon in the company.

⌒

While the coordinates and locations would change, we repeated the same deadly routine every day. Up at the crack of dawn, trudging for miles along ridgelines and saddles toward our next nighttime position. Clearing the areas en route. Setting out ambushes. Tension, C-rations, and too little sleep became my life as an infantry commander. The Marines called this "The 'Nam." Back home was not the United States but "the real world." I quickly lost track of days and weeks. All that mattered was morning, noon, and night. My world revolved around my patrol: the weather, the light, whether it was going to rain, and how much chow, ammo, bullets, and water we had to last until the next clatter of helo blades somewhere above the ever-present canopy meant another resupply had arrived.

Like the others, I quickly discarded my underwear, which was a sure recipe for the fiery, infected chafe we called crotch rot. With no way to wash except when it rained, and little clothing in the resupply, we began to stink, like . . . well, like grunts in the field probably always have. Field sanitation consisted of heading off the trail a few feet, taking a crap, and wiping as best we could. It was impossible to follow the field sanitation manual.

Serving under Van Riper meant never spending two nights in the same place. The jungle was incredibly hot during the day, as close and humid as a commercial laundry. Somehow, though, it managed also to be freezing cold at night, cutting through our thin utilities and light ponchos. Each day, we were up and on the line long before dawn, in case of attack. Then would ensue a long, slow, grueling day of cutting our way to the next night position, where we'd dig in all over again and throw out our LPs and ambush parties. Occasionally, as ordered, we would clear villages, or try to ambush NVA on a trail intel said was heavily traveled.

⌒

If you like Fourth of July fireworks, you would love a B-52 Arc Light Strike, the granddaddy of explosions. They would drop their 108 500-pound bombs in a one- to two-mile string and the explosives looked like a tsunami fireball moving across the valley. You could see the shock wave coming across the valley before you heard the ear-shattering sounds.

After a while, our ceaseless patrolling was interrupted by a message from Lima Six. Our next major activity would be to join up with Mike Company, 7th Marines, for a combined operation with some of the Vietnamese Popular Forces, or "PFs," as they were called. We would work with tanks and have air support. Van Riper told us to link up with Mike by moving down a "red line," a cleared road, until we hit a "blue line," a stream.

This was the first time I'd moved the platoon in the open, on something more than a trail, since we'd left the firebase. The impenetrable jungle had hidden the NVA from us, but it had also concealed us from our enemies. Just the thought of open sky made me feel like a mouse with hawks circling overhead. As we filtered down off a hill, the unmistakable growl of a heavy diesel engine came from somewhere ahead.

"Tanks," said Kruithoff, behind me. The guys seemed to perk up, like kids going to a circus. I felt the same way. With heavy armor around, we should be safer. No one would screw with us then.

As we neared our rendezvous, though, a tremendous explosion blew leaves down off the trees around us. We hit the deck and prepared for a firefight. I aimed my point man ahead. In the strange, hunchbacked, crouching jog men quickly learn in battle, he disappeared in the direction of what had now become a strange, muffled popping, like a string of wet firecrackers going off.

When he passed the "all clear" back, we rose and continued our march, more alert now. When we emerged onto the red dirt road, a huge, olive drab monster was burning and smoking fiercely, sloughed off to the side. The M48A3 Patton had hit an antitank mine dug into the roadway and was being consumed by bright orange, fuel-fed flames. The turret lay several yards distant, also burning. We detoured around it, warned off by the popping, which was machine-gun ammo cooking off. We threw a perimeter around the burning armor and waited for the medics. There was no sign of the crew. Later, after the vehicle had been towed to recovery, we heard that all that was left of them were the steel plates in their boots. We continued to the linkup. Once there, I was told my platoon was to provide security for the Mike Company CP, since its own platoons were already tied into the Popular Forces farther out. The commander had picked terrain that would not have passed the TBS test on Company in the Defense. I did the best I could to prep. Fighting holes, gun positions, and claymores . . . as usual. I also checked to ensure that the company's forward observer, FO, had planned his protective fires. (The FO was a lieutenant who, I was told, was the son of a famous actor.)

In the middle of the night, our LPs notified us that enemy sappers were moving on our position. NVA sappers, combat engineers, usually assaulted dragging satchel charges, which they either armed and threw, or left near bunkers or combat positions.

I woke the entire platoon and all the CP personnel. We fired illumination flares to try and spot the enemy, and soon an intense firefight erupted. This was the worst-case scenario: sappers in your outer perimeter. I loosened my KA-BAR in case we went hand to hand, scared shitless at the thought of close combat.

We had to keep them at a distance; sappers typically tried to close with us, hugging American troops, so we couldn't bring our firepower to bear. This time, it didn't look like the enemy was making it into our position. But before we could call off the attack helicopter support that had been requested, artillery shells began bursting . . . *within our perimeter.* The shock and flame was far worse than Dante's description of hell. Incredible, shattering noise, flying metal shredding everything it hit, and screams from Marines mauled by our own guns. The smoke of the high-explosive rounds was choking, even if the shrapnel didn't kill you. I was close enough to the CP to hear someone screaming, "Check fire, check fire." This was the command for an artillery battery to stop firing.

But then, I heard "Fire! Fire! Fire!" and in a matter of seconds, a second barrage from our 105s was howling in. The lieutenant had given the arty bad coordinates, and they were firing directly on *us.* In all the noise, the Fire Direction Center couldn't hear his frantic "check fire." They'd come back over the tactical net with "Say again, everything after check—" and the FO had yelled, "Fire, fire, fire." An error that tiny had sent another round of hell, death, and destruction onto us.

The sappers never got close to our defenses that night, and they didn't have to. Our own FO had single-handedly killed or wounded twelve of our Marines. We spent the rest of the night taking care of the wounded, medevacing the worst cases, and toe-tagging those killed in action.

The next morning we moved out. I never heard what, if anything, ever happened to that lieutenant, other than that he was ordered from the field back to the rear-area fire direction center. I just hoped I never got him on the other end of the fire control net supporting my platoon. There was nothing scarier than being on the receiving end of artillery or mortars. You couldn't outrun them, and the fragments shredded buildings and human flesh into tiny bits of scrap steel and meat. The NVA had a lot of Chinese-made mortars and knew how to use them.

The inaccuracy of artillery FOs got so bad that division put out an order requiring a white phosphorous air burst and ground burst before you could fire high-explosive rounds for effect. This was to ensure that Marines would not fire on other Marines, but when the air burst came, the enemy knew what was coming and got out of the area.

One night several days later, we'd reached our objective and were digging in for the evening in an area of high ground with some large rock formations, huge gray granite boulders, nearly the size of houses. The battalion's new supply officer, Second Lieutenant Deal, was spending a couple of days with my platoon to get a feel for the field.

All of a sudden, we heard the distant, hollow thunk of incoming mortars, then the unmistakable whistle of the rounds coming in. If you don't have a hole to jump in during an arty attack, the best bet is to get your ass as low to the ground as possible with as much cover as you can find. My guys were jumping behind the rocks and making like linoleum on the ground. Our own fighting hole was dug, however, so Kruithoff, Deal, and I rolled in. We pasted ourselves to the muddy bottom and waited.

Suddenly, inexplicably, Deal stood up. To look around? To see what was happening? We never knew. In an instant, while we were grabbing at him, another round went off almost in our fighting hole. It splintered him from the waist up. He'd been in country for only three days but would be heading back in one of those silvery coffins that were in such ample supply at Da Nang.

I didn't really know 2nd Lt. Oliver Evans Deal Jr. I'd had only a few words with him before his death. But what were they teaching them at TBS? As I sadly helped slide him onto the medevac chopper, I recalled my DI's admonition: you don't eyeball the area.

⁓

That death can come quickly and unexpectedly in a war zone should have been obvious. But in Vietnam, we never knew who was an enemy or who was a friend. And sometimes, whether an individual was a threat or a friendly depended on when and where you encountered him. The harmless civilian and the Viet Cong dressed the same. You had to be careful when you came up on an unfamiliar clearing, paddy, tree line, or village. There could be booby traps, punji pits, ambushes, or other death traps.

This was a war without a front line. We were trained to deal with snipers. What we weren't trained on were the soda girls who'd hawk Coca-Cola in the red and white cans for fifty cents. The Cokes were black market, stolen from U.S. supply. From time to time, even in the field, they'd find you. Their high, youthful voices would sing out in Vietnamese-English, "Kol sota." But the very first time we came across the soda girls, one of my guys spotted a Chicom grenade disguised as a Coke can. After that, anytime they came near, we put down warning shots and yelled "*Di di mau*," or "Get the fuck out of here."

I was also suspicious of the Chieu Hoi or "open arms" program. Designed by some idiot in the rear, it worked like this: if we came across an enemy soldier who might be persuaded to give himself up, we were supposed to yell "*chieu hoi.*" If he responded with the same phrase, we had to let down our guard and beckon him to approach. After the first couple of fake *chieu hois* who came into our lines with grenades strapped under their black pajamas, I put in my own program: No *chieu hois* after 1800, because we couldn't see what they were doing. After that hour, anyone approaching was treated as hostile, no matter what they called to us.

I couldn't feel it at the time, or didn't want to think about it, but I was changing. Yes, I was saddened by the death of the Vietnamese family. I didn't want to kill anyone else by mistake. But after experiencing the indiscriminate hell and destruction of war up close, I was now determined to protect my Marines at all costs.

❧

The northeast monsoon begins in September in central Vietnam. By early October, I don't think we'd been dry for a month. Days of intense rain during that first week prevented the helos from flying resupply, and I had several Marines coming down with malaria. The docs were busy.

Despite a downpour so heavy you couldn't see individual drops, just sheets, we trekked up a steep draw to flush out the enemy. To our surprise, we stumbled over Vietnamese living in bunkers under some enormous rocks on the hillside. The heavy rain gave us cover and enabled us to sneak up on a hooch undetected. Our discipline—and good fortune—was rewarded as we captured an NVA soldier. In two months of patrolling, we only rarely saw them. He had a kit bag full of medical gear, so we surmised he was a doctor. His mess kit contained a lot of rice that we kept and cooked for ourselves. Covered with C-rat cheese and combined with some cucumbers we found, we had quite the meal!

I always dreaded working with the Popular Forces even though their training was supposedly our ticket out of the war.[7] My rudimentary language skills helped us communicate, but they didn't always understand my accent.[8] I tried to teach them some of the fundamentals like noise and light discipline at night and the proper setup of the claymore mines, since they were always pointing them the wrong way. The only thing that made me really nervous was when they used fragmentation grenades to kill the fish in the streams. Back in Georgia, we just used bamboo poles, but then, we didn't have the PFs' brains.

One bright spot throughout the endless patrolling was Moe. He was a twelve-year-old Vietnamese boy who became my sidekick while we were protecting a bridge about four thousand meters from LZ Rock Crusher. He spoke great English and was smart as a whip. We ended up giving him much of our chow to bring to his mother and sister since his dad was wounded and in the hospital. To him, our C-rats were a top-notch meal. Most of the kids stole anything they could get their hands on, but Moe never did. He loved school and dreamed about going to college. He told me he wished there was no more fighting in his country so that the Marines would go home because, "U.S. is Marines' home; they want to be there. Vietnam is my home; I want to be here." Moe was definitely right about that.

$$\sim$$

November 10 is the birthday of the Marine Corps, the date it was established in a tavern in Philadelphia in 1775.[9] On November 9, I got the word to be at a certain position no later than 1000 hours the next day. We would be getting a Corps birthday cake, a pause from our fighting to remember the glories of the wars of the past.

We were all more than ready for a respite from the two extremes of boring, monotonous patrolling and the adrenaline-fueled blast of high-intensity firefights. A cake? Bring it on! We arrived early at the assigned coordinates, which turned out to be a clearing. I set up a hasty perimeter and we got our smokes ready to mark the landing zone for the CH-46 that would bring our treat.

Then we waited.

And waited. We kept getting traffic as the sun rolled downhill into the afternoon: "Stand fast, the cake is on its way." I cleaned and oiled my rifle and wrote a letter to home. My troops were smoking, shooting the breeze, and playing cards. Typically, during a lull it would be chow down, but we'd already missed one resupply and most of the troops had eaten all their six entrees and were down to gnawing their pack straps.

Eventually, I got nervous. There was no way we could dig in here for the night; it was lowland, wide open, and there were way too many avenues of ingress. I called Kruithoff over and got on the horn. "Skipper, we need to haul ass to our nighttime position. Somebody in the rear can eat our flippin' cake."

"Lima Six. Sure you don't want to wait? Chopper's on its way."

"Skipper, I've been hearing that since sunup. We're gonna saddle up."

"This is Lima Six. A reluctant green light on that. Out."

I was swinging my pack on when we got the word that the chopper actually *was* on the way, but they didn't have time to land. So it would be an airdrop, and we should pop a smoke to guide Capt. Glenn "Smoke" Burgess in.

This I had to see. Cake, airdropped? Sure enough, right then the growl and clatter of the chopper echoed through the valley.

The receiving unit always called the smoke color, so that if the enemy was listening he couldn't pop one too and lure the aircraft into a kill zone. "Advise, red and yellow," I told Kruithoff. To celebrate the red and gold colors of the USMC. Burgess came over the horizon low, but going flat out at about a hundred knots. Some hundreds of meters from us, the crew kicked a small pallet out the back. It fell so fast it must have had a rocket engine on it. With no parachute, at least we didn't have to worry about the NVA watching it floating to the ground and pinpointing our location that way.

When my troops got to the pallet, they sent word back. We'd waited all day for a five-gallon tin of ice cream that had turned into soup from sitting on the tarmac at Da Nang. After a terminal-velocity impact, it was now nothing more than vanilla paint splattered on the green foliage.

"Okay, saddle up," I yelled. "We gotta hurry to our nighttime position and dig in. Maybe we can ambush something more useful than melted ice cream."

⌒

The days became weeks, and the weeks months. Saddle up, move out, dig in, ambush . . . then start all over again. Constant danger blended with constant lulls. It was winter now. The weather turned rainy and much colder, and at night Kruithoff and I crawled under our "Snoopy blankets," our GI-issue poncho liners, and huddled spoon-fashion for warmth. Who said this was a tropical climate? Our utilities grew ragged, frayed at the legs and crotch, and rotted off us. My men became hollow-eyed, vitamin-depleted scarecrows. And still we patrolled. Had Codispoti forgotten about us? What great strategic goal were we accomplishing, out here?

You get to know people when you live together 24/7 in the most inhospitable conditions. We grew to respect each other, and my Marines gained confidence in my leadership for two primary reasons: I never got lost, and they knew I wouldn't put them in more danger than absolutely necessary. Although constantly alert, I gained an inner peace after I accepted that death was more likely than not and came to see that dumb luck was as important as sound tactics. Our entire world was our small platoon, our only tether to the larger universe a radio link to our company CP. We didn't see the bigger picture and we received no news.

As I concluded my fourth month in the bush on Christmas Eve 1969, and slid down a muddy mountainside on my backside into a B-52 bomb crater flooded by an orange liquid,[10] I thought things couldn't get much worse.

Boy, was I wrong. A few days later, Van Riper gave me the word. Division suspected they had a major element cornered on Hill 953. Regiment wanted us to move to contact and check it out.

Things were going to get a lot worse. For me, and for many of my Marines.

HOSPITAL

1970: Japan and Okinawa

After our helicopter landed, Corporal Hammonds and I parted company. They put me on a gurney with white sheets and rolled me out of the airlift. He got zipped into a black plastic bag and carried off into the night. A good Marine, going home.

I'd heard bad stories in the field about the 1st Medical Battalion, the major medevac destination for 1st Marine Division.[1] First Med "alumni" talked of chaos, confusion, and carelessness. And, true to the scuttlebutt, the corridors were busy. Still, I was almost immediately wheeled into a surgical suite, and doctors and nurses attached an IV and began to stick me with syringes. I snidely muttered, "Glad I'm not at First Med."

At that, one of the nurses leaned in to my face and hissed, "Welcome to First Med, Marine." The anesthesia kicked in then, and I was flat-out gone, unable to apologize to the people who held my life in their hands.

⌒

I woke the next day in what looked like a squad bay from back at OCS. It was long and narrow, with cots along both sides of the room, bone-white walls, and a puke-green tile floor. My lower back, backside, and right thigh burned like a steam iron was pressing them at high heat. Something was jabbing my cheek. I only gradually realized that someone had pinned a Purple Heart on my pillow while I'd been unconscious.

Some indeterminable time later, my battered brain, observing the rat's nest of tubes and needles leading in and out of my torpid self, slowly arrived at the conclusion that I must have had some sort of operation. Under the crisp white sheet, I was no longer wearing tattered, blood-soaked utilities, but was wrapped in a clean blue hospital gown. Nor was I alone. First Med was busy, my ward filled with other wounded men.

Not long after I woke up, a nurse came by. Leaning over me, she said, "Lieutenant, you're at Da Nang. But you're not staying here. We're going to medevac you to the hospital."

I blinked, puzzled. If this wasn't a hospital, where was I? As best I could figure, she must have meant I'd be flown out to one of the hospital ships off the coast. That would be a good deal: hot chow, hot showers, and a dry bed. And I didn't feel like hanging around this crowded ward full of moaning men any longer than necessary.

Within a few hours, the attendants had whisked me onto another gurney and were rolling me through the hallways. They loaded me on a C-141 Starlifter and we were on our way, not to a ship, but to Japan.

The aircraft had been converted to carry wounded. They slid my litter into a rack attached to the interior fuselage and somehow locked it in, or on. Several IV bags hung above my head. At least four plastic tubes still ran from my body in various directions, snaking out of my line of sight. One of those IV lines must have contained a pretty powerful opiate, since I don't recall much about the flight, though the groans from the other wounded on board are still seared into my memory.

⤿

When we landed, the crew carefully detached our litters and carried us to yet another helicopter. This next flight took us from Yokoda to the Naval Hospital at Yokosuka, our largest base in Japan. It would be my home for more than sixty days. Of course, I didn't know any of this then, nor, with the morphine drip, would I have much cared. It wasn't until I was in a nondescript (but more private) hospital room that I was eventually informed where I was and what was happening. A stony-faced surgeon told me my wounds were serious. First Med hadn't been able to do much more than stabilize me for transport to a dedicated facility, where I could actually be taken care of properly.

There were two other guys in the room. Next to me lay Lt. Eric Chase, the Lima Company 3rd Platoon commander, who'd been shot earlier the same day as myself and whose platoon had been folded into mine. Our third roomie was Lt. Bert Farley, from 2nd Battalion. Eric had a through-and-through gunshot wound in his leg. Bert had ugly, constantly bleeding shrapnel slashes and punctures all over his upper torso. All three of us had been in the bush for months, and we looked and smelled like it. We were unshaven, our hair as long as any of the hippies I'd sneered at. We had jungle dirt and sores everywhere that could be seen and places that couldn't.

I received strict instructions from the head nurse not to get up. Fine, I didn't feel like dancing. Still, without a bite of anything for two days and the pain meds starting to wear off, I was heartily pleased to see a "room service" mess attendant deliver three trays with metal covers.

Unfortunately, what was underneath the lids must have been hijacked from the pediatric ward. It was nothing more than pablum and Jell-O. My roommates hadn't fared any better. We exchanged outraged glances. Time for a food riot! All three of us pushed our call buttons at the same time. A couple of nurses scrambled in, assuming we were in distress. Our outraged demand for real food was the first of several actions that would land us at the top of the hospital bad actors list.

We cemented this position the next day when the commandant of the Corps visited our floor. The head nurse—a woman I only remember as Sam—told us that we were too unsightly and smelly, not to mention obstreperous, for the commandant to see. Since we couldn't stand at attention, he wouldn't be coming to our room.

But my bed had a line of sight to the hall. When an entourage of colonels and light colonels passed by, accompanied by physicians in white coats, I let out a very loud Marine Corps yell: "OORAH!"

Gen. Leonard F. Chapman Jr., the 24th commandant, was a World War II veteran, with decorations from Peleliu and Okinawa.[2] He'd seen his share of bloody, wounded men, I'm sure. And maybe that was why, when I called, this small man with the tired-looking eyes turned on his heel from the doctors, who were still talking to him, and walked into our room.

We couldn't come to attention, but we could sound off. "Sir! Lt. Punaro. Lima Company, 3rd Battalion, 7th Marines," I snapped out, or at least tried to.

"Lieutenant, what the hell happened to you?" the general asked.

I started to go into my story, but Nurse Sam interrupted. "General, this room was not on your stop. You need to get moving on to the wards."

Bert piped up then. "Sir, the nurses said we were too dirty for you to visit. Plus, we're too weak to stand at attention. But it's no wonder, they don't give us any real chow."

This got Chapman's attention. He turned to his aide and, reaching into his attaché case, pulled out three Purple Heart medals. He presented each of us one and thanked us for our service. Now I had two. "You look like combat Marines to me," Chapman said. "Get well quick. We need you lads back in action." He looked sharply at Nurse Sam. "And get these men some damn chow, if that's what they want!"

‿

A couple weeks later, I headed into surgery for wound repair. They were going to give me a spinal anesthetic, not general since both my wounds—the entry in the lower back and the gaping exit wound in the right thigh—were too large for standard sutured closures. Two yellow happy pills elevated me to euphoria. I lay on the operating table contentedly listening to the medical team discuss step by step how they were sewing me up with metal wire.

After I was wheeled into the recovery area, the post-op nurse told me that under no circumstances was I to get up and move around. But I was feeling no pain, and I had noticed some young enlisted guys in recovery with me. Why not check on them? I did a handshaking tour, and then climbed back onto my gurney before I was caught, gloating over how quickly I'd recovered from surgery. Stupid nurse.

Once I was back in my room with Bert and Eric, though, a dull pain built inside my head. My skull was preparing to explode. It was a spinal headache, created by the differing pressures from the tap and by getting up and cruising around. No matter how well-intentioned, I'd set my recovery back. I rang for the nurses and told them, "My head is killing me!" They knew right away what had happened. "The doctor has no pain medication on your chart. You're shit out of luck, Marine," Nurse Sam gloated.

"Call him. Please," I begged. "This is awful. My head feels worse than my wound."

"No, Lieutenant. We *told* you not to get up. This is not an emergency."

All night long I was moaning and groaning.

But even that agony paled in comparison to the mental anguish I continued to suffer lying in bed at night and reliving the attack on the hill, thinking primarily about Hammonds' sacrifice. What could cause a man to choose the life of a fellow Marine over his own? Why would someone so close to going home risk his life for a guy he'd never met, who wasn't even in his unit? I had no doubt that the bullets that had torn through his protective gear would have ripped me to shreds had he not thrown himself between me and the snipers. Greater love hath no man than this, that a man lay down his life for his friends.[3]

But we weren't friends. Just fellow Marines.

Night after night, lying there, this was the only answer I came up with: Hammonds had done what warriors have done through the ages: take care of their comrades, no matter the cost.

His sacrifice would remain seared in my soul forever.

～

A couple of days later, when I was finally able to limp to a phone, I called my parents, collect. Dad, on the other end, said, "From who? Where?" He yelled to my mother, "It's Arnold . . . how much is this gonna cost?"

"Dad, just accept the call!" I muttered.

Mom got on the line. The first thing I told them was that I was basically okay, but was in Japan because I'd been shot.

They received the news with the stoicism of spartan parents. Sure, they asked about my well-being and recovery, but they remained so calm, as if I'd just gotten home from school and they were wondering how my day had been. Probably they were just relieved I was still alive. I asked them to send money, since I'd been separated from my pack and other belongings sometime between being shot and arriving at First Med.

I also asked them to get the word out back home so folks could start mailing some care packages our way. The chow hadn't improved, outside of that one meal the commandant had ordered. But the packages weren't just for us. We weren't the only Marines in that hospital, and a lot of the others didn't seem to have much of a support system back home.

∽

I recovered. Slowly, the wounds began to heal. Rehab was rudimentary, but we had to show up or get put on report. The wounded never stopped coming and there was never enough equipment or personnel.

We spent a lot of time with the enlisted, including those from my and Eric's platoon who'd been wounded in the same action. Several of the pilots who'd been hit trying to medevac us were also at that hospital. In the course of our conversations, we pieced together what had happened. We'd come across the forward element of a large enemy concentration that had gone on to attack our battalion headquarters at LZ Ross two days later.

In that later battle, Ross had been pounded by hundreds of rounds of mortar fire, followed by an overwhelming assault. Thirty-eight NVA had been killed, some inside the wire, with thirteen Marines KIA and sixty-three wounded. Many of those Marines were in the hospital with us. Clearly, the enemy had been determined to keep my platoon from discovering their massing of forces for the attack.

To this day, I still don't understand why regiment didn't send in a force after our contact to determine exactly what the NVA were doing. Maybe they could have prevented those thirteen Marines from dying at LZ Ross.

∽

Two months after arriving at the naval hospital, I finally talked the doctors into releasing me. They wanted me to stay a few more weeks, but my wounds had healed enough for me to return to full duty. I was headed to Okinawa, then back to Vietnam. After all, I still had six months left on my in-country tour.

Or at least that was what I expected until I arrived at the same airfield in Okinawa where we'd refueled seven months earlier. When I got off the plane, though, the liaison at the clerk's desk said I needed to catch a bus to the HQ Marine Corps Base, Camp Butler. I'd get further instructions there.

Camp McTureous, about twenty-seven kilometers from Kadena Air Force Base, was the location of MCB Camp Butler HQ. There I discovered I was being assigned to the G-3 shop, responsible for operations of the Marine bases on Okinawa, with the 3rd Marine Division, as an assistant training officer.

I gaped at the lance corporal in the personnel office. "I'm supposed to go back to 1st Marine Division!"

He eyed my medical records. "Not anymore, Lieutenant. Orders from LBJ himself. Any wounded troop hospitalized for more than sixty days out of country can't go back to the 'Nam."

"Okay . . . I guess . . ." I felt both guilty and relieved, a strange combination. I'd expected to return to my men, and to combat. But now I wasn't? "Then when do I go back to the States?"

"When your overseas control date's up in September. About six months from now."

This wasn't good news. The medical board said I was ready for full duty again, and I'd worked hard at therapy to get there. But now, because of a no-doubt well-meant political decision, I was nondeployable and couldn't go back to combat. But since I hadn't completed my thirteen months overseas, the Corps wouldn't send me home, either.

I protested, but the clerk just shrugged. "Ain't no good kicking it upstairs, L-T. This here is cast iron. Sorry."

⟋

This desk job on Okinawa was the worst half-year of my life. Boring, tedious paper pushing. Busywork. The only action I saw was against some of the local residents who were protesting the Marine presence on Okinawa. I put in Administration Action forms time and time again to go back to Vietnam and even requested mast with the commanding general, Brig. Gen. Bob Barrow. The answer was always the same. No.

The only duty there I didn't really mind was escorting senior officers who were transiting Okinawa on their way back from Vietnam to the States. One day, I shared that job with another lieutenant who'd been in my Basic School company, Frank Neubauer. He'd been wounded serving with 2nd Battalion. The Code 6, which is for a full bird colonel, on the plane was our former regimental commander, Gildo Codispoti, the one who had gruffly welcomed me to Vietnam, given me the "dry socks" nonadvice, then sent my platoon straight into an ambush. Neubauer and I met him planeside and said, "We're from 7th Marines." He seemed glad to see us, but he also acted overly concerned with making sure his luggage made it onto his United States–bound plane. So Frank escorted him to the waiting area while I took care of the colonel's luggage.

I'm very much afraid that I gave way to temptation and decided to *really* take care of him. I located his sea bag and several trunks and pulled off all their destination tags. Then I slapped on new ones, forwarding them to the "dead luggage" section at Camp Hansen. Dead luggage was where belongings from Marines killed in action were sent to be sorted before being expressed home to the next of kin. We put the good colonel back on the plane after a couple of drinks, and he expressed himself pleased that I'd made sure his luggage went to the right place.

I never heard any more about this until decades later, when I was the staff director of the Senate Armed Services Committee and my old company commander—then Colonel Van Riper—and I were reminiscing. Somehow Codispoti's name came up. Van Riper said, "You won't believe what happened to him . . ." Somehow, Codispoti's luggage had gotten misrouted coming back from Vietnam. The dead luggage section on Okinawa had gone through it and found a lot of contraband, including automatic weapons he'd been trying to sneak back into the States. Codispoti had gotten in a lot of trouble and had been forced to retire from the Corps.

For those Marines wounded and killed on January 4, 1970, some small measure of justice had been meted out, after all.

As the end of my thirteen months in country drew closer, I decided I wanted to return to the Washington, DC, area because it was on the East Coast and close enough to home. Plus, Van Riper had told me Quantico was an ideal place for first lieutenants. Since I had more than two years left on my four-year obligation, I worked my butt off to get back to TBS.[4]

At last, my next set of orders arrived. I was to report to MCB Quantico.

BACK IN THE REAL WORLD

1970–73: Quantico, Virginia, and the University of Georgia

The spirits of the nearly two hundred Marines lifted faster than the aircraft itself as we took off from Kadena. Nearly all of us had completed thirteen-month combat tours. As the wheels went up, a cheer erupted, with high fives and smiles all around. But it was also sobering to think we'd survived when so many of those who'd come over with us had not.

As a senior first lieutenant, I'd been designated the plane commander. But my only order on that thirteen-hour ride came right after takeoff. I yelled, "The smoking lamp is lit."

⌒

We touched down near Seattle, Washington, before our final destination, Norton AFB in Los Angeles. I visited with a few high school friends in the area who'd also fought in Vietnam. From there, I stopped in New Orleans to pick up my car from my younger brother Vincent.

It's a seven-hour drive from New Orleans to Macon. All through it, I mulled over the past year, wondering if I'd made the best decisions in combat. I wasn't inclined to second-guess my actions, but as excited as I was to get back to my loved ones, I found myself pulling over and sobbing uncontrollably several times on the way. Weeping for those Marines who'd never make it back. But eventually I got a grip, and as I pulled up the driveway at last, relief settled over me like an air-conditioned breeze. I no longer had to worry about tripping a booby trap or becoming a target for a sniper. I was no longer constantly cold, wet, and hungry. Nor bored with a meaningless job, as I'd been on Okinawa.

In my room at home, all my gear was in the same place, and the daily routine of Mom and Dad heading out to work hadn't changed. Visiting my high school classmates quickly snapped me back into early 1970s America. Everyone was glad I was back safely, but no one seemed interested in what it had been like over there. Dinner-table conversation with my parents and Frank, Michael, and Trudie, my only siblings in town, revolved around family and friends, never anything military.

After a week in Macon, I headed to my next assignment.

⌣

September 1970. Unlike the first time I'd driven through the gate at Quantico, reporting to OCS, I had zero apprehension as I drove the same Chevy past the sentry. This time, instead of barking orders, he snapped off a salute at my shiny silver first lieutenant's bars. The base HQ assignment officer said, "Welcome aboard, Lieutenant Punaro. You've actually been assigned to the Basic School, so you need to go check in over at Camp Barrett."

MCB Quantico is bisected by I-95. East of the interstate is mainside: the sleepy little town of Quantico, and the PX, commissary, and a number of administrative commands strung out along the shore of the Potomac. At this point, the river is wide and slow, serpentinely meandering its way down to the Chesapeake. West of I-95 is Camp Barrett: TBS, Weapons Training Battalion, the FBI Academy, and hundreds of acres of dense, thick, tick-crawly woodlands. These woods make up the training areas and live fire ranges. The terrain is steep and hilly, and in the summer the undergrowth fills in with azalea, wait-a-minute, blackberry, and plenty of poison ivy.[1] Aside from the low elevation, it didn't look all that different from the Que Son Mountains, actually.

I was glad to discover that Eric Chase and Jay Kerney, both now lifelong friends, would be coming to OCS when their overseas tours were up. Jay had been in both my OCS and TBS platoons, and we would become roommates. At OCS, Eric and Jay would turn candidates into officers, and at TBS I would transform them into warriors.

I drove over to Camp Barrett and reported in with the NCO in Heywood Hall. "Lieutenant, you've been assigned to Alpha Company 1-70. Major Downs is the commander. The company office is right down the hall."

TBS company commanders were handpicked by the CO of TBS, who was handpicked by the commandant. It's one of the most prestigious billets in the Corps. Many go on to make general, such as Maj. Michael Downs, my new CO, who was married to Martha Puller, daughter of the legendary Marine Lewis B. "Chesty" Puller. Compared to Chesty's five Navy Crosses, memorable quotes, and ever-present cigar, John Wayne was a wimp.[2] I never met Chesty, but Marines revered his warrior legacy. The executive officer, or XO, was Capt. Dick Trapp, a ramrod-straight no-nonsense Marine, the all-consuming, make-it-happen action officer. Trapp told me I would be the training officer for Alpha Company, since the previous occupant of that billet had just left active duty. Alpha had started earlier in June. It was the first training company of the year and was filled with recent Naval Academy and NROTC graduates.

The mission of TBS is to "train and educate newly commissioned or appointed officers in the high standards of professional knowledge, esprit de corps, and leadership to prepare them for duty as company grade officers in the operating forces, with particular emphasis on the duties, responsibilities, and warfighting skills required of a rifle platoon commander."[3] Just being selected to be on the staff was an honor. I later learned that my battalion commander had rated me as the top second lieutenant in 3/7. It took luck and connections to get to Quantico, but my combat record got me to TBS.

The captains and first lieutenants assigned to TBS were all hardened combat veterans and masters of their profession. One of Alpha Company's staff platoon commanders, or SPCs, was Toby Strange, a Silver Star recipient (the nation's third highest award for valor). He would be another of my roommates. Toby looked so much the part of a Marine he was featured in recruiting ads by J. Walter Thompson. Also in the Instructor Battalion were two Medal of Honor recipients, Capt. Harvey "Barney" Barnum and Capt. Wes Fox. They taught mortars. Platoon-level tactics was taught by Capt. Oliver North and Capt. Lee Gound. Lee had been one of my own TBS class's staff platoon commanders.

I didn't fit the mold of the stereotypical TBS staff officer: a career-minded lifer who saw the assignment as a fast track to the top. When I'd signed up in '68, I'd never intended to make the Corps a life's work. With a little more than two years on my short-timer's clock, I took my duties seriously but knew I would be returning to the civilian world, and so I didn't get too caught up in the careerism I saw around me.

The majority of the officers on staff were bachelors, with apartments in Woodbridge or Occoquan, just north of base, up I-95. I formed the WOBOC, the Woodbridge-Occoquan Bachelor Officers' Club. Back in those days, before the crackdown on alcohol abuse, the officers' club was filled every night for happy hour. Our standard operating procedure during the week was to buy several cases of Rheingold Chug a Mug beer and a couple of Manny Moon's pizzas and drink until we were blitzed. As a training officer, I honchoed the daily schedule, making sure the classroom academics, field training, military skills, physical training, chow, and study halls were run with precision. I coordinated all the "supporting fires": instructors, audio-visual equipment, training camps, transportation, and field gear. The job required close attention to nitpicking detail, and it was good training for some of my future duties.

After Alpha graduated that November, I moved over to headquarters and became the assistant student activities officer to Major Nebel, an aviator who was being pushed out of the Corps. He was a victim of the "up or out" promotion system, as he'd been passed over twice for lieutenant colonel.[4] Nebel didn't care what we did, so it was a cushy job, and we had a full-time civilian who did all the real work.

Col. George Smith assumed command of TBS in June 1971. About the same time, Maj. Gen. Louis "Lou" Wilson took over as director of development and education on the mainside. Wilson was a World War II Medal of Honor recipient whose nickname was "the Cobra."[5]

Colonel Smith always wanted events to go smoothly when General Wilson was involved. I'd shown some knack for planning and working social events, so once Nebel left I became the acting head of student activities, though it was a lieutenant colonel's billet. I worked directly with Smith and Col. Billy Max Adrian, the new XO. I was in charge of all the nontactical activities for all the companies. This included welcome aboard mixers, wives' tours, graduation receptions, and the student Mess Night, a formal dinner in dress uniform.

I probably wouldn't have made a good tactics instructor since I'd so often discarded approved tactics in Vietnam. But I soon mastered the art of running social events. This required diplomacy, understanding protocol, and making sure parties and dances weren't just properly catered, but enjoyable. I learned then that officers' wives command a lot of influence. I made sure I had their ear. It was an early lesson in Washington ways: if you don't mind kissing some butts, you can go far. There were actually many such events, but they were baked into the schedule, so I knew in advance what had to be done when. My routine was to get to work between 0700 and 0800. Around 1130, I'd head over to the gym to play some pickup basketball. After that, I'd PT on my own, usually running either the three- or five-mile loop. I still hated running, but I made myself do it. Afterward, I'd either do a quick swim or relax in the sauna before lunch on the mess deck and then back to my desk by 1330.

The Marine Corps has always been fanatical about its members staying in shape. So no one ever complained when we were out of the office midday for several hours doing PT. In fact, it was expected. If there wasn't a dinner or event that evening, I could leave work late in the afternoon, since no one would be looking for me. At least that's what I thought.

The TBS training schedule condensed two years' worth of instruction into six months. With multiple companies on deck, at various stages, the instructors and SPCs were busy morning, noon, and night. Because there were so many field exercises, there was always a need for alternate instructors, or AIs. Everyone on staff was supposed to pull AI duty for the company tactics section, which was by now run by Maj. Roger Simmons and one Capt. Oliver North, a popular, charismatic officer. Both were squared-away Marines who looked and acted the part. They had the high and tight haircuts, impeccably starched utilities, spit-shined boots, and gleaming brass. They worked and acted like studs. Unfortunately, Simmons was also a by-the-book officer, inflexible and stuffy, representing everything bad about lifers. Ollie was the opposite: the most popular instructor, outgoing, and with an endless stream of war stories. But when my name came up, my assistant, Linda, would always tell Simmons, based on my instructions and on my feeling I'd been miserable enough in the Vietnamese jungle for ten lifetimes, that I had a "student activity" that precluded my participation.

I had a squawk box in my office so Smith could hit a button and talk directly to me. One afternoon, his voice crackled over it, "Lieutenant Punaro, come down to my office right away." This wasn't unusual. I figured it was a pop-up VIP visit or something similar. I hustled down and his secretary waved me in. And there was the XO, Colonel Adrian, with Simmons and North. All looking as judgmental as the Spanish Inquisition, with triple rows of colorful ribbons: two colonels, one major, one captain against a lowly first lieutenant.

Smith murmured ominously, "Ah, here he is. Arnold. Major Simmons here says you're our only staff officer who refuses to do any alternative instructor duty. Can that really be true?"

I had no response ready, so the truth was my only possibility. "Yes, sir," I said. Simmons and North beamed at him triumphantly, like they'd just nabbed Al Capone.

Colonel Smith didn't look pleased. "Why exactly is that, Lieutenant?"

For some reason, I figured a quip might go over better than the unvarnished truth. I just couldn't tell an iron-hard Marine like George Smith that I hated field-work. "Sir, I don't have any utilities." This is the standard USMC field uniform and every officer is required to have at least six starched and ready to go at all times. Which, of course, I did.

The moment of silence felt like a lifetime.

"There you have it. He doesn't have any utilities. So he can't do it. Thank you, Arnold," Smith said, squinting at me in a manner that suggested I was dismissed. I hurriedly left.

I asked Linda to find out, girl to girl, from Smith's secretary, Dottie, what had been said after I left. Smith had told Simmons and North that I was his direct report and my activities were important to our standing with the command. They were to leave me alone; I would not be standing in as a tactical instructor as I had evening events to run. The word got around, and from then on I had folks kissing my butt instead of vice versa.

⤿

As bachelors, we definitely drank too much. I don't know if it was just a different time, before Mothers Against Drunk Driving changed the perception of heavy drinking, or if we were all just trying to blow off steam after combat deployments. Because antiwar sentiment was still strong, it was awkward to hang out in civilian bars. With our telltale "high and tight" haircuts, it was never long before some sort of riot ensued. We did find one dive that welcomed us with open arms, Matt Kane's Bit O'Ireland at the intersection of Thirteenth and Massachusetts. Kane ran an old-school pub that smelled of stale cigarettes and Guinness. A lot of mid- and senior-level officers from Headquarters frequented it after work and on weekends, including P. X. Kelley, a future commandant.

I almost didn't survive one such evening.

One of the charter members of the WOBOC was driving his sleek green Stingray convertible. I was riding shotgun. We were headed home from a night out when the cops pulled us over on Sixteenth Street, a couple blocks from Kane's. Clearly they'd targeted us because we'd just come from there. He spectacularly flunked the sobriety test and was cuffed and hustled away on the spot. For reasons still unknown, the police left me sitting there in the passenger seat.

I was, obviously, going home in his Vette. With my heart still thumping after such a close brush with the law, I carefully navigated to I-95 south and began the twenty-minute drive back to my apartment. After several miles, my shakiness subsided and the law faded from memory. I decided it was a great night for getting some air. I pulled over just south of the Beltway—the highway that encircles DC—after which point the traffic on I-95 lightened considerably, especially at that hour, and put the top down. Before long, I was standing, hands braced on top of the windshield, steering with my knees. I blew past a truck stop at a hundred miles an hour.

The next morning I crouched in my apartment, hungover as hell, and remembered lying face down in that creek in Vietnam. Then parting ways with Corporal Hammonds for the last time when we disembarked the helicopter. I owed it to him, and to every other Marine who hadn't come home, to do more with my life than this.

This kind of behavior wouldn't be tolerated in today's Corps. In some areas, however, we've overcorrected. In the field, our officer corps is made up of magnificent warriors. In the rear, they can be magnificent bureaucrats. Would those who were hell raisers but aggressive leaders, like Pappy Boyington, Chester Nimitz, or Chesty Puller, be tolerated in today's military? Probably not. But there's a difference between poor social behavior and the check-the-box personnel management system that governs today's military. An organization that promotes only non-risk-takers will end up with sheep for its senior officers.

⌒

Just before my tour at TBS was set to end in August 1972, I reconnected with Jan Fitzwilliam. My uncle, Father Frank Benedetto, head of the physics department at Loyola, came to Washington several times a year on business. He'd grown up with Jan's mother, Anita, and remained close to her. My mother was one of Anita's closest friends. Whenever Uncle Frank came into town, he'd have dinner over at the Fitzwilliams' house in Falls Church.

~

JAN

My parents told us that since they had six daughters to educate, they'd take care of the first two years of school and the rest was up to us. I decided to take liberal arts courses to keep my options open. After receiving my associate's degree on a work-study program at Immaculata Junior College, I worked for the Tariff Commission doing statistical analysis. I was determined to finish my bachelor's, and I went to school part-time while working full-time. I found I enjoyed economics and decided to major in that.

After working for a couple of years I received a scholarship to Loyola University in New Orleans, as did my sisters, Monet and Fran. I loved finishing my last two semesters in the Big Easy. Although the scholarship paid for room and board, tuition, and books, I had no regular income. I had some money saved but definitely not enough. I still wanted to shop, eat beignets and sip coffee at Café Du Monde in the French Market, visit the local watering holes while listening to jazz, and try all the famous restaurants. It was also traditional to take out-of-town guests to Pat O'Briens, a tourist place, for Hurricanes; so much fun! I ended up incurring what was at the time serious credit card debt: $5,000.

After college, I moved back to DC, worked full-time at the newly named International Trade Commission during the day, and nights and weekends at Lansburgh Department Store. That, plus saving money by living at home, let me pay off that crushing debt.

Arnold and I finally crossed paths again when I was twenty-two. He was twenty-four at the time. His uncle Frank was often a dinner guest at my parents' home. Just before one such visit, my mother realized that Arnold was stationed close by in Quantico, and since his uncle was already invited, he got an invitation too.

Arnold looked sharp, with his "high and tight" haircut, pressed khaki pants, and dark blue golf shirt with the Marine insignia. As soon as he walked in the door, he cracked, "Anita, I'm happy to be coming here of my own volition rather than being coerced by Clifford." As soon as I saw him, it brought me back to that summer night in Macon when we were both teenagers. The dinner was filled with jokes, reminiscing, friendly banter, and great food and wine.

One Saturday, a month afterward, Arnold showed up at the Lansburgh Department Store, liberally doused with Brut. He told me, "I'm helping my buddy

Pat shop for a birthday gift for his wife, Trish." That's when I knew he was interested. Pat and Arnold lived practically across the street from a shopping center, but they'd driven an extra half hour to buy the gift from me.

‿꙼

ARNOLD

I hadn't seen Jan since high school, when she'd come to Macon to visit her grandmother. We started dating a couple of months before I got out of the Corps. At first neither of us was serious about anything but having fun. Jan fit right in with our party-hearty crowd, whether it was bar hopping, dinner parties, or the military social events.

As I said, I'd never intended to make the military my life. I wasn't a gung-ho, Oliver North type. I'd known from day one that I'd do my time, serve my country, and leave. Nothing I'd seen so far had shaken this plan. Even though I'd been advised by Colonel Smith and other senior officers that I could have a good career in the Corps, it had never appealed to me.

The reason was simple. I'd realized, particularly during my stint on Okinawa, that in the service your impact and respect were so closely tied to rank that little room remained for intelligence, energy, or initiative. No amount of effort would get me promoted faster than my peers. There was no incentive for top performers. Three-plus years to captain, five more to major, six more to lieutenant colonel, another six to full bird colonel. This timeline generally holds for every single officer. And because when I saw something stupid I tended to *say* it was stupid, that was a handicap. Despite encouragement from my seniors to stay, I was going to follow my original plan to get out when my obligation was up and finish my education.

I'd been interested in journalism from my time on the high school paper and as editor of my college paper. I wanted to be an investigative reporter. I longed to uncover misconduct, particularly in government, and expose it; to right wrongs. I researched graduate work at Columbia, Northwestern, Missouri, and, of course, the University of Georgia Grady School of Journalism. Frankly, I didn't have my pick, since my undergraduate grades weren't great, but I'd scored well on the graduate record exam. Not that it mattered, since I couldn't afford most of those schools anyway, even with the GI Bill.

Since Georgia was my home state, though, that meant I could get in-state tuition at UGA. Plus, it was close to Macon. I'd be lying if I didn't say the UGA team, the Bulldogs, didn't also factor into my decision. Georgia accepted me with the understanding I'd have to take a quarter of undergraduate classes.

I left TBS on a sunny Saturday morning, after saying goodbye to Jan. We'd promised to visit each other often. Leaving Quantico in my rearview mirror was as exhilarating as when our flight had lifted off from Okinawa two years earlier.

I was a civilian again. I was free.

$\backsim$

Since I needed to excel to be admitted into the master's program at Grady, I spent my first semester engrossed in study. This time, I wanted good grades.

I spent all my free time during the week and on weekends at the main library, at the edge of a hill on the north side of campus. Halfway down the hill, the Grady College of Journalism is covered in glass, its modernism a stark contrast to the classical facades of North Campus. At the bottom lies Sanford Stadium, where the Bulldogs play "between the hedges." To the north spreads the idyllic North Campus. Red brick buildings frame quads shaded by towering oaks. Abraham Baldwin, developer and founding president of UGA, was a Yale grad. He modeled the campus plan on that institution. At the very top of North Campus is the Arch, the most recognized symbol of the university. It was an unwritten rule that current students couldn't walk through the Arch if they wished to graduate on time, so it was a rite of passage to finally pass through those three iron pillars after graduation day.[6]

My grind paid off. I made straight As and was admitted to grad school. I continued that year with an almost perfect record; my only blemish was a lone B. When I wasn't in class or the library, I wrote sports reports and columns for the *Red & Black*, the daily student newspaper. I also wrote a humor column. I liked seeing my byline in print.

Jan often came down to visit me in Athens that year, and any time I had a break, I'd hop in my Vega and drive ten hours up to Falls Church. Over the year of grad school Jan and I had gotten more serious. As graduation day neared, we both sort of knew we'd get married. This made me think about getting back to the Washington area, where she had a good job with the International Trade Commission.

My dreams of being an investigative journalist focused on the *Washington Post*. The Watergate scandal dominated coverage during 1972–73, and I fancied myself a future Woodward or Bernstein. Then one day in the Tate Student Center, I spotted a flyer on the job board about an internship with Georgia's freshman senator, Sam Nunn. Could this get me to DC? Or even increase my chances of getting a job at the *Post*?

The application process included an interview, with both faculty members at the public affairs school and people designated by Senator Nunn present. One of the questions they asked was what I would do if I saw some wrongdoing by a fellow senator. Call the papers? Go public? Being a chain-of-command Marine, I simply said I would tell Nunn and let him sort it out.

The news arrived via phone from the senator's office. They wanted me to start on October 1, 1973, a month after I finished school. So I had to decide, and fast. Jan still lived at home, and I knew her mother would invite me over for dinner most nights. We still hadn't informed our parents, but we came from similar backgrounds and had similar interests. Our families were close and we were both ready to settle down.

Should I accept? If I did, I'd have it all: a beautiful fiancée, free meals, and a lily pad in the Senate from which to hop to a real job in the Big Pond. I packed my rusty, trusty Vega with my meager belongings and headed north.

THE ORDER OF BATTLE

October 1973: Washington, DC

When I'd been in Hong Kong on liberty, I'd taken advantage of what seemed an unbelievable deal. Kim's tailor had handmade suits for a bargain price. I was feeling good about my sense of style and thrift when I walked out the door with five "hand-made Italian suits" for $50 each. As soon as I tried one on before my first day at the Senate, Jan's laughter revealed I'd been had. Thread began to pull from the seams and the thin material showed creases where there shouldn't have been any. Thus, I reported to work in a striped blazer bought at the last minute from the Marine Corps Exchange.

The Russell Senate Office Building on Constitution Avenue is a Beaux-Arts limestone block with a Doric colonnade in white marble. When I saw the massive white dome of the Capitol looming beyond it, I knew I was somewhere important. Sparkling crystal chandeliers lighted the lofty, frosty-marbled corridors.

Room 110 was a five-room suite, shoehorned with desks and file cabinets. But the clutter did nothing to hide the majesty of these high-ceilinged spaces. The gilded, sculptured crown moldings looked like an architectural detail from Versailles. Assembled with me were three others selected for Senator Nunn's first academic internship program.

I was from Georgia, true, but didn't know a lot about Sen. Samuel Augustus Nunn Jr. I hadn't even voted in the previous election. I did know, or at least had gleaned during an orientation meeting, that Nunn was from Perry, Georgia, a small town twenty-five miles south of my hometown of Macon. He was related to the powerful Georgia congressman Carl Vinson. A basketball player in high school, Nunn had graduated from Emory. After that he'd worked several careers—Coast Guard, congressional staffer, family farmer, and private law practitioner—before getting elected to the Georgia House. He'd gone from there to the U.S. Senate, a meteoric rise, by defeating the incumbent senator in the Democratic primary, a Jimmy Carter crony whom Carter, governor at the time, had appointed to fill the remainder of Richard B. Russell's term after Russell died in office. Nunn had then shellacked Republican representative Fletcher Thompson in the 1972 general election. He'd been in office less than a year when I arrived.

My first day was all paperwork and forms, a task I had mastered during my military experience. I didn't actually meet the senator until several days later, when the four of us interns had our pictures taken with him in his personal office.

Nunn was seated behind a looming mahogany desk, wearing a dark lawyer's suit and a blue striped tie. He wore big, round glasses, which the *Wall Street Journal* would later describe as giving him an owlish look. His well-groomed but thinning hair receded ever so slightly.

He greeted us in a warm, Southern lilt: "You're my first set of interns, selected because of your academics, and I have high expectations of you. I see this as a key program in my office, to benefit from your expertise but also get you more interested in government." I felt both excited and a bit nervous because I'd never been around politicians, certainly not any as high up on the food chain as a senator. But his calm demeanor and candidness put us all at ease.

Nunn struck me as a serious, driven individual with a clear focus on serving the citizens of Georgia. Yet even with a busy schedule, he tried to meet with us at least once a week during our ten-week program. We respected that.

Because of my journalism background—and, to be perfectly honest, my speed with an IBM Selectric typewriter, which proved as essential to a Senate office as a bayonet is to a Marine in the trenches—I was drawn into the world of the press secretary. I still don't know, though, how we answered the one thousand letters Nunn received every day in those early years with no automated word processing.

The senator's press secretary, Roland McElroy, was affable and jovial, the polar opposite of the ever-serious Nunn. He always looked rumpled, more like a reporter run ragged from chasing down sources than an influential aide. A diehard Bulldog fan, Roland came from tiny Quitman, Georgia. He had worked with Nunn's campaign from day one. He knew everything about local radio and news media but was more than just the press secretary; he was a trusted political adviser. Because he'd traveled all over the state with the senator during the campaign, Roland knew someone in every small town. He would ask, "What part of the state are you from?" Once he knew, he could say something like, "Did you ever eat at Finchers Bar-B-Q?" Because he knew all the local food joints, he fit right in with the "bubba network." It was easy to see why everyone loved him.

As interns, one of our duties was leading visitors on tours of the Senate, so we had to learn our way around. Due to my map-reading skills, I found lots of hidden areas, such as where President Lincoln's catafalque was kept in the basement under the Capitol dome. I would take constituents to these out-of-the-way spots and make sure they knew they were seeing something special.

We also had to deliver paperwork to other offices and do administrative chores like copying and filing. The permanent staffers encouraged us to learn as much as we could by going to hearings and debates on the Senate floor. We also had to help respond to correspondence and write some press releases. Nunn did a weekly radio and TV program in the recording studios. My job was to package the tapes and send them to all the Georgia stations.

The senator's large personal office was one door down from the reception area. Martha Tate, his personal secretary, had the requisite accent. A traditional "Georgia peach," she could've come from central casting in *Gone with the Wind*, with her Dixie charm and hospitality. Martha was always perfectly coiffed, with bright red lipstick, and she referred to everyone, from foreign dignitaries to senior generals, as "honey" or "sweetie." She sat outside with the receptionists, who greeted visitors and answered the phones that rang incessantly.

The next office housed the legislative team, who worked on policy issues. Next door was the press section: Roland, his personal secretary Rose Johnson, and me. Between the additional legislative staff and caseworkers, the rickety desks and battered green metal General Services Administration file cabinets, and the stacks of papers that teetered like derelict smokestacks, there wasn't a lot of room. Rose took great care of Roland and me. She was a motherly type with a sharp wit—fast, precise, and always ahead of us. That first year, she surprised me with the most delicious, buttery pound cake on my birthday. Jan still uses Rose's recipe forty years later.

Roland assigned me a green steel desk toward the back of this crowded office. It was next to a space I nicknamed "Grant's Tomb" to mock the Union general and because it was as small and dark as a burial vault. Originally, it had been a shoebox bathroom with sink and toilet, but now it held file cabinets and the Autopen. This simple machine would sign Senator Nunn's name with either a *Sam* or a *Sam Nunn*. Somehow, the staff had also managed to squeeze in a TWX, an early, electromechanical e-mail. The "Twix" was a hulking teletypewriter on a stand, in a crackle gray finish, that looked like it had probably sent code messages during World War II. It made a deafening racket during the rare times it received anything. I used it when the various government agencies would notify us that a locality or county in Georgia was getting a federal grant. I had to draft a notice and send it to local officials announcing their good fortune so Senator Nunn could receive proper credit. There I sat in my swivel chair, entombed, turning left to work the Autopen and right to work the Twix.

Neither assignment was exactly glamorous, so it became my challenge to make them exciting. I decided to set the world record for signing the most letters with *Sam* in a minute. This wasn't easy. You couldn't set a record with *Sam Nunn* because it took the Autopen a lot longer to sign his full name. I had to make sure the letter was clamped down securely before I started, or the *Sam* would look as if the senator had been drunk on the job. That was undesirable, for obvious reasons, but also since Nunn was extremely particular about both content and appearance. I was only allowed to sign his letters after they'd been through an extensive review, including his personal approval. Nothing half-assed or half-done ever went out of Nunn's office. He was so thorough that one time, after we had printed and mailed thousands of reports, he spotted a tiny factual error, one that hardly anyone else would notice. Nonetheless, he had Roland and me go down to the Washington main post office and dig through hundreds of orange congressional mailbags to collect all of the erroneous reports. After several hours of work, we retrieved every last one, and then our office reprinted and sent out the corrected reports.

I had other tasks. My days also included copying, filing, sending out information to radio and TV shows, processing press releases, and researching and drafting answers to constituent inquiries of all sorts. It was certainly a thorough introduction to staff work, and in those ten weeks, I'd been too busy to look for another job.

As my internship neared its end, Roland called me into his cubicle one day and offered me the position of assistant press secretary, at the princely salary of $17,000 a year. I thought it over. Seventeen thousand? Not a lot, and a lot less than Jan's salary. But I had no reporting job lined up, and it was beginning to look as if finding one wouldn't be easy. The work in Grant's Tomb was sometimes boring and occasionally menial. (In retrospect, though, Roland probably hired me because I'd shown some dexterity with those two antediluvian mechanical adversaries.) But I liked the staff, and I definitely liked being where the action was. After leading Marines, I felt up to any assignment that came my way. Plus the only hostile fire I had to duck here was lengthy phone calls from constituents, some of whom could drawl a five-minute problem into a five-hour dramatic monologue. On any given day I might talk to a Nunn supporter who was a hard-core conservative that saw communists behind every tree. Or the schoolteacher who lectured me about my grammar and pronunciation. Then there were the calls insisting that "Machine Gun" Ronnie Thompson, then the mayor of Macon, was buying armored boats to patrol the Ocmulgee River.

"Thanks, Mr. McElroy," I said at last. "I think I'll stay on with you."

Little did I know I was signing up for a decade's tour on Nunn's personal staff and then another fourteen years on the Armed Services Committee . . . nearly a quarter-century with the Senate and the senator, in one way or another.

᠁

JAN

When Arnold proposed, it wasn't the typical get-down-on-one-knee event. Though we were certainly in love, he told me, "I don't have enough money to buy you an engagement ring."

I was fine with that, but when Arnold went home to tell his parents, his mother, Annina, wasn't. She retrieved her engagement ring from a safety deposit box. She'd originally planned to give it to him so he could use the stones for his chalice; believe it or not, he'd gone to seminary out of grade school. But he'd decided the priesthood wasn't for him, luckily for me.

The ring is stunning—a center diamond, surrounded by smaller diamonds and two baguettes on each side—and one of the most meaningful presents I've ever received. Annina couldn't have given me a warmer, more meaningful welcome. I've worn it every day for forty-two years and love it even more now.

⌒

ARNOLD

Jan and I set our wedding date. I felt I had superb organizational skills, honed by planning social events at TBS. But I was no match for Jan and her mother. Anita was a combination of southern charm and Navy protocol who ensured that every event was memorable and enjoyable. She would only serve dinner by candlelight on the most delicate, meticulously pressed tablecloths, her favorite being the Army Navy tablecloth, alternating squares of embroidered linen and handmade lace, edged with scalloped lace.[1]

Saturday, February 23, at the small but charming Navy chapel on Nebraska Avenue, turned out to be a brisk but sunny day. Jan's five sisters, along with my two, Mary Angela and Trudie, plus Jan's grammar school friend, Debby, wore beautiful matching floor-length red velvet dresses. But none of them could hold a candle to Jan in her ivory satin and lace-trimmed dress. I'd asked my dad to be my best man, staying true to the Italian tradition. My brothers, Michael and Vincent, and a few college buddies were the groomsmen.

My uncle, Frank Benedetto, performed the service along with Father Tom Donaher, the Naval Academy chaplain who'd served with my father-in-law. The ceremony included a Mass. The guest list was mostly relatives and close friends, but with large families on both sides and many friends as well, it was still a large wedding. By the end of the lengthy service we couldn't wait to go on to celebrate at the O Club. Since my buddies had already overimbibed at the rehearsal dinner, they were on their best behavior that evening. A more intimate party at Jan's parents' house followed the formal reception. We stayed up celebrating until four in the morning.

We spent our honeymoon at Seven Springs Ski Resort, a four-hour drive from our home. As newlyweds on a tight budget, we had a blast just eating Cheez Whiz and peanut butter on crackers in our room with a bottle of cold duck. We skied all day and relaxed in the lodge's hot tub at night. The week flew by.

But all too soon we were back to daily commutes to downtown Washington. From our apartment in Falls Church I drove fifteen miles to the Senate side of Capitol Hill. Most days that took about twenty minutes. So I was quickly back into a battlefield sort of routine: up at dawn, weave through the traffic obstacle course to the office, engage in nonstop and unpredictable activities, then secure after 7 p.m. to head home.

We spent weekends on grocery runs, house cleaning, and seeing friends and family. Fortunately Jan's parents and most of her sisters lived nearby, so it was easy to get together. These gatherings reminded me of the family dinners of my youth in Georgia. Jan's dad liked nothing better than taking us shopping at the Post Exchange. And I liked nothing better than wearing his leather Navy flight jacket. After six daughters, I think he was happy to finally have a son close by to pal around with!

꩜

As a full-time staff member, my duties changed. I still had to process mail, write releases for the weekly radio and TV shows, and run the Twix, but I didn't do much filing anymore. Instead, I did more writing, and since Roland wanted me to get to know the media, I worked closely with the press, radio, and TV. He also wanted me to share the travel duties when the senator went back home. One of us would always accompany him on these trips.

In those first two years as assistant press secretary, I spent a lot of weekends traveling back to red-clay Georgia with Senator Nunn. We'd fly down on a Thursday or Friday evening and spend the weekend driving around in an area staffer's car; unlike the military with their government vehicles, we had to rely on local staff's personal cars. After a particularly bumpy ride in my Vega, Nunn's administrative assistant issued guidance on minimal transportation standards.

When the senator traveled, the logistics had to be perfect. My Marine five-paragraph-order training came in handy: careful planning, coordinating, and making well-researched backup plans in case enemy or terrain didn't turn out the way we expected. I briefed the senator ahead of time on key people scheduled to attend each event and kept detailed records of new supporters we met along the way. If I didn't know this essential information, Nunn would grill me like a drill instructor until I felt like I was going to be sent before his firing squad.

"Arnold, who all's going to be at this barbecue?"

I looked frantically through the stack of papers on my lap and on the bench seat between the driver and myself. "Uh . . ."

"Arnold, what did you say?"

"Yes sir, I'm trying to find the materials I prepared for this event, but it must be with the stuff from the first four we've done today."

"Just brief me on the details, then."

My road days would start with me rubbing sleep from my eyes, often knocking over the alarm clock blaring at 5:30 a.m. These were long days with five events each. We oriented the big ones around breakfast, lunch, and dinner, squeezing smaller, less formal meetings or appearances in between. I'd fight to keep my eyes open driving us home in the dark, more than ready to collapse on my hotel bed. I'd thought my days of getting up before dawn, moving at first light, and drudging until I dropped were over.

I remember an early trip when the senator did a fundraiser at the home of a guy named Ted Turner. Unlike the big-money events that would typify fundraisers in later years, these were small, informal gatherings where a supporter would invite friends and acquaintances to his or her home for a cookout or cocktails. Then the senator would speak briefly and answer questions. Guests were expected, though not required, to make a donation to the re-election campaign. I was familiar with Turner because he was CEO of Turner Advertising. Now it seemed he wanted to start a worldwide, all-news TV channel. He struck me as a quirky individual, floating from topic to topic and person to person. His thoughts seemed off the wall, and after the fundraiser I remarked to Roland, "This wacky CNN idea will never amount to anything. Who would ever want news *all the time?*" But Senator Nunn saw his potential.

Back in DC, political reporters and media sought out Nunn. He wasn't in the business of publicity for publicity's sake, but he still prepared for each interview intensely, reading and relentlessly quizzing the staff and outside experts.

Typically, a news show such as *Face the Nation* or *Meet the Press* might call on Tuesday and ask him to go on that weekend to talk about something like our relationship with Russia. Roland, Rose, and I would hustle to prepare multiple briefing books: multitabbed binders of everything related to the subject, including answers to the most likely questions. He would read every word and take notes on yellow legal pads. Actually, he often ended up with three or even four full pads. To my amazement, he'd boil these down to one, then reduce and summarize that to just one sheet. And yet it all still made perfect sense. Unlike many politicians, he would actually answer the question that was asked.

The Senate in the early 1970s was a very different place than it is today, mostly because of the senators themselves. Today, the tyranny of the twenty-four-hour news cycle reigns. Cable news and social media dominate, and they penalize even minor gaffes. Part of this, too, is an increasing need for political correctness. Today's gaffes were yesterday's lovable eccentricities. Senators weren't expected to be perfect; foibles were seen as harmless and readily accepted. Sen. Strom Thurmond's legendary butt pinching was overlooked, as was other senators' habit of voting on the Senate floor while intoxicated.

Still, some staffers worried about their bosses going to meetings or media interviews on their own. If a senator said or did something stupid, that could blow his or her public image, giving the opposition ammunition for the next election. These senators had to have handlers who'd accompany them everywhere. Some were getting up in years and only needed prompting. Others simply were not prepared, or not effective, without staff members hovering at their elbows.

Nunn wasn't one of them. We never worried about him going anywhere alone. He was a demanding boss, sure, but none of us worked harder than he did. He didn't keep a nine-to-five schedule. Sometimes the days felt as long as those I'd spent on patrol in Quang Nam: up before dawn, on the move early, and always on alert, and you could never really take your pack off.

෴

I met many of Nunn's early supporters from all over Georgia. They were successful businessmen or farmers or small-town lawyers, Chamber of Commerce types. Most were Democrats, but there were Republicans and independents too. Some were pastors, like the Reverend Martin Luther King Sr., whom we met at the famed Ebenezer Baptist Church. The senator made sure I knew that nothing was more important than keeping up with his earliest supporters. I was to make sure they had my phone number and that they understood they had a friend in his office to talk to if they ever had a problem or a suggestion.

Pleas for his help weren't limited to supporters. Our office got requests from constituents and business leaders on a regular basis. Most were routine. A visiting Georgian might want a tour of the Capitol or a flag that'd flown above the Senate. Some requests crossed the line to ridiculous or even unscrupulous, though. A contractor once asked us to ensure he won a Pentagon bid. Another person asked us for his competitor's pricing information for a job at Robins Air Force Base.

Needless to say, requests like these were not honored. In twenty-four years of service, Nunn never had an ethics scandal, because he employed and associated with people who knew where the line between help and undue influence fell, and he did not cross it.

෴

One of the staples (and sometimes curses) of all congressional offices is casework. Because the federal bureaucracy can be a stone wall to its citizens' requests, Congress has become a middleman of sorts. Every congressional office has people whose job is to solve its constituents' problems with the executive branch. Each executive department and agency also has a staff that interfaces with the congressional caseworkers. (When you hear proposals to "trim the federal bureaucracy," by the way, it's typically these lower- to mid-level folks—the ones who actually help you—who tend to get laid off first.)

On a typical day, the Senate postman would bring more than a thousand letters to our office alone. Let's say someone's not getting a Social Security check. We would put a "buck slip" on that complaint and route it over to the appropriate office in the Social Security Administration. The slip would say, in effect: *Here's correspondence from one of my constituents. Please look into this problem and send me a response I can get back to him or her with.* They'd reply, and we'd send that answer, with a polite cover note, back to the constituent. If the problem was solved, we wanted the good news to arrive with Senator Nunn's name on it, Autopenned, of course.

If the news wasn't good, though, if we couldn't get them their check, we'd try to figure out another way to help. Sometimes, unfortunately, we just had to tell them, "ain't gonna happen." Those letters always went out with an assistant's name on them, not the senator's.

Casework took up at least 60 percent of my time. As I've said, the senator and Roland were adamant about answering all the mail we received, no matter how weird or incoherent. I didn't grasp why until one day Nunn told us the advice passed on by Herman Talmadge, the senior senator from our state. Nunn had voiced his exasperation because so much mail appeared to come from nuts and kooks whose letters made little sense. He'd decided it would be better to answer only the serious ones. The staff certainly would've welcomed that decision. Nunn asked, "Herman, I am getting a lot of 'nut' mail with questions about space aliens and all sorts of wild conspiracies. Do you reply to those types of letters?" Talmadge had told him with a perfectly straight face, "Sam, answer every one of those letters! If you don't carry the 'nut' vote, you won't carry a single county in Georgia!" So every letter got answered, no matter how insane.

Of course, the biggest executive department, and one we often had to go to with complaints and questions, was Defense. Each service had an enormous staff devoted to congressional case inquiries. Because I had a military background, others in the office asked, or maybe expected, me to handle some of those cases.

Sometime around 1976 or 1977, Nunn decided to beef up his military section, since he was on the Armed Services Committee and Georgia had a large number of bases. He hired a noted expert from the Brookings Institution, Jeffrey Record. Jeff was posted as the military legislative assistant, which meant he was responsible for following and writing all legislation and policy regarding the Defense Department and national security writ large.

Senator Nunn quickly determined that Jeff needed backup because Record wasn't one to answer mail or phone calls or do anything else he deemed of a trivial nature. This was the beginning of my transition from the press office into defense policy. I learned a lot working with Jeff, who was an expert on military history and a superb analyst and also a prolific writer who, like the senator, could draft a final product on the first try. He'd provide incisive questions for hearings and his excellent memory kept Pentagon witnesses on guard. Soon I became involved in taking the lead for Senator Nunn's positions on specific military and foreign policy issues. Jeff couldn't handle them all and didn't care to fool with some. So I researched, drafted analyses, provided recommendations on the pros and cons of each position, and briefed the senator. I was also given the lead in protecting and expanding Georgia's significant military base structure.

I learned early on that the military wasn't always right. On numerous occasions, this huge bureaucracy showed no interest in helping a deserving individual. When cases such as rejected humanitarian reassignments, or being passed over for promotion with insufficient cause, came across my desk, I gave them special attention. I would work with the liaison officers personally and if necessary the Pentagon directly. Rarely would I take no for an answer.

The toughest cases were the humanitarian transfers, hardship discharges, or adverse fitness reports, because they were totally subjective. A service member who might need to get transferred to be close to an ailing loved one, or to get out early to help run a faltering family business, would often face hard-hearted Hannah. The typical response was that the needs of the service came first. But since these decisions *were* subjective, a member of Congress could generally convince the service to reconsider. One time, a lance corporal at Camp Pendleton, California, wanted a transfer to the logistics base in Albany so he could be closer to his dying mother. She had no other family to help her. He was an 0311, or infantryman in the 1st Marine Division. The USMC said, "We don't send riflemen to Albany" and "He's only one year into a three-year tour." I took great pleasure in taking his case to a general and beating the manpower bureaucracy.

The Pentagon could also be quite inflexible . . . particularly (and this *was* a surprise) its medical departments. For example, James Stone, the son of a prominent Georgian, had been accepted to the Naval Academy. He desperately wanted to be a pilot. As a boy he'd had bad reactions to bee stings but had been cured of the allergy. He had documentation from every health expert in the world, yet the Navy Bureau of Medicine refused to allow him into pilot training. Their rationale? He might be flying in the F-14 Tomcat at supersonic speeds and a bee could get in the cockpit, sting him, and crash the plane. While I thought this paranoid, if not totally irrational, we never did budge the bureau. James never flew as a pilot.

We ran up against that giant medical bureaucracy time and time again, and rarely, if ever, did common sense prevail.

Perhaps the most memorable case I handled was that of a Navy doctor. During the Vietnam War, the Berry Plan allowed people to go to med school and defer the draft—and the possibility of being sent to Vietnam—but they had to serve two years in the military medical services after graduating. This was a good deal when the war was at its peak, but some people used Berry to dodge being drafted, and then, when the war was over, tried to get out of their commitment.[2]

In 1980, Dr. John Hudson from Riverdale, Georgia, contacted our office asking for help in avoiding his obligation. I was eager to help folks when the government was wrong, but that didn't seem to be the case here. Although we were polite and worked with Hudson in an objective way to help him make his case to the appropriate authorities, ultimately we didn't go to bat for him. Still, he became something of a pen pal, and we'd talk on the phone from time to time. To his great credit, he honored his commitment and ended up as a battalion surgeon with the Marines.

Lieutenant Hudson called me the day before he deployed to Beirut, Lebanon, in 1983. We talked about how much he'd come to respect the Marines and how he was enjoying his work with them. In October, he was killed in the horrific bombing of the barracks there. We were devastated by his death. Of course I had to wonder . . . it's impossible to know with any certainty if our office could have helped release him from his obligation. And if we had, someone else would have died in his place. But I was glad Hudson had told me he was comfortable with his assignment.

୶

Because of Nunn's growing expertise, seniority, and thus clout, the services worked hard to cultivate a relationship with our office. They became a conduit for solving problems, offering assistance when a constituent called with a complaint about pay or benefits, and also a source of information about both military issues and military operations. The relationships I developed would prove invaluable when I became staff director of the committee.

I got to know the liaison officers who worked in the Senate. Their offices were just down the hall from us in Russell, so I spent a good deal of time there. Representing the Navy from 1977 to 1981 was a fit and wiry Capt. John McCain, USN, who would go on to become a congressman, senator, and presidential candidate. McCain cut an impressive figure in dress whites stacked with ribbons, including the Purple Heart and several awards for valor. He was best known on account of his nearly six years of captivity in North Vietnam. He'd been imprisoned in the infamous "Hanoi Hilton" after being shot down, at the same time his father was a full admiral and commander of Pacific Command. His forceful, high-octane personality gave him direct lines to key Pentagon leaders and made him a source of advice and counsel for senators and staffers alike. A dynamic advocate for the Navy, McCain forged close relationships with powerful senators like John

Tower, Henry "Scoop" Jackson, John Stennis, and Bill Cohen. During his years as a liaison, I never saw the flashes of temper for which he became notorious later as a senator. He certainly was more patient in uniform than in a coat and tie! Over many years and Codels—official trips of congressional delegations—McCain worked hard to make sure Senator Nunn and his colleagues always had the information and support they needed.

McCain's Marine counterpart, who shared the same office space, was a ramrod-straight former Georgetown University basketball player, then Lt. Col. Jim Jones. A major when first posted to the Senate, he served for five years. This unusually long stay normally would have been the kiss of death for a fast mover. But Jones' calm professionalism attracted senators and staffers, who scrambled for his involvement on key issues. He was knowledgeable without being a know-it-all, serious yet not stiff. Although he ran a tight ship leading the Codels, he was not overbearing. Everyone who worked with him realized Jones had a bright future. I predicted at the time—twenty years early—that he would become commandant of the Corps. He held that post from 1999 to 2003, then served as Supreme Allied Commander Europe and President Barack Obama's first national security adviser.

Jones and McCain were but two of the many dedicated officers who served in the liaison office. I became good friends with many of these men and women as we worked together early in our careers. As we rose in rank, stature, and power, friendships forged years before, based on shared work and trust, would prove beneficial. I still work with many of them today.

Another example of a young officer who would go on to become one of the nation's most powerful leaders was Carl Stiner, a young lieutenant colonel stationed at Fort Benning, Georgia. We worked closely to implement the one-station unit-training concept. Up until then, Army recruits did their basic training and advanced individual training at different bases. The one-station unit-training concept was more efficient, but it meant some bases lost personnel and facilities.

Stiner would go on to become a four-star general and the commander of U.S. Special Operations Command during the first Gulf War, when Nunn chaired the Armed Services Committee. He was one of the first leaders of the elite and secretive Delta Force and Joint Special Operations Command. We had access to a lot of sensitive information. Because of that trust, when either of us wanted information from the other, we knew we would get the gospel truth, not just the amen chorus, as we say down South. Carl shared his personal observations about several operations directly with Senator Nunn and the committee, and it led to some of the reforms in the Goldwater-Nichols Act.

I was thus fortunate to meet nearly as an equal the best of the best in the military, in private industry, and in the executive branch. The Senate has always attracted smart, driven individuals who—with hard work and a little luck—will make their way up the food chain. It was clear to me early on that, in large part, any given person's success or failure in Washington revolved around *personal relationships*. People remembered when you went out of your way to help them. They also, for far longer, remembered when you didn't, so I made sure never to burn a bridge by taking the short-term view. Years later, many of my good deeds would be paid back tenfold.

Meanwhile, I continued my own military career, but it was definitely on the back burner. When Creighton Abrams became the Army chief of staff after returning from Vietnam, he came up to the Hill to visit with Senator Nunn in 1973. Because I was the only person in the office with combat experience, I was allowed to sit in on this meeting. Abrams spoke at length on the need for a viable Reserve and National Guard. He impressed on us both that the nation should never again go to war without our citizens having "skin in the game." This was the lesson he'd learned when the Guard and Reserves had not been mobilized and instead the country had relied on conscription to fight an unpopular war. Abrams' passion inspired me to join the Marine Corps Reserves even though back then it was not seen as a prestigious move. As a Reservist, I only had to wear my uniform one weekend each month and two weeks in the summer. Initially, I did those drills with the 4th Civil Affairs Group at the Anacostia Navy Yard.

But reserve or active, deep down I would always be a Marine. One symptom of that was a certain difficulty mustering much sympathy for military members whose requests didn't seem to have a lot of merit. Whiners and grumblers who felt they deserved special treatment, such as not being assigned overseas or not liking their fitness reports; I didn't have patience for such cavils.

As assistant press secretary, defense policy assistant, caseworker, and general factotum and SLDO (sorry little duties officer), I gradually learned a lot over the next ten years about the nuts and bolts of the Senate and how things worked.

Like a metropolitan opera or a major corporation, the Senate requires an entire support structure, from carpenters to painters to cabinetmakers to a radio and television shop. The print shop was especially important—producing releases, newsletters, and mass mailings. Each senator had a paper allotment and the queue was strictly based on seniority . . . *unless* you knew the shop and took the time to visit it yourself—even just to chat—and maybe bring coffee or a sweet roll. I got close to a lot of the folks who worked hard to make us look good, and the personal touch made all the difference.

I also learned that time served is to the Senate what rank is to the military. Even more so, because unlike the Marines, Senate seniority is based absolutely and solely on years in office and not on any record of actual accomplishment. It determines everything, from the location of a senator's desk on the floor to committee and subcommittee assignments to parking spaces to leadership within the caucus. It also, I found later, controls the size of a senator's staff devoted to committee work.[3]

As the years went on I became fascinated by the ins and outs of how this amazing machine, the United States Congress, really worked. Herman Wouk once said the Navy was "designed by geniuses for execution by idiots."[4] Congress was designed by geniuses, all right—our Founding Fathers—but the people who ran it were ordinary men and women who ranged from brilliant to ignorant, from colorless to colorful. They were dedicated public servants who, like all of us, suffered from the frailties of ordinary mortals.

↜

In 1973 there was no C-SPAN and no broadcast of Senate proceedings. To watch them in action, we had to walk the long, marble hallways and bronze-railed staircases from the Russell building to the Senate side of the Capitol, where a separate gallery was reserved for staff. We could listen to legendary speakers like John Pastore of Rhode Island, Russell Long of Louisiana, Fritz Hollings of South Carolina, or Ted Kennedy of Massachusetts. The staffs had an informal early warning network; we flocked to listen and learn when one of the great orators was headed to the floor. Later, the Senate installed squawk boxes or mini-radios in each office so we could tune in from our desks. This was a real boon because we could follow the debate while continuing to work. Once, when the Senate was weighing the future of the B1 bomber, the Air Force liaison and the leadership were so anxious that Gen. "Moon" Mullins called to ask if I'd put my phone next to the squawk box so they could listen in.

As my career progressed, these older, larger-than-life senators with larger-than-life personalities began retiring, and younger, more staid politicians took their places. While less exciting, the new senators were still serious legislators focused on solving problems. As chairman of the Finance Committee, Russell Long was one of the most powerful members, if not *the* most powerful. He was the son of the infamous Huey P. Long, governor and senator from Louisiana. Senator Nunn went to see him soon after I joined the staff to talk about fathers who didn't support their children—a big issue during Nunn's campaign—and to glean some life lessons and career advice. When he returned from their meeting, I asked what Long had told him. He said the patriarch had offered lots of good advice, but the best was, "Sam, don't ever solve a problem for people before they know they have one."

What this meant, I think, is to spend time documenting and making sure you've convinced the public a real problem exists, or at least make sure the media has directed attention at some shortcoming, before you propose a solution that's sure to rile some vested interest in one way or another; it was sage counsel.

I also met the fabled Strom Thurmond in these early days. The Army's one-station unit-training decision led to our meeting. Georgia's Fort Benning and South Carolina's Fort Jackson were affected by the new policy. I was working hard to get the new barracks the Army would need for the program at Fort Benning.

But then I got a call from one of the staffers on the Armed Services Committee, Ed Kinney, Thurmond's point man. He said, "Come see me, Arnold. I want to talk about Fort Benning and Fort Jackson." A senior staffer was summoning me for a senior senator; that's the system. A four-star general does not go to a one-star's office. In the committee's offices, Ed sat me down and courteously explained, as if to a not-very-bright child, that Georgia and South Carolina should not be in competition. Instead we should cooperate. If we did, everything would work out well for both of us. He added, "By the way, I think Senator Thurmond wants to talk to you."

Everybody knew Strom Thurmond. When he was governor of South Carolina, he'd been so disgusted with the Democratic Party he'd run for president in 1948 on a third party ticket for the Dixiecrats. He'd been in the Senate since 1954, had stood like a rock against desegregation, and had spoken for twenty-four hours straight on the Senate floor in a filibuster—the longest in history—against the Civil Rights Act of 1957. He did this even though he'd fathered a child out of wedlock with a black woman. Thurmond became a Republican in 1964.[5]

I'd be lying if I said I wasn't nervous as Ed walked me to Thurmond's office. Because of his extreme seniority, it was much bigger than Nunn's. The walls were covered from parquet floor to elegantly molded ceiling with large framed photographs of the lean, leather-faced senator in the company of presidents and kings, princes and prime ministers.

The man himself rose slowly from behind a massive oak desk that dominated the spacious suite. Though in his mid-seventies, Thurmond had an iron grip as he shook my hand. He told me, in that long Carolina drawl, "Sam and I are good friends and we're gonna work together on a lot of important projects." He expected us to work out a compromise on this issue. At this less rigidly partisan time, being in different parties didn't matter much when you were talking jobs and the military impact in your state. Thurmond wanted Fort Jackson, South Carolina, to be a one-station unit-training facility too. He said he'd support infantry training at Fort Benning if we'd back personnel and administration training at Fort Jackson. I took the proposal back to Senator Nunn, who agreed wholeheartedly.

This began a long, productive relationship. Thurmond supported many projects in Georgia that today might be called pork, but which brought jobs and benefits, such as the Savannah River Site, a nuclear weapons plant and hydro-electric dam on Lake Russell near the South Carolina–Georgia border—projects that proved their worth.

On one trip I accompanied Thurmond and Jim Smith, a professional staff member on the Armed Services Committee, to Europe to tour some of our bases in England and Germany. Thurmond needed to check out their physical condition because he was the senior Republican on the Military Construction subcommittee. I went along so I could report back to Nunn. We arrived early in the morning and spent the day touring Molesworth Air Force Base, as it was slated to be one of the controversial ground-launched cruise missile sites. When we finally got to our lodgings—the Grosvenor Hotel, one of London's four-star locations and every bit as ornate as Buckingham Palace—I was exhausted from the overnight flight, a full day on the move, and the five-hour time difference. I hadn't slept in twenty-four hours.

Early the next morning, far *too* early for my tastes, someone hammered on my door. I opened it groggily. "Arnold, it's time for PT and running." There stood Thurmond, at seventy-five, thin as a rail and leathery as an old alligator. Ready to run in white cotton shorts and an Army T-shirt.

I was thirty, a fit Reserve captain who could still cruise the eleven-mile Quantico loop in a little more than one and a half hours. I figured I would use this as my warm-up and get a real workout in later. Unfortunately, none of my training cut the mustard in Grosvenor Park as the sun rose. Thurmond did a hundred pushups, and then ran Jim and me into the ground, making us look like the old-timers. Senator Thurmond was an Army Reserve major general who reveled in calling cadence and taunting Jim and me for our plodding ways. He chanted as we tried, unsuccessfully, to keep up: "I want to be an Airborne Ranger—I want to live a life of danger!"

Bill Scott, from Virginia, was another colorful senator. One of his personal staffers told how Scott requested that every letter they received be answered that very day. He would check by looking on everyone's desk to ensure no letters were left at the end of the day, so the staff hid them in their drawers, and Scott never caught on. Back in 1974, an upstart magazine called *New Times* published a cover story identifying the ten dumbest members of Congress. The scathing story, written by the magazine's Washington correspondent Nina Totenberg, bestowed upon Virginia Republican Sen. Bill Scott the dubious distinction of being the very dumbest. As a rebuttal, he called a press conference. He was short and to the point: "I am not the dumbest senator." Thus proving in many people's minds that he was, indeed, the dumbest member of the entire congressional delegation. Another senator said of Scott at an open committee hearing, "If he was any dumber, he'd be a tree stump."

The patrician Claiborne Pell, chairman of the Foreign Relations Committee, was noted for various eccentricities, such as his enthusiasm for the paranormal and for threadbare suits, despite his immense wealth. One time, in the middle of a serious discussion about the Middle East, Senator Pell started blaming unidentified flying objects for causing the ruckus. "Sam, you ought to get the military to show you all the UFOs they have stored in their secret location." Many years later, Nunn and I took a trip to this "secret location" out in Nevada, Area 51, and we never saw any UFOs. Of course, they had probably turned on the invisibility shields. (This was not the case with Pell's successor, Sen. Joe Biden. He was always in discussions in the majority leader's office on key foreign policy issues, and his ideas were thoughtful and persuasive.)

Herman Talmadge was first elected way back in 1956 (and not just by the nut vote). Talmadge might have stepped from the pages of a Robert Penn Warren novel. His folksy demeanor and country drawl belied a sharp intellect and keen political instincts. He smoked cigars and chewed tobacco, and even kept a spittoon under his desk on the Senate floor.

Although Nunn had technically succeeded David Gambrell, whom Governor Jimmy Carter had appointed to replace the legendary Richard Russell upon Russell's death in 1971, Russell's shadow still loomed over us. The very name of the building in which we worked testified to that. Talmadge, who'd known Russell intimately, was a source of great support and stability both for Nunn and Georgia. Talmadge supported each of Nunn's legislative initiatives, and the two formed a good working relationship based on a clear division of labor. Talmadge, as chairman of the Agriculture Committee and member of the Finance Committee, took the lead on agriculture and business, the twin engines of Georgia's economy. Nunn, meanwhile, focused on the military and foreign policy. Talmadge and his staff taught me a lot about how to work cases and the intricacies—and idiosyncrasies—of the Senate so we'd know how to get things done. I got well acquainted with his people.

In 1978 my first son, Joe, was born. Being a proud dad, I bought a box of large, but inexpensive, cigars from Dart Drug. You know, the *really* cheap ones with a blue wrapper saying "It's a Boy!" I knew the venerable senior senator from my home state liked cigars, so I took some over to his office and told Will Ball, his administrative assistant (and future secretary of the Navy), to make sure he got one. In my defense, though exhilarated, I was also exhausted after staying up all night with Jan to witness the birth of our first child, a truly amazing experience.

Several hours later, Will called. Talmadge wanted to see me. I hurried over, wondering what in the world he could want. Will escorted me straight in to where Senator Talmadge was standing with five of his most senior staffers. He was holding one of my drugstore cigars between two fingers as if it were a dried cat turd.

Not quite registering this, I waited for him to congratulate me, to thank me for my thoughtful gift. Instead he drawled, "Punaro, you must not be very proud of your new son, to be handin' out these lousy cigars!" Everybody in the room was hooting and hollering and I knew he was kidding. But, since they always seemed to have anything a senator might possibly need, I immediately went down to the military liaison office to ask about banned Cuban cigars. Col. John Campbell, the Army liaison, did not disappoint. Senator Talmadge got his upgrade: a Diplomatico.

＜‿ᔆ

JAN

In 1976, after years of renting, we decided it was time to buy a home, take advantage of the tax breaks, and possibly build some equity. We were also ready to start a family, and wanted to stay in the McLean area because it was convenient and had good schools. We finally found a one-story, red brick house with three small bedrooms, one bath, a tiny kitchen, and a combination dining and living room. Fifty thousand dollars sounded scary, but we finally bit the bullet and signed a contract.

The living room and dining room had what we considered, at the time, to be the height of fashion: red shag carpeting. Also true to the unsubtle style of the 1970s were the avocado-green kitchen appliances. The back wall was lined with huge picture windows, which made it seem more spacious than it actually was. There were peach trees in the backyard, but we were never able to get to that delicious-looking fruit ahead of the bees.

My brother-in-law, Gil, helped us plant tomatoes, lettuce, zucchini, peppers, and yellow squash. I was so pleased with my homegrown lettuce that one night I proudly served it to our dinner guests, some of Arnold's Senate colleagues we'd just met. I'll never forget the horror that spread across Arnold's face as a worm crawled out from under a leaf of his salad! For some reason he was always reluctant to eat my organic lettuce after that.

Our first child was born on May 8, 1978. Joe was a colicky baby. Arnold and I spent many a night driving up and down the George Washington Parkway with him in a carrier in the back seat. That was the only way we could get him to sleep. I also will never forget my first solo outing after Joe was born. It felt so freeing to finally be in the car by myself, even if it was only to drive to Safeway to pick up milk and bread. I'd been gone no more than fifteen minutes when I got into the checkout line. I happened to glance out the window at the front. There, lurking outside and peering in was Arnold, holding Joe, waiting for me! I paid for the groceries and sauntered outside. "Arnold. Why are you here?"

He replied, in that matter-of-fact manner he has, "Oh, I was just afraid you'd stand in line reading magazines and take too long getting home."

At that point I realized my former freedom was truly gone. Yet I was glad for the encumbrance of my small but growing family.

⌐◠

ARNOLD

Barry Goldwater was the most iconoclastic member ever. He was fearless, as befitted an Air Force Reserve general. He favored opening the military to gays and reforming the Pentagon long before such views were seriously considered, much less before they were mainstream. On more than one occasion, he told senior defense officials and generals that the U.S. military had its collective head up its ass and that the bureaucracy was far more focused on its own preservation than on any exterior threat. He really believed in individual freedom and was a huge champion of Native Americans. He drove a black AMX, a two-door muscle car like the one owned by the comic book hero the Green Hornet. He showed it to Col. Jerry Smith, the Air Force liaison, and me, insisting we climb in and take a look. We thought we were at the controls of the lunar landing module, gaping at all the dials and switches. Goldwater was particularly proud of the gauge that displayed the temperature of the exhaust as it exited the tailpipe.

John Glenn might've been the only senator more famous for what he'd done before he went into politics. Glenn had been a Marine fighter pilot in World War II and Korea and later, of course, one of the original Mercury Seven astronauts, the first American to orbit the earth in 1962. Because of his service, he had an understanding of the troops and families that eluded many other senators. On our trip to Beijing, the first Codel allowed to fly on a U.S. government aircraft into China, Glenn spent most of the trip in the cockpit, helping the pilots navigate. When we arrived in Beijing, he posed for pictures with some little kids only two or three years old. One, wearing a bright red and yellow outfit, reached up and poked the senator on the nose. He responded with a big smile and hearty laugh. But he was a serious legislator. He brought his astronaut "checklist" approach to the Senate. He was extremely thorough in his preparation for committee hearings, bill markups, or floor action, just like the legend from *The Right Stuff*.

But perhaps no other senator loved the Senate itself as Robert Byrd did. He'd risen from humble origins in West Virginia to become one of the most powerful statesmen of the era. During Nunn's early years, Byrd was the majority leader. Like Talmadge, his back slapping, joke cracking, and horsing around masked a voracious intellect and near-photographic memory. He could name all the emperors of Rome and the kings of England, and he could quote Homer in the original

Greek. He wrote several volumes of Senate history, which gave him knowledge of the institution and mastery of its arcane procedure that made him a first among equals. In fact, he knew the rules better than the Senate parliamentarians, wizened ancients who seemed to my young self to have been there since the first gavel came down in 1789. Watching Byrd in action taught me that process was often more important than substance. He could win votes on procedure that he couldn't on the merits. But despite the Greek and the mastery of parliamentary rules, Byrd had the common touch too. He once headlined a fundraiser for us in Dublin, Georgia, whipping the crowd into a frenzy when he grabbed his fiddle and played "Cripple Creek." This was a real crowd-pleaser; the locals saw a powerful Senate majority leader as simply one of them.

Like many senators back then, however, Byrd was not a man to get on the wrong side of. Once, Nunn had committed to support him in what everyone expected to be a closely contested election for majority leader. At the last minute, Nunn's good friend Lawton Chiles decided to enter the race. Even though the vote would be by secret ballot, Nunn went to see Byrd privately in the latter's inner office. Nunn told him about his long and close friendship with Chiles and asked to be released from his vote. Byrd, of course, gave permission and went on to win the election.

Shortly afterward, he told Nunn that when the final vote was much closer than anyone had predicted, it was obvious that a lot of senators who'd said they would vote for him hadn't. Many years later, Byrd mentioned to Nunn in passing that it had taken him a long time to figure out exactly which ones had broken their words. But he finally had, and he was still making them pay, one by one. As majority leader, Byrd not only controlled committee assignments, but also had tremendous input on what funding got added or subtracted from the appropriations bills. Crossing him was a sure way to get a backwater assignment like the Library Committee, have your earmarks deleted, and miss the boat on special assignments and Codels.

I can envision Byrd even now, having set an elaborate and foreboding scenario, waiting a few seconds and hoping to see his friend sweat, before adding gently, "You were the only one who came to me and personally asked to be released from your vote. I won't be making *you* pay, Sam." Byrd thought the world of Nunn, I believe because of his integrity, as he'd shown in that simple courtesy call, man to man. That kind of loyalty and mutual respect went a long way in the Senate back then. As majority leader, and later as chairman of the appropriations committee, Byrd always made sure there was enough time to amply debate the defense bill on the floor and that we sidestepped any procedural land mines, doing things like preventing senators from offering trivial amendments.

To sum up, I found the Senate a world of its own, a fantastic, expansive world of dinosaurs, giants, titans, and wizards. But also more compact and familiar than one might expect, a sort of hyperpowered small town. One through which, as my family grew, I would accompany Nunn as he steadily ascended in power and influence, and one through which I would ultimately gain a bit of my own.

THE WASHINGTON BATTLEFIELD

1973–80: Washington, DC

When I arrived at 110 Russell Senate Office Building around 7:30 a.m., I didn't need the marble columns or gold-leafed ceilings or brass stair rails to remind me of its importance. All I had to do was look around to see that morning's headlines come to life: the Watergate hearings were underway on the third floor, in the historic Russell Caucus Room.[1]

The lines for the hearing snaked down two flights of marble stairs, around the first floor corridors, and out onto the sidewalk. The Capitol complex was wide open in those days, and the Nixon administration witnesses would use the Delaware entrance. It was common to spot some of Bob Woodward and Carl Bernstein's targets coming and going. The Delaware entrance was also the closest to the Senate Armed Services Committee main hearing room in Russell 212. So it was the perfect location for celebrity watchers.

It was always interesting to see who caught the public's eye. I recall one day Barry Goldwater and Hubert Humphrey were chatting in the corridor. All of a sudden, a group of tourists started pointing and rushing toward them. Goldwater and Humphrey primped to receive their accolades, but the tourists stampeded past them to catch a glimpse of Ted Kennedy, who was coming down from his fourth-floor office.

Those early years were a blur: answering letters, dealing with the media, traveling with Nunn, helping with casework, and tackling difficult policy issues. But even the grunt work felt familiar. The unpredictability, the intensity, and the clash of opposing views reminded me of another combat zone, but this was the Washington Battlefield.[2]

In those years, John Stennis of Mississippi chaired the Armed Services Committee and one of its most respected members. He'd followed Richard Russell in simultaneously chairing the SASC and the Defense Appropriations Subcommittee, a feat no senator has repeated since. Controlling both the Defense Department's policies and budget, Stennis wielded immense power. In early 1975, he was concerned about the fledging all-volunteer force. He asked Nunn, whom he'd taken under his wing to chair the Manpower and Personnel Subcommittee, to examine whether this experiment might stand the test of time.

He also asked Nunn to go to Vietnam in January 1975 to make a firsthand assessment of our operations there and give his recommendations for further action. The last U.S. combat troops had come home in 1973 once the war had been fully "Vietnamized." Senate support for the Saigon regime was eroding, but it was still more supportive than the American public, with whom the war was deeply unpopular. Only SASC professional staff members could travel with senators to a war zone, so, as a personal staffer, I couldn't go along.

Unfortunately, that protocol did not apply to writing the twenty-page report due on his return. Roland McElroy and I were drafted to help write *Vietnam Aid— The Painful Options*, which basically concluded that there were no easy answers in year nine of U.S. involvement in a war that had started between the French and Viet Minh in 1946. During this trip, Nunn had grown skeptical of the rosy scenarios senior Vietnamese and U.S. military and civilian leaders painted. This skepticism would stay with him throughout his career whenever military and civilian leaders would suggest an easy fight. As he did with all issues, Nunn completed his homework: briefings from experts on all sides, reading and researching every detail, and sending staffers in advance to investigate on the ground.

All Nunn reports were chock full of facts, charts, and unassailable documentation, which often contradicted the Pentagon's positions.[3] They were based on input from individuals whose expertise and credentials were unchallenged in their respective fields, and they went through numerous rounds of revisions.

It was very difficult for me to work on the opening section of this report, which started with:

> History has already recorded the continuing war in South Vietnam as a series of misjudgments, political and military mismanagements and tragedy. Total combat deaths are estimated at over 1.2 million with U.S. combat deaths recorded at over 46,000. In monetary terms, this war is the most expensive for America, costing over $140 billion. Compounding the tragedy, each year the American people are told that next year will be better, the end is in sight, and this contributed to a growing cynicism about government.[4]

The U.S. military deaths in Vietnam weren't just numbers to me. I still saw their faces, I knew their names, I mourned their loss.

I was pleased that Nunn recommended against either cutting off all aid or providing massive open-ended aid to South Vietnam. He also felt the practice of looking at aid on a year-by-year basis, with no relationship to the past or future, was unsound. He recommended that after a two-year transition, we should match whatever level of arms the Soviets and Chinese were providing to North Vietnam, with the ultimate goal, if the other side reciprocated, of reducing the overall flow of armaments. A transition was necessary to allow the South Vietnamese to regroup and develop their own war-fighting style, after we'd "Americanized" their military with sophisticated equipment and massive supplies. Though I remembered the constant lack of food and ammo and Kruithoff scoffing "we never have any fucking *dry* socks, L-T." Where had those "massive supplies" ended up? We sure hadn't seen them in the field.

The senator accompanied this recommendation with ten specific steps forward, one of which had an additional twelve elements, which goes to show Nunn's thoroughness and attention to detail. The report had a very short shelf life, however. Just two and a half months later, Saigon fell to North Vietnamese forces on April 30, 1975.

∽

My first exposure to the service academies was in April of 1976, when a cheating scandal rocked West Point. More than a hundred cadets had worked together on an electrical engineering take-home. The instructor forwarded 117 names to the Honor Committee, a panel of cadets that reviewed violations. As time went on, more and more violations were uncovered, including bribery allegations. By the end of that year, an internal review had investigated 235 cases spawning from that original take-home, and 151 cadets had either resigned or were involuntarily separated.[5]

As chairman of the Manpower Subcommittee, Senator Nunn was charged with investigating, and I took my first trip to the campus of the Long Gray Line.[6] The sense of history, merged with the scenic location, was overpowering. But I was representing the Senate, and as a Marine I already had plenty of experience in enemy territory. The superintendent at the time was Lt. Gen. Sidney Berry, and the commandant of cadets was Brig. Gen. Walter Ulmer.[7]

The leadership initially tried to downplay the problems by suggesting that honor violations were not pervasive. As our investigation continued, though, we found they were more widespread than anyone had thought. Because of their refusal to admit that their prestigious institution could be plagued with such problems, I nicknamed their approach the "West Point Protective Association." When I met with General Ulmer, he was inflexible and arrogant, not at all the kind of leader required during a time of transition. Berry, too, was overprotective of the institution.

Senator Nunn put pressure on the Pentagon to do its own independent investigation, under the committee's watchful eye. The Army acquiesced, and the Borman Commission was created. The Borman Commission was quite critical, recommending comprehensive reforms to both the Honor Code and the environment at West Point. As a result, the secretary asked a legendary leader, Gen. Andrew Goodpaster, to return from retirement to implement the reforms. Goodpaster, a World War II hero, had been a presidential adviser, NATO supreme allied commander, and recipient of two Purple Hearts and the Distinguished Service Cross.[8] Though Goodpaster had retired as a four-star, he served for four years at West Point with the rank of lieutenant general, because that's what the billet called for. Senator Nunn and I visited with him often, and under his leadership West Point rebuilt its reputation as one of the finest institutions in our nation.

$\backsim$

1976 was an election year. President Gerald Ford and former Georgia governor Jimmy Carter were going at each other. We knew Senator Nunn and Mr. Carter weren't on the friendliest of terms after Nunn defeated Carter's handpicked replacement for Senator Richard Russell in the 1972 primary. (Back then, it was unheard of to challenge an incumbent senator in your own party, but Nunn had, and he won the Democratic primary as well as the general election.)

Nunn was concerned about Carter's reductions in the defense budget, which Nunn felt needed to be increased again due to shortfalls in capabilities, despite general public antipathy toward anything military following the Vietnam War.

Carter, on the other hand, was very pro–arms control. After he beat Ford in a close election, he nominated Paul Warnke to be both head of the Arms Control and Disarmament Agency and the lead negotiator of the Strategic Arms Limitation Talks (SALT II). Nunn had his reservations about Warnke and voted against him, but he was still confirmed by the Senate.[9]

The SALT II debate was another bone of contention between Nunn and Carter. President Ford and Premier Leonid Brezhnev of the Soviet Union had laid out a framework for the treaty in 1974, but it had never become official. The completion of the task fell on President Carter. SALT II required both the United States and the Soviet Union to limit strategic nuclear delivery vehicles and Multiple Independently Targetable Reentry Vehicle (MIRV) systems. It also prohibited the construction of new land-based intercontinental ballistic missile (ICBM) launchers and limited the deployment of new types of strategic arms.[10] Considering the huge number of weapons the United States and Soviet Union had amassed during the Cold War, and their catastrophic potential, verifiable limits seemed to be a reasonable approach, at least on paper.

There was just one problem with this: the Senate. Nunn wasn't sold on the treaty. His biggest reservation was that it limited our ability to modernize our arsenal, even at the lower limits. So he put together a bipartisan group of senators to work on improvements. There was also bipartisan concern over verification in case the Soviets cheated. It was clear the treaty needed significant changes before it could pass. John Warner, John Glenn, and Bill Cohen would typically meet in Nunn's office. But one morning, the group was invited for breakfast at Senator Warner's home in Georgetown.

Warner's military legislative assistant, Chris Lehman, and I got there early to ensure everything was ready. It took a long time for Warner to answer the door, and once inside the dimly lit home we couldn't see any breakfast preparations. Warner went back to finish getting dressed, leaving Chris and me wondering about the food, just as the other senators began arriving. No coffee, no juice, nothing; just yelling from the back of the house that culminated in a woman's voice ringing out, "If you want breakfast, fix it yourself!" Warner wandered out looking sheepish, and Chris and I were immediately dispatched for bagels, coffee, and juice. Toward the end of the session, as we were discussing MIRVs, Warner's then-wife, Liz Taylor, actress and legendary beauty (and unabashedly half-dressed in a flimsy robe), came out to greet the senators. They were mesmerized, and Chris and I were awestruck. She was as beautiful close-up as she was on the big screen. There was no hint of the earlier harsh words, and even though they later divorced (Liz went through seven husbands), to this day I've never heard Senator Warner utter an unkind word about his famous ex-wife.

There was much infighting in the committee, as Senators Jackson and Tower wanted to release a report criticizing SALT II, and Nunn was one of the few who opposed the release of that report based on timing. But Nunn still refused to sign on to SALT II until the administration made a sincere effort to increase defense spending. Others wanted the MX deployed as a "mobile missile" that would be harder to target before they would agree to any deal. None of this was helped by the fact that Brezhnev was fighting yet another proxy war in the Horn of Africa, where Somalia had invaded Ethiopia. Congressional unease and distrust grew with the increasing Soviet intervention in Africa.[11]

Nunn kept up the pressure. He gave speeches and met with administration officials indicating he would not support SALT II without a commitment to increased defense spending. His was a swing vote, so this created real leverage for Nunn, whose vote as a conservative southern Democrat was often sought by presidents of both parties.

At one point, Carter asked Nunn to come down to the White House and update him on the arguments for increased spending. Carter had apparently come to office believing he could govern without fostering the relationships on the Hill and around Washington that were traditionally ingredients for success. He felt he was above the personal touches and courtesies extended to congresspersons and other influential Washingtonians. He also didn't see the need to improve relations with the man who'd defeated his handpicked senatorial appointee, or anyone else in the very experienced Georgia delegation.

But Carter did understand vote counts. He also knew that when it came to national security, he needed Nunn to serve as a bridge between hard-liners who totally opposed any agreement and the pro-defense southern Democrats who controlled the Senate in that era. Nunn, however, wasn't going to play nice just because Carter was from Georgia. He didn't believe in that kind of automatic favoritism.

We were notified on a Friday to prepare for a Monday meeting with the president and his national security team. I thought, *There goes my weekend.* I had to work with the Armed Services Committee staff to put together a hard-hitting case. I needed reinforcements, so I set my sights on the grunts of the Pentagon. I needed someone below the secretary's level to get the cold hard facts, so I called up Maj. Gen. Max Thurman,[12] then head of the Army budget shop. I told the general the mission: I needed information, but the political appointees could not be brought into the loop since they would just repeat the White House's talking points. Thurman put together a compelling case for an increased budget, with lots of charts and graphs printed neatly on poster board (this was before the days of PowerPoint).

Attending the session with Carter were Harold Brown, the secretary of defense; Russ Murray, the head of Pentagon Program Analysis and Evaluation (PA&E); Zbig Brzezinski, the national security adviser; and a number of other key White House staff, including chief of staff Hamilton Jordan. Nunn seemed right at home in the Roosevelt Room, but for me it was like getting into the conclave of the cardinals when they were picking a new pope. Nunn gave the introduction, then had Jeff Record talk about the deficiencies in the nuclear forces. To this, Hamilton Jordan quipped, "Thank you, Dr. Strangelove." I did a summary of the problems with readiness, the "hollow Army," the lack of modern equipment from ground vehicles, helicopters, artillery, and tanks, to individual fighting gear, and lack of sufficient lift compared to the conventional threats we faced. Russ Murray's face turned beet red; he knew the only place I could have gotten those specifics. He growled, "Where did you get this information?"

My reply: "Friends of conventional forces."

Carter looked at Secretary Brown. "Harold, is Sam right?" Brown said, "I'm afraid he is, Mr. President. We need to increase defense spending." Carter had campaigned on a promise to cut defense spending by $7 billion and balance the budget by 1981, so he was more reluctant to increase spending. Brown was one of our best secretaries of defense in terms of what he did for the military, but publicly he never deviated from the president's policies. Behind the scenes, however, he pressed hard to beef up defense.

Not long after this meeting, Carter announced his plan to raise the defense budget by 3 percent per year, with an emphasis on conventional readiness instead of strategic weapons. Considering that he'd campaigned on a pledge to cut, this shows how his desire for an arms control agreement resulted in a change of heart on defense.[13] I don't know if Carter was really convinced by the facts, but he knew the SALT II vote was coming up. He also knew he'd be facing a tough re-election battle, and former California governor Ronald Reagan was spreading the word that Carter was weak on defense. This was another motivation for his about-face.

Though Nunn and his colleagues won that battle, Carter still ended up losing when it came to SALT II. He and Brezhnev signed the treaty on June 18, 1979. Carter handed the treaty off to the Senate four days later for advice and consent, but it went nowhere. The following January, he asked the Senate to hold off on consideration since the Russians had invaded Afghanistan. Carter and Stansfield Turner, his CIA director, could not ignore this invasion, though they'd turned a blind eye to all the other evidence the Soviets were increasing the military capabilities of the Warsaw Pact and couldn't be trusted. Thus, SALT II never entered into force.

～

JAN

When I was expecting our second child, Julie, we decided we needed more room. We moved to a white brick split-level with blue shutters. The new house, in a child-filled neighborhood on Baldwin Drive, had four bedrooms and an unfinished basement, which we later turned into more bedrooms when our next children were born: Meghan in 1984 and Dan in 1986. Its large backyard, with a swing set and later a basketball hoop and soccer and lacrosse goals, became the gathering place for the neighborhood kids. There was also a large, messy, sap-filled pine tree they climbed and sometimes fell from. I didn't know until much later that they also shot bottle rockets out of it.

The births of our babies were, without a doubt, four of the happiest days of our lives. Back then fathers weren't expected to be as involved with child rearing as they are now. But when he wasn't working long hours—and once I convinced him they wouldn't easily break—Arnold was a natural with the kids. I was surprised, however, considering all he'd seen and endured during the war, at how anxious he became even at a slight cough from one of the children. He'd seen men killed and wounded on the battlefield and been wounded himself. But when it came to his children, he was far from stoic.

Since we'd decided I would stay home, I acquired all kinds of useful skills: painting, putting up wallpaper, stenciling walls, fixing washing machines, dishwashers, and various other appliances . . . and then there was ironing shirts, not my favorite pastime.

Even though Arnold's were "permanent press," they still had wrinkles. I completed this chore nightly after the kids were in bed. I'll never forget, however, the last day I ever ironed for him. He wanted a particular oxford that day, one that had yet to be ironed, of course. He was in a hurry, anxious to get out the door, so I simply pressed the front and collar and said, "Here, you should probably keep your jacket on all day."

But he was meeting later with Sen. John Warner, who was always impeccably dressed, and forgot my advice. At some point he slipped off his jacket. Warner remarked, "Arnold, it looks like you slept in that shirt." He came home and relayed the story as an amusing incident. But I was mortified. It took years for me to actually find it funny. Needless to say, his shirts all went to the cleaners from that day forward.

∽

ARNOLD

Carter appointed retired admiral Stansfield Turner director of the CIA in 1977, and Turner quickly began dismantling much of its operational and analytical capability. As chair of the Manpower Subcommittee, Senator Nunn decided to increase the workforce at the Defense Intelligence Agency (DIA), adding more than eight hundred analysts as a counter. While Nunn was willing to make sure our intelligence establishment was manned and funded, he felt the Department of Defense's (DOD's) officer corps was bloated, in particular at the general-level ranks. He had us do an analysis.

Nunn held several hearings on this issue, including one with the abrasive head of the Navy nuclear propulsion program, Adm. Hyman Rickover. Rickover was known for his crusty personality, bucking naysayers and red tape to create the nuclear Navy.[14] By dint of his success and sheer longevity, he had the final say over all matters relating to nuclear propulsion. He was legendary for indoctrinating his juniors with absolute loyalty, not to the Navy but to him personally. His staff worked with us and it was always the same story: Rickover wanted something done, his way, and because of the success of his programs and his irascible style, he usually got it. So when he stated his disdain for the large number of flag and general officers, Senator Nunn paid close attention, as he too questioned why we needed more admirals and generals to wage peace than we had at the height of the Vietnam War. (In 1978 the military had 1,165 generals and admirals, or 1 per 1,800 military personnel. In 1968 the ratio had been 1 for every 2,600 personnel.[15]) Rickover's recommendation was to take half of the generals and admirals, lock them in a room, and give them some crayons and coloring books to keep them busy. Nunn followed a more objective track, looking at all the billets and requirements. He concluded we could cut 20 percent of the generals, a 4 percent reduction a year over five years, and substantially improve the ratio of generals to troops.[16]

I was at my desk when Rose Johnson, now Nunn's personal secretary, buzzed and said Secretary of Defense Brown needed to see the senator. I told her to make it happen right away; you don't keep a SecDef waiting. Later that afternoon, Brown showed up, accompanied by his deputy, Graham Claytor, and the chairman of the Joint Chiefs, Gen. David Jones. Roland and I were wondering why all three had come in for a meeting, a rare event. I surmised, "We must be going to war somewhere."

Brown started the sit-down by saying, "We're here about one of the most serious problems we've ever faced, one that could seriously degrade the fighting capability of our military." I assumed the Soviets must have finally invaded West Germany or sent missiles to Cuba again. Brown continued that the reduction in general officers Nunn had proposed would wreck the military as we knew it. Clayton and Jones added similar arguments.

I was stunned. We had a hollow Army, the Soviets were rearming, Warnke was negotiating away our nuclear forces, and the top three people in the Pentagon were worried about losing a few admirals and generals. I was both amused at their priorities and impressed that we'd located a major tender spot. I always kept this meeting in the back of my mind once Nunn became chairman and I was the committee's staff director. We used the Pentagon's irrational concern for their generals to leverage lots of key issues in our favor.

‿

Nunn did prove helpful to the president when it came to advice and consent on another treaty, this one regarding control of the Panama Canal. This issue was hotly contested throughout the country, and it hit close to our home: Jan had lived in Panama when her dad had been stationed there from 1962 to 1964. Back then, it was a duty station that came with lots of perks, including cooks, cleaners, and seamstresses for the military families. The Fitzwilliamses believed, from firsthand experience, that Panamanians were incapable of operating the canal without the United States.

Back in 1903, President Theodore Roosevelt and Philippe Jean Bunau-Varilla had signed a treaty that allowed America to build and operate the canal. Bunau-Varilla wasn't an elected representative, so many Panamanians never fully accepted this treaty, even though it had also assured and protected their own long-desired independence from Colombia.[17] In 1964, protests over their right to fly the Panamanian flag over the Canal Zone led to tension between the two governments. Panamanians resented having to show identification and being harassed trying to cross the zone. Both countries realized the original arrangement was no longer sustainable.

The canal fight started to really heat up in the late 1970s. In the 1976 campaign, President Ford was the only candidate to support negotiations with Panama. Both Carter and Reagan were vehemently opposed. Reagan's campaign became famous for the line, "We built it, we paid for it, it's ours, and we're going to keep it!"

Well, campaign promises are made to be broken. When Carter stepped into office, he made it his mission to cede control. He had the weighty task of not only shifting senators' views, but also convincing the American people that this wasn't a surrender of our rights or a compromise of our strategic position. Many conservatives in the Senate, notably Strom Thurmond, falsely believed that Panama's leader, Brigadier General Omar Torrijos-Herrera, was a communist. The Senate tried its best to derail the negotiations, with senators adding amendments left and right that they knew others couldn't vote for or that would cause Carter or Torrijos to head back to the negotiating table.

While the treaty was under the jurisdiction of the Foreign Relations Committee and its chairman, John Sparkman, there was no way it could pass without the support of key members of the SASC. Nunn did his usual due diligence. He attended all the hearings, took all the briefings, and finally decided he could only support the treaty with certain reservations. He supported a provision that would allow the United States to keep a military presence, if both countries wished it so, after the official turnover in 1999.

Because of the complexity of the issue, the SASC general counsel, John Roberts, proved a key player. John Stennis, chairman of the SASC, was a treaty opponent, and Roberts was writing his point papers and speeches. At the same time, he was helping us draft the Nunn provision. This is a great example of the professionalism of the SASC staff; they're there to support the members, not push any personal agendas.

While everyone was deliberating the specifics, Carter's administration led a full-on lobbying and information campaign to get the public on board with the new treaty. Thurmond led a group of forty senators who opposed it, and the treaty required a two-thirds majority to pass, which meant Carter had to persuade up to ten senators to change positions, including Howard Baker, a favorite for the Republican nomination for president. (Baker ended up voting "for," but it cost him the nomination.) Torrijos started hosting senators in Panama to prove he wasn't a communist.

Even John Wayne, the cowboy actor and an icon of the right, weighed in, supporting the negotiations and his longtime friend, Torrijos. But we were still facing a lot of opposition. At the height of the debate, our office was getting a thousand letters a day, 95 percent of them against. Most were from out of state, some were hostile, and a few were even threatening. We had to turn a couple over to the FBI. But in 1978 Carter's efforts paid off.[18] The Senate just barely approved two treaties, one establishing the canal as neutral territory, open to any nation (but allowing the U.S. military to defend it if necessary), and the other giving control to Panama by December 31, 1999. Nunn voted in favor, and the vote was 68–32, one above the two-thirds requirement.[19]

Even ten years down the line, some people never forgave Nunn for "losing" the canal. A popular bumper sticker around Georgia read "Once we had a canal; now we have Nunn." But this was a great example of the senator looking at long-term national interests rather than just voting with the back-home popular instincts.

∽

On November 4, 1979, a mob of Iranian students attacked our embassy in Tehran. Unwilling to use deadly force, the United States was unable to prevent them from gaining access to the compound. Several hundred students streamed in and began ransacking. Some personnel managed to escape, but many did not. Fifty-two Americans, including Marines, became hostages of the revolution.

President Carter exercised restraint. He tried to secure their release through negotiations with representatives from the revolutionary government. But as the days became weeks and weeks became months, Carter's approval ratings nosedived. His restraint was interpreted as weakness.

Unrelated to the events in Tehran, an Army colonel and fellow Georgian, Charlie Beckwith, had spent years raging against the bureaucracy to create a special antiterrorist unit that would specialize in hostage rescue and direct action raids. After several successive high-profile terrorist events, he was tasked with creating the 1st Special Operations Detachment Delta, or Delta Force. Selected from the ranks of Army Special Forces and Rangers, these men were the best of the best.

Beckwith's unit hadn't done much but train since its inception in 1977, but the hostage crisis gave the unit an opportunity. The White House directed him to come up with a plan and begin rehearsals, and by early April 1980, President Carter was ready to pull the trigger.

The plan was complicated and dangerous. Six Air Force C-130s, carrying troops and fuel, and eight RH-53D Sea Stallion helicopters would rendezvous at a remote, makeshift airstrip in the desert south of Tehran under the cover of night. The helicopters would refuel, embark the Deltas, and proceed to the capital's outskirts, dropping the commandos at a waiting position. From there, they would assault the embassy the following night. The helos would then pick up both the assault teams and the liberated hostages, spiriting them to where the C-130s could pick them up and fly them out of Iran.

There was one major problem: the separate units had never really trained together. When they all finally arrived at the departure airfield in Egypt, there was no time for a full rehearsal, despite Beckwith's and others' requests for one.

No plan survives contact with the enemy. In this case, the enemy was Murphy's Law. On their flight to the desert strip, code-named Desert One, the eight helicopters encountered a haboob, a phenomenon where the sand particles from the desert floor became suspended thousands of feet in the air. The dust wreaked havoc on the choppers; one was forced down and another had to turn back. At Desert One, another encountered other mechanical problems that would prevent it from continuing the mission. The assault force required a minimum of six helicopters, but suddenly they only had five.

Maneuvering aircraft around one another on the ground requires a certain choreographic skill. It's a complicated dance even under good conditions. In the Iranian desert at 0200, with dust clouds kicked up by rotor wash, it became deadly. A helicopter was maneuvering away from a C-130, both laden with fuel, when it crashed down on top of the plane. The explosion rocked the desert. A number of the Deltas and aircrew were able to escape, but eight servicemen died, including a Marine staff sergeant and an Air Force captain from Georgia.[20]

The overall commander of the operation was Maj. Gen. Jim Vaught. Nunn and I knew him from his time as commanding general of the 24th Mechanized Division at Fort Stewart. We always worked hard to ensure Georgia bases and personnel had everything they needed, so we were close with all the senior military at each of our bases. I remember Vaught as a gruff mud soldier who knew infantry basics like the back of his hand but disliked operating outside of the school solution. As one of the few staffers with combat experience, I asked Vaught during the SASC investigation how he'd done his training. He told us he'd kept all the units separate for security reasons. This lack of teamwork was one root cause of the tragedy.

Just as in Vietnam, a good leader can make all the difference; a poor one can cause untold harm. Vaught was a good division commander, but he failed at Desert One, just as Colonel Codispoti was a poor leader in Vietnam. I constantly found myself thinking, *Who puts these people in charge?* Whoever it was, they were just as much to blame.

⬿

In 1969, the Gates Commission, chaired by former secretary of defense Thomas Gates, had been set up by President Nixon to assess whether or not our country should continue to use the draft or convert to an all-volunteer force (AVF). Due to the unpopularity of the Vietnam War and the many instances where those with connections dodged the draft, "universal service" was universally despised, except by the military, as it guaranteed a ready supply of new recruits. The commission found that the draft was no longer sustainable, for several reasons. First, because of demographic changes it was no longer "universal." Second, they argued that volunteers would be more cost-effective because paying a higher wage meant attracting more competent people. Third, there were moral arguments against a draft from both sides of the aisle. And, finally, the Army had experienced significant drug and discipline problems among draftees.[21]

Thus, in 1973, the United States ended peacetime conscription. A lot of people were skeptical about replacing the draft, but I wasn't in their ranks. I'd seen firsthand what it did to both our country and men who never should have been put behind a trigger. With Nunn as chairman of the Manpower and Personnel Subcommittee, we gradually began to notice a different side to the AVF. It seemed to us in the middle to late 1970s that it was on the verge of collapse. The services could not meet their recruiting goals, retention was suffering, and quality was deteriorating. Nunn conducted hearings to get at the facts. Was the AVF attracting and retaining the talent needed for a modern military, one of the fundamental premises of the Gates Commission?

I shared his concerns about quality. No one could have been in favor of the Army's recruiting practices; both their end strength and their overall quality was slipping fast in the late 1970s. Though the Army asserted that this was only temporary and they could easily fix it with additional funding, by the end of fiscal year 1979 the end strength was more than 15,000 short of the congressionally authorized number. To make up the shortfall, Army recruiters had resorted to targeting less desirable candidates, such as seventeen-year-olds without high school diplomas, and dipping into the lower mental categories to try to reach their quotas, which they still couldn't meet.[22] In some years, the Army was experiencing 42 percent non-end-of-active-service attrition, meaning almost half of those enlisted couldn't complete their tour because they were unfit for service.

This was both expensive and destructive. Nunn was determined to fix it, but he found himself at odds with the Pentagon, which was trying to cover up the AVF's shortcomings. The Department of Defense (DOD) always has a difficult time admitting that something isn't working. Secretary of the Army Clifford Alexander even tried to remove the quality scores from the books, claiming test scores didn't matter; but he really wanted to ensure these trends couldn't be uncovered. The Senate blocked his attempts.

Nunn was determined to get the facts out. He organized a series of hearings on the AVF. To help make his case, he asked the General Accounting Office

(GAO, now the Government Accountability Office) to investigate the problems as well as to do a cost analysis, because he didn't believe the numbers the Gates Commission and the DOD had projected. The Pentagon was caught in their own rhetoric. They'd argued the AVF wouldn't cost more than the draft, so they didn't want to admit there were increased advertising, recruiting, and retention costs and needed increases to basic pay and benefits. Yet, at the same time, to ensure these costs were managed, they refused to increase basic pay and other benefits.

The GAO found that since 1973, the AVF had actually cost $3 billion more per year than the draft.[23] With facts and evidence from GAO, the Congressional Research Service, and experts like Charlie Moskos and Marty Binkin in hand, Nunn came out guns blazing. The AVF was headed for the rocks, and a major course correction was necessary. After these hearings, the only ones still in denial were John White and Richard Danzig, the heads of Manpower and Personnel.[24] Within the DOD, it's common practice to stick with the party line and not admit problems. The hearings revealed that the AVF could not meet its recruiting goals in either quality or quantity and could not retain midcareer personnel, nor could anyone fully comprehend all its hidden, downstream costs.

Once word got out that Nunn was serious about identifying the problems and finding solutions, the closet patriots—individuals who would be fired if they criticized the party line but who were willing to provide information off the record—brought us many examples that confirmed Nunn's worst fears. He took a dual approach to fixing the problem: first, require the military to increase its quality standards, and second, develop a benefits package to help attract, motivate, and retain higher quality personnel. The quality of the force was more important to him than the price tag.

Our office was helped immensely by Capt. John McCain. He came to me one day and said that the chief of naval operations, Adm. Tom Hayward, was concerned about the AVF too. McCain wanted the chief to come in and talk to the senator, but they couldn't ask for a meeting because the Carter administration kept the military on a short leash. Nunn was always happy to speak with a service chief, but he would not ask for a meeting unless he had something specific on his agenda.

McCain and I decided to pull a fast one. He reported to Hayward, "Sir, Senator Nunn needs to see you," just as I walked into Nunn's office and remarked, "Senator, the chief of naval operations requests a meeting."

They met in Nunn's private office in the Capitol, where he rarely took visitors. After they exchanged pleasantries each waited on the other to start. Silence. For a moment, nothing happened.

Almost simultaneously, both turned sharply and glared at McCain and me. Our sheepish expressions gave us away as we decided it would be politic to quickly dart out of the room. But from that meeting came the foundations of the legislation that would save the AVF.

Senators Nunn and Warner, and Chris Lehman and I at the staff level, worked to put together the Nunn-Warner benefits package. This included the largest pay increase since the inception of the AVF, specialty pays to get more doctors and dentists into uniform, pay for deployments at sea and for those who served in technical specialties, and the variable housing allowance, a massive increase in how service personnel and their families received their housing allowance. Other changes included an increase in enlistment and re-enlistment bonuses, special bonuses for enlisted personnel with more than ten years' service, and increasing pay for flight and sea service.

The Carter administration opposed the package. The administration didn't want to admit to all the problems, as it would further underscore their poor record on defense. But the SASC and the Senate approved it anyway, and the House was receptive. Carter was really feeling the heat as he headed into the general election, and he finally decided to support the legislation after all.

Coupled with the later Reagan-era defense buildup, the benefits package reversed the downward spiral of the AVF, and it remained in solid shape through the 1980s. But as the active force was substantially reduced at the end of the Cold War (going from 3.5 million at the peak of the Korean and Vietnam Wars to 1.4 million[25]), the cost per person was increasing due to the cumulative effect of added benefits and programs such as TRICARE for Life and the reversal of the retirement reforms we put in place in 1986.

Today, the AVF is again unsustainable from the standpoint of fully burdened life-cycle costs. The Department of Defense spends more than half of its budget supporting people.[26] I'm amused when some label me as a critic of the AVF. I was there back when we first saved it and were called its critics then. I'm still a supporter of the concept, but our force *as it stands today* is no longer sustainable over the long term. This is primarily due to its long-term costs, particularly for those no longer serving—more than 2.4 million retirees whose retirement pay is more than $100 billion a year. Their Pentagon-provided health care costs more than $30 billion a year. On the active side, costs have doubled from 2005 to 2015 for a slightly *smaller* force. Because of those increased costs, we continue to reduce the size of our active and reserve fighting forces, and thus both our readiness for war and our ability to deter it.

The Gates Commission foresaw this circumstance, stating in 1970 that a volunteer force would not be sustainable unless lawmakers eliminated the twenty-year cliff retirement, reformed the "up or out" promotion system, and changed the basis of pay and compensation from a simple time-in-grade system to a skill- and performance-based system. None of these recommendations were ever adopted and reforms in these areas are long overdue.

〜

Senator Nunn developed a close working relationship with senior Marine Corps leaders, but not without a few bumps. As part of his detailed examination of the problems with the all-volunteer force, Nunn had highlighted the fact that quality in the Corps had significantly decreased and the Marines were not making quota even with some significant recruiting scandals. The leadership had incorrectly assumed that since they'd had more volunteers than draftees during the Vietnam era, this would continue.

In actuality, many had been draft-motivated volunteers, like me. The number of courts-martial, nonjudicial punishments, and others problems were off the charts. Several studies found that the Corps had the highest rate of unauthorized absences, desertion, and drug abuse of any of the services. Racial tensions were also high, with gangs and violence rampant on bases. But like the Army, the Marine leadership was intent on keeping up their authorized end strength at all costs, even when they didn't meet their recruiting goals. Senator Nunn decided to cut the Marine Corps by 25,000 to force them to focus on quality.

Gen. Bob Barrow, who served as the head of Manpower and Personnel, had worked with the subcommittee on this issue. He had a hard time understanding why I, as a Reserve Marine on whom he'd pinned my major's leaf, wasn't supporting the HQ position. So I made a personal case to him that we needed to set and meet high standards of quality. In like manner, Nunn also remained adamant that the Corps needed to emphasize quality over quantity. My civilian boss and I were of one mind.

Unfortunately, my sit-down with Barrow didn't take, and the Corps went into attack mode. They were used to getting their way with Congress. General Wilson, the commandant and Medal of Honor recipient, had previously served a tour as the head of legislative affairs and still had strong ties in Congress, particularly with his fellow Mississippian, Chairman Stennis. But despite their intense efforts, Nunn held firm. When Wilson learned Nunn had been the one who'd convinced Stennis that the Marines needed to shift from quantity to quality, he requested a one-on-one meeting.

This took place in Senator Nunn's personal office. Wilson and Barrow both came to the meeting and made their case to give them more time to improve before reducing the Corps's numbers. I was thinking, as they spoke, that this had been one of my reasons for leaving active duty: the inability to bring about change from within. Senator Nunn did not relent. He told Wilson that if the USMC would make a major shift and hold recruiting and retention to higher quality standards, he would allow the Corps to have a higher end strength. But Wilson would have to live with a smaller Corps if the quality didn't improve.

Wilson eventually swung around to Nunn's point of view. He gave Nunn his word, and said he expected General Barrow to follow him as commandant. Barrow, at the same table, made the same commitment. Nunn accepted their assurances and removed the cut in the end strength, but he put a requirement into law for a better percentage of high school graduates and more recruits from the higher mental categories.

Marine historians note that one of Wilson's most important accomplishments was the shift to quality standards in the Corps.[27] The senator who made it happen and the staffer who supported him are, of course, not mentioned in these annals.

~

While President Nixon and Henry Kissinger are credited with opening China, Carter made the most significant strides toward normalizing relations with that nation. On December 15, 1978, he concluded secret negotiations with the People's Republic, which agreed to establish formal diplomatic relations if the United States would no longer recognize the sovereignty of Taiwan. This was a landmark development, so naturally Nunn wanted a firsthand report about its effect on our allies in the region. He was also concerned about Carter's desire to remove U.S. troops from South Korea and growing unrest in the Philippines.

We put together an itinerary: the Philippines, Thailand, China, South Korea, and Japan. I went to McCain and asked him to be our escort. We flew from the 89th Airlift Wing at Andrews Air Force Base on the blue and white United States of America official jet. The trip included Nunn as the leader of the Codel, along with Gary Hart, John Glenn, and Bill Cohen. Howard Baker, then the minority leader, had called Nunn and asked him to include Cohen, one of the most promising new senators. It was the beginning of a productive relationship between Nunn and Cohen, who went on to be one of our most accomplished senators and ultimately secretary of defense. The staff support included myself, Jeff Record, Jim Locher, and the escort officer. As with all other trips, Nunn required advance briefings from the DOD, the State Department, and our intelligence agencies, as well as the preparation of papers on every issue related to that part of the world.

During his campaign, Carter had pledged to withdraw all ground troops from South Korea, though he'd made this pledge without consulting South Korea, China, Japan, or Congress. This was causing distress. Japan and others feared the vacuum a U.S. withdrawal would cause. Thailand and the Philippines in particular were looking at Vietnam's invasion of Cambodia with apprehension. The United States was interested in keeping up good relations with the Philippines, home of critical naval and air bases. Relations with Japan were also tense because of our trade deficit. Congress was becoming more protectionist and was debating limits on our imports from that nation.[28]

I spent a lot of time working with our staff and with the various agencies to make sure we had a solid agenda, that we would see all the key foreign leaders essential to a productive trip, and that the logistical details were in place. We were picked up by Pentagon transportation and taken to Andrews, where we got to wait in the distinguished visitors' lounge, the one used by the most senior personnel, including the privileged passengers of Air Force One. It would be a long and demanding trip: five countries in eleven days, covering more than 20,000 miles there and back.

The pilots of the 89th take great pride in taking off and landing exactly on time, and the flight crews provide first-class service. Still, for the staffers, the trip, while comfortable, was all work and no play. We had to respond to questions from the senators' review of the briefing materials. At each stop we coordinated with the ambassador, the political officer, and the defense attaché. Nunn also liked to meet with the CIA station chief at each stop to understand our intelligence community assessments. We organized more briefings on the issues that would be raised with the various leaders. We met both career and political ambassadors and worked with Foreign Service officers, diplomats every bit as knowledgeable and capable as their counterparts in the Pentagon.

Our first stop was Manila. As in most Asian cities, the downtown traffic can only be described as a cacophony of chaos, with bicycles, motor scooters, cars, festive trucks, ox-drawn carts, and rickshaws. Our cars wound among food stalls and outdoor markets and an endless throng of people. Our most important meeting would be with President Ferdinand Marcos, whose kleptocratic government was marked by brutality and extravagance. The United States had looked the other way for years, but Carter had started to push back against Marcos's dismal record on human rights.

The formal meetings were uneventful, with each side making standard points. The highlight was the formal dinner that First Lady Imelda Marcos attended, wearing a pair from her very expensive collection of more than three thousand shoes. Opulence glittered, from the golden candelabra to the golden silverware to the finest china and more wine and toasts than one could count. The dinner was a sharp contrast with the poverty we'd seen en route to the palace. Various organizations over the years have estimated that the Marcoses looted their country of more than $10 billion.

Next, we headed to Bangkok, Thailand. Our ambassador then was Morton Abramowitz, one of the stars of the Foreign Service. In early 1979, Thailand was struggling with refugees from the Vietnamese invasion of Cambodia and the escalation of the fighting with the Khmer Rouge forces.[29] The refugee population peaked at more than a million. Until 1975, Thailand had been a key staging area for U.S. airpower, from the reconnaissance and fighter planes at Udorn, only forty minutes from Hanoi, to the huge B-52 bomber base in U-Tapao in southern Thailand. Thailand had been a good ally during the war, but in 1976 it was back under military rule after the Thammasat University Massacre.[30]

One thread running through all my foreign travel with Senator Nunn was my personal resolve never to return empty-handed. I was always either filling a "request" list from Jan and her sisters or surprising her with something special. Thailand was known for its Baht necklaces, which are almost pure gold, and for their ornate multistone rings. Staffers didn't have much free time, but I was usually able to bring home the goods. Thailand was jewelry, China was the handwoven, floral rugs in favor then, South Korea was jewelry chests, Japan was pearls. On a government salary, I couldn't exactly focus on the high end, but sometimes I got it right.

$$\backsim$$

JAN

Arnold often traveled overseas, especially when the Senate was out on recess between Thanksgiving and Christmas. After one trip he came home to a hero's welcome. It was 1984, the year of the Cabbage Patch dolls. Customers were stampeding the stores to purchase those "must have" dolls for Christmas. There was a huge shortage, so whenever a few hit the shelves, they sold out in an instant. That year Arnold had been traveling in Europe, with a layover in Ireland. He called to say, "There are plenty of dolls at a store here in the airport. How many should I buy?" He came home with dolls for our children, nieces, and nephews, even some of our friends' children. A true hero!

$$\backsim$$

ARNOLD

From Thailand we flew to China. We were the first U.S. government plane allowed to land in Beijing. Our pilots were nervous about navigating, so they asked Senator Glenn up to the cockpit to help. We landed with no incidents at an antiquated airport. On the drive into town, I was taken aback by the number of ox-drawn carts, the lack of automobiles, and the dreary, outdated buildings. The city looked run-down, with none of the glitz or bustle of Manila or Bangkok.

We were put up in a government hotel that fit the pattern of old and tired, but it was handy for my morning PT. I put on my Marine Corps sweat gear and took a run through the Forbidden City, which wasn't that "forbidden" after all;

plenty of locals were strolling along. The air, though, quickly gave me a coughing fit, forcing me to stop and catch my breath. It was laden with choking pollution.

This freedom of movement didn't prepare me for our meetings with their foreign ministry, defense minister, and others, leading up to a highlight with Deng Xiaoping himself. There was also an elaborate state dinner. I was unprepared for the rigid sequence of events, with multiple musical numbers, toasts, and a twelve-course meal. To keep from getting bored, we played a game of trying to figure out what we were eating.

Since this was the first U.S. delegation to visit after the normalization, all meetings were of intense media interest. We were fortunate to have Ambassador Leonard Woodcock at our side; he'd been there in a liaison capacity prior to the opening of official diplomatic relations.

The get-together with Deng Xiaoping was different than we expected, since he didn't spout the party line we'd heard everywhere else. He was a chain smoker who didn't abstain while he was with us. The sit-down was held in a nondescript office building and Deng occupied a large, comfortable-looking armchair with the other Chinese leaders to his right and Nunn, the other three senators, and Woodcock to his left. Interpreters sat close by the leaders. The U.S. side had skillfully prepared the issues they would raise; the staff was relegated to the sidelines.

Nunn wanted to determine if there were areas to put pressure on the Soviets to divert them from concentrating all their forces on NATO. It was good for us to keep them nervous about Mongolia. The other issues we covered were Taiwan, the conflict in Cambodia, the U.S. naval presence in the Pacific, and Beijing's views on international security and economics. Since China had been closed off to the United States, we were all curious to better understand this important nation.

After all the official meetings, the senators were slated for a press conference back in our hotel. There was a tremendous demand from the world media as to what we'd discussed and what the Chinese had said. Being from Georgia, the birthplace of Coca-Cola (which, like many other companies, was interested in the potentially vast Chinese market), I wanted to make sure they saw back home that Sam Nunn helped open China to Coke. So as the conference started, I took one of the Coca-Colas the Marine Corps had brought along for our control room supplies. I held it out, so all the cameras could see it, and set it down right in front of Senator Nunn. Wearing my red and black University of Georgia tie, I placed the red and white can for all to see. Carter may have opened China to the United States, but I helped open China to Coca-Cola.

The next stop, South Korea, was just as important, since our key ally was concerned about the opening of the dialogue with Beijing, our relationship with Japan, and Carter's promise to withdraw troops. In Seoul's eyes, such a move would diminish our commitment to protect them from the always unpredictable

North. We visited the demilitarized zone, the no-man's-land between North and South Korea, where the war had stalemated in 1953. Both sides of the DMZ were on full military alert 24/7, staring each other down. We'd received all the intelligence briefings and analyses and knew about the tunnels that were deep and wide enough to move huge amounts of supplies and weapons into the South undetected. Our delegation was received with open arms by our military and theirs, since Nunn supported keeping U.S. forces in place.

We met with Seoul's political leadership as well, assisted by Ambassador William Gleysteen Jr. A formal dinner hosted by President Park Chung-hee was held in a palace that put the Senate's most ornate rooms to shame. There was a long table with the American delegation on one side and the Korean on the other. I enjoyed eating with goldware and being served by my own waiter. No detail was out of place and there was no idle chatter. We were with the senators, the senior military, and the state officials, though the staffers were far down the table. But it did not escape attention when one of our escort officers handed me a note for Senator Nunn. I opened it and realized it needed immediate attention, but I was concerned about the glare he'd give me if I got up and took it over. Nor was passing it up the table an option.

I finally got Jim Locher, the senior staffer, to deliver it. He gulped, rose, and walked down the long line. All eyes on both sides were fixed on him. Nunn opened it, took one glance, and held up two fingers in the victory sign.

I think everyone assumed there must have been some huge victory for the United States. But to understand, you need to know that earlier that day we had all gone to get the famous one-day custom-made suits. Nunn had placed an order, and the note was from the tailor, who needed to know if he wanted three buttons or two on his suit coats. Nunn proved again how decisive he was; he made the decision in less than five seconds. (I should add that the suits had a very short half-life, like the ones I'd ordered in Hong Kong.)

Nunn and the delegation were reinforced in their views as to the need to keep U.S. troops in South Korea. And we were directed to write up a report that made the case for continuing our long-standing commitment. At our other stops, we found the same support.

From Korea we headed to Japan, where the ambassador was former Senate majority leader Mike Mansfield, who'd served in the Navy in World War I, then in the Army and Marine Corps. Nunn wanted to talk about better coordination between U.S. forces and the Japanese. Japan hadn't changed much in the ten years since I'd been in the hospital there. The traffic and hustle were still there, so I decided to do my PT around the emperor's palace, which had a lot more security and more uptight guards than the Forbidden City.

The trip seemed both a blur and a long march since we covered so much substance and had so many meetings. On the trip back, we were busy writing drafts of all the reports Nunn and the others wanted for a variety of audiences, from their fellow senators to the CIA to the State Department and, in particular, for Carter and his national security team. As with all other Nunn reports, these would go through multiple drafts, but we knew his demand for timely debriefs would pressure us to complete them quickly.

I also had to ensure that the staffs of the other travelers, as well as many executive branch offices, were rapidly made privy to our information and impressions. I spent time with our DIA intelligence analysts, since we were not on the favorite list at CIA, given Nunn's decision to increase the DIA workforce. We also had to file reports on our expenditures with both the Senate and the Pentagon. I made sure they were accurate and timely. In all the years we were in the Senate and with all the travel we took, there were never any reports returned for inappropriate expenditures or poor accounting.

The meeting with President Carter was already set. The staff was not invited to this one, but we armed our senators with the talking points from each stop and with the specific report Nunn and the others were giving him directly.

It concluded that our Asian allies were watching our actions with increasing concern, from our abandonment of Taiwan to the promise to withdraw troops from South Korea. There were growing tensions and the possibility of a number of conflicts: between China and the Soviet Union, China and Vietnam, and North and South Korea. Other allies also worried about a resurgence of Japanese power. The United States simply could not ignore Asia and the Pacific. It was home to over half the world's population. Yes, we'd probably made too many commitments there. But pulling back would unleash many devils. True, those commitments were expensive. Yes, they could involve risk. But we could only hope that the president would take the negative consequences of his actions, as well as his rash campaign promises, into account. Carter did reverse his decision to withdraw U.S. troops from South Korea.

⌒

Heading into the fall 1980 elections, Carter had a full plate.[31] He was dealing with the Iranian hostages, the invasion of Afghanistan, a boycott of the Moscow Olympics, and the unpopular decision to reinstate draft registration. The polls had predicted a close race, but November 4th was a shocker. Ronald Reagan's coattails swept in the first Republican majority since 1954. A number of "safe" senators, such as McGovern, Church, and Talmadge, went down in defeat. Howard Baker replaced Robert Byrd as majority leader. John Tower replaced John Stennis at the helm of the Armed Services Committee. But the same tough national security issues were unresolved and would continue.

IN THE BELLY OF THE BEAST

1980–85: Washington, DC

The Reagan Revolution brought in a wave of Republican senators as well as a new president, flipping the Senate from Democratic control for the first time in more than twenty-five years. The Armed Services Committee had a new and powerful chairman, John Tower of Texas. Tower had served in the Navy in World War II and would retire from the Reserves in 1989 as a master chief boatswain's mate. As ranking member, Tower installed a separate staff for the minority. Traditionally, the minority and majority had shared one unified, bipartisan staff. While the split was controversial at the time (1977), he put a highly capable staff in place with Rhett Dawson as his staff director and chief counsel and Ann Sauer as the budget and policy expert.

Tower had been critical of Carter on many issues and was a prominent adviser to Reagan during the election. His new majority staff would work closely with Defense Secretary Caspar Weinberger to increase the defense budget. This climbed so fast under Reagan that Weinberger's previous nickname "Cap the Knife" (from his budget-cutting days in the Nixon administration) became "Cap the Ladle." He shoveled so much cash that the Capitol Steps, a well-known Washington singing group that pokes fun at all things political, made a parody of the *My Fair Lady* song: "immense expense is mainly in defense."

Senator Stennis became the ranking minority member on the Appropriations Committee, replacing Warren Magnuson, who lost his re-election, and so Henry "Scoop" Jackson, a Democrat from Washington State, took Stennis's place as ranking member of the SASC. Jackson was hawkish on defense and foreign policy yet liberal on social issues. Senator Nunn shared Jackson's views on defense but was more conservative on social issues. Jackson and Tower had both been critical of Carter and saw eye to eye on most issues, so they had a good partnership at the top of the SASC.

While Tower supported most of Reagan's requests, he broke ranks when it came to the deployment of the MX missile. This was an upgrade to our nuclear triad of strategic bombers, submarine-launched missiles, and intercontinental ballistic missiles.

The MX would have ten MIRVs and would counter the massive Soviet SS-18s. During Carter's initial foray into arms control negotiations, his administration vehemently opposed the MX, which would have undermined the ongoing talks. The Pentagon, on the other hand, felt that the Soviets could destroy almost all of America's Minuteman missiles, housed in fixed silos, in a first strike. Thus, all through the 1970s, the Pentagon had argued that the MX needed to be mobile to survive, like the Soviets' SS-20s. Several senators leveraged Carter to support the MX in exchange for more support of SALT II. But how to deploy the big new missile remained controversial. Carter's plan was to constantly shuttle 200 missiles among 4,600 shelters throughout the West, in what the Air Force called a "racetrack" mode. During the campaign, Reagan blasted Carter for supporting the missile, then switched course when he took office. He even renamed it the "Peacekeeper" missile.[1]

Since the system would be mobile, there was a lot of opposition from westerners, who weren't thrilled about nuclear warheads constantly shuttling around and among their states. The two most prominent were Republicans, both close to the president: Paul Laxalt from Nevada and Jake Garn from Utah. They lobbied for a different deployment mode, which the Air Force converted to dense packs, clusters of underground silos that defeated any pretense of mobility.[2] The "fratricide" theory, as it was called, was that the silos would be so close together that Soviet MIRVs would hit each other before they hit the silos, a theory that was ridiculed by most every expert. The press picked up my nickname for the harebrained idea: the "dunce pack."

Tower was upset about the dunce pack and decided to ask the Joint Chiefs to testify on it.[3] The SASC had a long-standing tradition of requiring the personal views of the military, even if those conflicted with those of the administration.[4] Tower asked each of the chiefs for his personal view on the new basing mode, and the Army, Navy, and Marine Corps were opposed, while the Air Force supported it, since it was their proposal. The chairman also supported it, as he felt he had to represent the secretary of defense and the president.

This, however, was the end of dunce pack basing and yet another setback to the decade-long efforts to field the MX. In the late 1980s, the United States finally deployed fifty Peacekeepers in traditional silos at Warren Air Force Base in Wyoming. Each still carried ten warheads, making it a powerful weapon, but they were vulnerable to a first strike. Just a few years later, the START I and II treaties banned land-based multiwarhead missiles entirely, and the Air Force began eliminating them from our arsenal.[5]

There are other examples of expensive weapons once needed for deterrence or other capabilities that eventually were eliminated through agreements and treaties. The Pershing II ballistic missiles and Tomahawk ground-launched cruise missiles, deployed in Europe to offset overwhelming Warsaw Pact conventional forces, were instrumental in bringing the Soviet Union to the negotiating table on the Intermediate Nuclear Forces Treaty. That treaty was signed by President Reagan and General Secretary Gorbachev in 1987.[6]

The MX was a lesson in how the Air Force would say almost anything to justify a system they wanted, and this stain on their credibility would follow them for decades as they struggled to justify other platforms. It was also an example of the SASC's nonpartisan independence; Tower, as a fellow Republican, could have gone along with Reagan's proposal, but instead he followed the path he knew to be right. The battle indicated once again that the SASC and an administration would not always agree.

Tower was a proactive supporter of the Navy, given his prior service. He was lucky to count the new secretary of the Navy, John Lehman, as an ally. Lehman was one of the most effective and powerful secretaries in history. He convinced Reagan to support building a six-hundred-ship Navy (there had been about five hundred combat ships in the fleet under submariner Jimmy Carter) and articulated a new, aggressive strategy that would take the fight directly to the shores of the Soviet Union.[7] Lehman had strong support in the uniformed Navy for his six-hundred-ships proposal, but there were many critics of taking aircraft carriers within range of Soviet air, naval, and missile power.

Lehman also came up with a plan to build two nuclear-powered carriers in one year, to take advantage of a quantity discount from Newport News Shipbuilding (in the end we spent around $7 billion to save $750 million[8]). Lehman's plan was popular in the Pentagon since they believed we needed as many as twenty-five carrier battle groups to fulfill Reagan's strategy. This was a laughable number; at the time the Navy had thirteen and Lehman had advocated for only two more under the six-hundred-ship plan. Tower was, however, worried that there would not be sufficient funds for both carriers and the new B-1 bombers. So he decided to provide for only one carrier. This started a battle royale in the committee, particularly from the Virginia senators, Harry Byrd and John Warner, who were also naval advocates, and not just for the business it would bring their home state.

The vote was tight, and Tower followed a tradition that left things open until the close of business that day. Nunn spent that time making sure he knew all the arguments on both sides. He'd gotten to know the Newport News folks thanks to the newest *Nimitz*-class carrier, CVN 70, USS *Carl Vinson* (Senator Nunn's great-uncle). Nunn wasn't a big fan of restarting the B-1 line, since the B-2 was coming down the road, but he was a proponent of naval forward presence. So he cast the deciding vote in favor of the two carriers, which became the USS

Abraham Lincoln (CVN 72) and the USS *George Washington* (CVN 73). The B-1 was also approved in a separate vote and was not crowded out by the carriers.

The committee continues to this day a long history of challenging presidents and the Pentagon when it believes they are wrong.

↜

The Senate Committee on Armed Services was created in 1946. Until that time, responsibility for defense oversight had been divided between the Military Affairs and Naval Affairs committees. From its inception, Armed Services was one of the most prestigious committees in the Senate, and also one of the most bipartisan. This was a result of its initial roster; all the senators were serious, well-respected legislators, such as Richard Russell and Edward Gurney. That began a tradition that has carried through to the present day, despite periods of partisan tension.

The new committee immediately weighed in on some of the most important legislation of the twentieth century. It reported the National Security Act of 1947 and several follow-up amendments two years later that transformed the national security apparatus and laid the foundation for the modern-day Department of Defense and intelligence community.

In fact, the committee approved and sent to the full Senate 173 of the 460 bills and resolutions concerning national defense referred to it between 1947 and 1948. The committee conducted 216 hearings during that Eightieth Congress. President Truman signed 145 of the public and private bills the committee passed. The volume of legislation alone illustrates the diligence of the committee. Under subsequent chairmen, it always rated in the top tier in number of meetings, hearings, legislation, and nominations considered and measures passed into law.

In dealing with the landmark "unification of the armed forces" proposal from President Truman that merged the Department of War and Department of the Navy into the Department of Defense, established the Air Force, and created the Central Intelligence Agency and the National Security Council, the fledgling committee faced the same tensions and struggles in the executive branch and the interservice rivalries that would manifest themselves thirty-nine years later when we tackled the reforms that resulted in the Goldwater-Nichols Act.

The SASC counts among its ranks such titans as Lyndon Johnson, future vice president and subsequently president, future vice presidents Dan Quayle and Al Gore, and presidential candidates Barry Goldwater and John McCain. Other powerhouses include Robert Byrd, Ted Kennedy, Trent Lott, John Tower, and such well-known defense experts as Sam Nunn, John Warner, John Glenn, Bill Cohen, Jack Reed, and many, many others. A good number of the professional staff of the SASC have also gone on to the most senior places, from deputy and undersecretaries of defense to senior White House and National Security Council positions.

The golden age dawned when Richard Russell became chairman in 1955. Due to the immense respect he commanded both in the Senate and the national security establishment, Russell steadily increased the committee's power and jurisdiction. He began by creating an annual piece of legislation known as the National Defense Authorization Act. This one act transformed the committee because it could now provide both policy and budgetary guidance to the department using a vehicle that had the force of law. To the displeasure of the Eisenhower administration, Russell slipped in an amendment to the 1959 Military Construction Act that required Congress to authorize missiles, aircraft, and ships prior to appropriations, which solidified the SASC's paramount role in the policy world. This legislation is still passed annually and, due largely to the committee's bipartisanship, it's never failed to pass.[9]

Jackson unexpectedly died from a heart attack on September 1, 1983. Senator Russell's outsized legacy, plus the fact that Nunn held his seat, made Nunn's promotion to ranking minority member that much more significant. Nunn held that position until January 1987, when the Democrats regained the majority and he became chairman.[10]

In Nunn's mind, it was not automatic that he would promote me to be his staff director, even though I had been by his side every day for ten years. I had not served on the committee staff before and my leadership experience consisted of my time as a platoon commander in Vietnam.

But I knew and understood how the senator thought and how he operated. In the end, his confidence in me and our professional relationship must have compensated for my lack of experience. For the next three years, I learned everything I could from the more experienced majority staff, particularly Carl Smith.

I would serve the committee for the next fourteen years, either as staff director or minority staff director, and would be involved in every major issue and piece of legislation, such as Goldwater-Nichols, the creation of the Special Operations Command, acquisition reform, intelligence increases, the drawdown after the Cold War, the first Gulf War, gays in the military, and expanding billets for women, to name a few. I would be directly involved with the confirmation process for secretaries of defense, chairmen of the Joint Chiefs of Staff and service chiefs, hundreds of civilian nominations, and tens of thousands of military nominations.

Being staff director for the minority meant not only a substantive shift in my daily duties—from individual adviser for a single senator to running the staff, being integral to all committee matters, and supporting at a minimum all the Democratic senators—but also a change of scenery. I graduated from Grant's Tomb to a large new office in the Russell building; it even had a marble fireplace and its own bathroom! The private office was right off the SASC's second major hearing room, Room 232. I started my tenure there, then moved across the hall to the majority staff director's office with its more ornate fireplace when the Senate flipped in 1987. In 1995 the Senate flipped again and I was back where I'd started. People asked, "What's the biggest difference between being in the minority and majority?" My answer: "The fireplace is on the other side."

The first three years taught me there really were significant differences between being a personal staffer and the leader of the committee staff. I learned about floor procedures, which can be more important to success than any fact or figure. For example, an amendment to a provision in the underlying bill is called a first-degree amendment and is open to a subsequent provision called a second-degree amendment. These are voted on first, and it is common that the first vote on the substance usually wins. So to have the first vote, if we were concerned about the outcome, we would tack on a second-degree amendment to someone else's initial provision and change it enough to pick up votes. And if senators were not going to be present for a vote in committee, we made sure to have their proxies vote with the leader, since a tie is actually a loss. We won several of Nunn's amendments to force our NATO allies to increase their military and monetary contributions by getting the first vote when we offered a second-degree amendment.

⤳

JAN

With Arnold's long, unpredictable hours, I did most of the planning and implementing of daily events with the children. On several occasions I told him I thought we should take the family camping. Not that I was an experienced camper. I *had* been on a weekend trip once when I was a Girl Scout. But camping was something I was convinced our children should experience: the bracing smell of pine resin, the fresh air, being at one with nature.

But whenever I broached the subject, Arnold's response was, "Jan, I 'camped out' in Vietnam. Slid down muddy terrain in the middle of the night, in torrential rain. I slept on sticks and twigs and roots in horrendous weather. I will never, in my life, ever go camping. But take the kids, if you like."

I turned to my sisters, who were always willing to try anything. Fran lived out in the country, so we decided she must be the expert. Monet and I purchased everything Fran told us we needed. We prepared a hobo stew: beef, carrots, potatoes, and onions. Instead of packing our food on ice, we froze the stew and then put everything else in the cooler with it, feeling smart and efficient, letting it do two jobs: refrigeration and dinner.

We arrived at the site in Williamsburg where Fran and her children were anxiously waiting, ready to help set up camp. That part went well. The tents, though slightly askew, appeared as if they were going to stay up. We fired up the grill and started heating the hobo stew. After quite a long wait, we realized we shouldn't have frozen the huge block, because it was never going to thaw, at least not *that* night. I remembered noticing, on the drive in, a 7-Eleven about a mile down the road from camp. So much for roughing it. We went immediately to Plan B.

In the chaos and excitement of heading to 7-Eleven with a large crew, I forgot to secure the rooftop carrier. As I peeled out onto the highway, the huge plastic container flew off like an oversized Frisbee. I'm still thankful it didn't cause an accident. We stopped, backed up, and retrieved it. We then drove on to the 7-Eleven for the most delicious hot dogs I ever tasted!

The next morning, before heading off to Water Country USA, our Cub Scout, Joe, suggested we put up a rain guard on the tent in case the weather turned. I glanced up at a clear blue sky. It didn't look like rain, so we ignored his advice.

After a long day at the water park and a nice dinner at a restaurant, we were ready to get back to roughing it. As we headed for the tents, though, it became clear that it had, in fact, rained that day. A good three inches of water was left in the tents. Furthermore, some animal had gnawed through the side of mine; he seemed to have especially enjoyed a whole jar of peanut butter. By then it was 11 p.m. No discussion was needed this time, as we threw sopping-wet tents and sleeping bags into the rooftop carrier, latched it securely, belted the kids in, and headed for I-95. Maybe Arnold had the right idea about camping, after all!

⌐

ARNOLD

One of our earliest challenges in Reagan's presidency was the administration's decision to sell five E-3 Air Force Airborne Warning and Control System planes to Saudi Arabia. The AWACS, built by Boeing, could detect and track aircraft over a 175,000-square-mile area at any altitude, over any terrain. U.S.-Saudi military sales had been going on since 1974 as a way to develop a closer relationship with our largest supplier of oil. In 1978, Congress had just barely approved the sale of sixty F-15 fighters, at the time the largest sale of advanced warplanes to anyone other than a close U.S. ally. The Carter administration had lobbied hard to get the sale approved and had to make promises not to sell other equipment, such as fuel tanks and air-to-air missiles for the F-15s, or advanced surveillance aircraft like the E-2C Hawkeye or the E-3A Sentry.

Then, in 1979 and 1980, Carter sent American AWACS to patrol the Saudi border during a conflict in Yemen and the Iran-Iraq War. The Saudis so liked the system that they put them on their wish list, and the Reagan administration complied. The sale also included six to eight KC-707 tanker aircraft to refuel the F-15s, conformal fuel tanks to boost the range of the fighters, and more than a thousand Sidewinder air-to-air missiles.[11]

The proposal was strongly opposed by Israel and the powerful pro-Israeli lobby, as well as by much of the public. An intense campaign from both sides unfolded for more than six months. It was clear to Reagan and his team that he would have to win over some Democratic votes if he wanted to stop Congress from killing the deal. But some of the strongest opponents of the sale came from the Republican side, including Congressman Jack Kemp of New York and Sen. Bob Packwood of Oregon. More than a dozen Republican senators came out in opposition, in a Senate where the Republicans enjoyed only a slight majority.

One of the strongest early supporters of the deal was actually John Tower, who traditionally put national interests ahead of political ones. Nunn's proved to be a pivotal vote as usual, and the SASC was a powerful advocate, while the Senate Foreign Relations Committee, headed by Sen. Chuck Percy, was bitterly divided. Even though it did not have jurisdiction over the matter, the SASC voted 10–5 in support of the sale, with Nunn voting with Tower. The SASC ranking member, Senator Jackson, was opposed. He was one of the staunchest supporters of Israel, even though the $8.5 billion deal would bring in a lot of business for his home state (one of his nicknames was "the Senator from Boeing").

Nunn, however, took his time to make up his mind, listening to the arguments and testimonies in the various hearings. Public opinion in Georgia was generally opposed, but, like Jackson, Nunn took a position that wasn't necessarily reflective of his constituents. At one point, Reagan's chief of staff, Jim Baker, came to Nunn's office and sat down at his large round table to discuss the senator's concerns. Nunn felt that Saudi Arabia was a key ally and very important to our overall security in the Middle East. He said he wanted to ensure that any country we sold AWACS to had six specific safeguards in place for their use. He wanted the president's support for an amendment he authored with Senator Warner, and got it. The passage of this helped to ease some other senators' worries about the deal.

The floor vote was very close on a resolution framed to disapprove the sale. Fifty-two voted against the resolution—that is, in favor of the sale—while forty-eight voted for the resolution, or against the sale. On the final vote, twelve Republicans voted against the sale and ten Democrats, led by Nunn, voted for it. Thus the sale was approved.

The AWACS and other equipment we sold to the Saudis were essential to the Desert Shield/Desert Storm operation in 1991. Virtually all of our military operated out of Saudi Arabia, a move that would not have been possible had we not cemented our relationship. Also, our overwhelming use of air power in the initial days of combat was greatly aided by Saudi AWACS patrols.

〜

Also in the early years of the Reagan defense buildup, we learned a valuable lesson in what really counts in the U.S. Senate: votes. For years, the Air Force had been planning to replace the Lockheed C-141 Starlifter (the same jet that had medevacked me out of Vietnam) with what would eventually become the C-17. All the major manufacturers were in the bidding, but completion of the system was still far off and we had a serious airlift shortfall at the peak of the Cold War. To make up the difference in the meantime, the Defense Department decided to buy fifty more Lockheed C-5B Galaxys, manufactured in Marietta, Georgia. The C-5 was the largest cargo carrier operated by the United States; it could carry more than twice the load of the C-141 and two rows of vehicles could drive straight through it as the nose of the plane swung up.[12] It was an airlifter decades ahead of its competitors. But that didn't stop Jackson, the senator from Boeing, from arguing that the Boeing 747 commercial freighter, built in Seattle, was a better alternative. He mounted a major campaign to use DOD money for the commercial freighters instead of the military C-5B. It became not only a major fight between the DOD and Congress and Boeing and Lockheed, but between senators from two states: Washington and Georgia.

Senator Nunn and I were at a bit of a disadvantage. We didn't have the committee staff or longer service in the Senate, as Jackson did, but we did have the full support of the Pentagon. We focused on the substantive arguments for why the C-5 was superior to the 747 from the military requirements perspective. The 747 would require lifting equipment up into its cargo doors, while the C-5 had roll-on/roll-off capability. The C-5 could land on more airfields, and even unpaved runways, with its unique twenty-eight-wheel landing system. We printed off all the equipment that could be carried on a C-5 (and not a 747), and the printout itself was several feet thick. Senator Nunn, the Pentagon, and Lockheed worked on this day in and day out.

The day before Senate floor debate on Jackson's alternative, Braniff International, another commercial airline, went bankrupt, fueling Jackson's argument that the airline industry needed Congress's help. Even though Nunn had the more substantive arguments, Jackson still won the vote, 60–39. But we still had hope in the form of the House. The House defeated a similar proposal by Rep. Norman Dicks of Washington, 289–127, and we worked out a compromise in conference.[13] We agreed to buy three 747 freighters for the Air National Guard, and the rest C-5Bs. C-5s are still flying today, while the military 747 program never got off the ground, proof that a factual argument *can* beat congressional pork barreling, as long as you have the votes.

〜〜

Two years after we normalized relations with China and convinced President Carter to keep U.S. ground troops in South Korea, Nunn decided to head back to the Western Pacific, with stops in Taiwan, Hong Kong, Malaysia, Singapore, Indonesia, Australia, and New Zealand. He wanted a better grasp of the security situation: what were the concerns and challenges of these nations and how did they understand our involvement, militarily and otherwise, in the region.

It's important for members of Congress to go on these trips occasionally, to obtain firsthand information on foreign policy and military issues. Just as an officer should lead from the front on the battlefield, there's no substitute for walking the terrain and discussing issues face to face with both allies and adversaries. This trip was just Nunn, his wife Colleen, Sen. John Glenn and his wife, and myself as both the professional staffer and the escort officer.

We flew from the east coast to Japan for a quick meeting with Ambassador Mike Mansfield, then we were on our way to Taipei, Taiwan, another four hours on top of the fourteen-hour flight from New York. We'd been up for more than twenty-four hours. I thought I had left those sleepless days behind me! We did have time when we landed to check in to our hotel prior to our meetings with the top three leaders of Taiwan: President Chiang Ching-kuo, son of the legendary Chiang Kai-shek, Vice President Hsieh Tung-min, and Premier Sun Yun-suan.

One of the main issues on the agenda in Taiwan was our arms sales to that country. The normalization of relations with China had come at a price: we no longer diplomatically recognized Taiwan. In order to strengthen one relationship, we had to back off on the other. The United States could only keep up unofficial relations with Taiwan, which, to Congress at least, included continuing arms sales to the island. China viewed these sales as a violation of its sovereignty, but we saw them as essential to a balanced relationship. The United States officially supported the "well-being of the people of Taiwan," leaving the interpretation of "well-being" up to the president.[14]

Because we no longer had diplomatic relations with Taipei, though, State Department officials weren't allowed to participate in any of our meetings. So it was just Nunn, Glenn, and me, and the State Department insisted I take detailed notes. No problem, I said. I'd learned from working with Nunn to always take detailed, verbatim minutes.

We were ushered into their Oval Office equivalent and I took my seat next to the senators. My notebook and pen were out and at the ready . . . then before I knew it, the meeting was over. The senators and I got up and there was the typical exchange of gifts (common in the Asian traditions and well within the congressional gift rules).

As soon as we left the room, I was cornered by State Department officials eager to see my notes. I reached for my notebook and gasped in horror. There was a total of two words followed by a long scrawl down the page. I flipped through it but everything was blank. I asked Nunn whether he'd taken any notes. He said, "You were the designated note taker." I was dumbfounded.

Then he chuckled. "Arnold, within thirty seconds of the start of that meeting, you fell sound asleep. It would have been too awkward to try and wake you up. So we all pretended not to see it, but it was clear to everyone you were out of it." The State guys were furious. They had nothing to send back to Washington. Lucky for all of us, Nunn saved the day. "I'll debrief you on all that happened, and you can take notes from that." Prior to his career in politics, he'd been a trial lawyer and had the memory to prove it. He relayed all the issues that had been discussed in great detail, down to direct quotes and their source. The bulk of the meeting revolved around Taiwan's security situation and its open but cautious approach to the normalization of relations with China. Senator Nunn defused what could have been an awkward situation, and one that was embarrassing to me personally. But he seemed to think the incident was hilarious, and I now consider it a badge of honor to have slept through a presidential meeting, just like Brent Scowcroft. Thank goodness we were headed to Malaysia for an opportunity to rest up in Penang prior to our official meetings in Kuala Lumpur.

We met with key leaders at each stop, including Lee Kuan Yew, president of Singapore. This meeting went much better than a later one when President Yew met with Senator Nunn in his Senate office. At that later session, I was there with these two larger-than-life leaders, staying mostly quiet and taking detailed notes. They were in the middle of a serious discussion when Nunn's vote clock—which told senators they had five minutes left to go vote on the floor—went off and he dashed out without any explanation. This was clearly the first time Yew had ever had someone walk out of a meeting on him. To break the constrained silence, I blurted out, "How 'bout them Dawgs!" and went off on a tangent about Georgia football and the Dawg Nation. Yew stared at me, still silent, as I listed off trivia about my college football team to one of the smartest leaders in the world. Mercifully, Nunn came back soon, and they picked right back up where they had left off. Later, Yew's foreign minister, Suppiah Dhanabalan, told us that Yew said learning about the Dawgs had been a "quaint little diversion."

In each country, we discussed the role the United States should play in this strategic region. For our last leg, Glenn and his wife left us as we headed to Australia and New Zealand. Australia has always been one of the United States's most reliable allies. We'd fought side by side in both World Wars, Korea, and Vietnam, when other allies sat on their backsides. Australia also allowed the United States to maintain important intelligence-gathering facilities on their soil.

Though Sydney was more of a rest stop before we headed to Canberra, it was strikingly beautiful. The Sydney Opera House was breathtaking. We left the vibrant metropolis for the quiet, small capital of Canberra. The ambassador's residence was on the grounds of the embassy, complete with a pool and tennis court. I thought, *What a gig—you can walk to work, you have a pool and tennis court, you're in a country where they speak English, there are no major international problems, and they love Americans.* I knew from my Vietnam days that Australia had been the most popular R&R spot for our troops.

This was still a business trip, however, and Nunn had substantive issues to discuss with Prime Minister Malcolm Fraser, such as our request to allow B-52s to operate from his continent. In return, Fraser wanted Nunn's help asking Reagan to invite him to the United States for an official state visit. In the end, we got our B-52s based and Fraser got to meet Reagan early in 1982.

As was his practice on every trip, Nunn met with what he called the country team: all the U.S. representatives in the country under the auspices of the ambassador. In their chief of mission hats, the ambassadors direct and coordinate all executive branch personnel, from the Departments of Agriculture to Commerce to Drug Enforcement to all the State Department representatives. He then met separately with the military attaché and CIA station chief. Their viewpoints were not always the same as those representing the State Department or the business representatives of our government.

One of the most impressive aspects of our Canberra visit was the War Museum. The Australian War Memorial is designed to honor all those who died in service of their country. It includes their Tomb of the Unknown Soldier and is one of the world's most respected military museums.

I came back wondering why we don't have a national military museum in the United States. We have individual museums for specific services, components, or battles, like the Infantry Museum in Fort Benning and the D-day Museum in New Orleans. But we don't have any joint museums. I think Australia has it right when it comes to honoring all who served in whatever uniform or conflict, without taking away from those who are service-unique.

～

One of the darkest developments in our military's history occurred during Reagan's first term. In the early 1980s, he was working hard to prevent an all-out Arab-Israeli war in the Middle East. Throughout 1981, Syria and Israel exchanged blows over Syria's aid to the Palestine Liberation Organization, based in Lebanon. Syria, under the leadership of Hafez al-Assad, sent surface-to-air missiles to the

Biqā' Valley in Lebanon, a terrorist hotspot, which interfered with Israel's ability to monitor the PLO. The Reagan administration calmed tensions for a while through Philip Habib, the emissary to the Middle East, but that didn't last. Syria refused to remove the missiles from the valley and the PLO was increasing its terrorist attacks in the West Bank and Gaza and against Jews in Europe, culminating in the assassination of Israel's ambassador to the United Kingdom, Shlomo Argov, in London. Three days later, Israel invaded Lebanon.

Reagan feared Syria would get drawn into the conflict as well, so he sent Habib to negotiate withdrawals on all sides. The PLO demanded an international force be deployed in Beirut to protect the Palestinians there. U.S. Marines, as well as French and Italian troops, were deployed as a multinational force to keep the peace. There were problems on all sides with the withdrawal process, with delays from the PLO and the Israelis initially refusing to allow the MNF into Beirut until the PLO was out. Finally, on September 1, 1982, the PLO left Beirut, and Secretary Weinberger announced the Marines were coming home soon.

And then the situation got worse. On September 14, Lebanese president-elect Bashir Gemayel was assassinated, and Israel stepped back in to try to keep the country from plunging into chaos. On Israel's watch, a Lebanese militia massacred around eight hundred Palestinian civilians in a refugee camp, causing international outrage. Reagan deployed Marines to a new MNF in Beirut on a UN peacekeeping mission. Secretary of State George Schultz was busy trying to negotiate a peace deal between Israel and Lebanon, while at the same time trying to ease Assad's opposition to the agreement.

On April 18, 1983, a suicide bomber drove a pickup truck full of explosives into the U.S. embassy in Beirut, killing sixty-three, including seventeen Americans. The attack was perpetrated by Hezbollah, with support from both Syria and Iran. Though it was a tragedy, there was no additional military action as a result of the bombing. Iran wanted to drive the United States out of Lebanon, but it would take one more straw to break the eagle's back.

Israel unilaterally pulled out of Lebanon in September 1983, causing rival Lebanese and pro-Syrian forces to renew fighting. Reagan dispatched USS *New Jersey* and authorized gunfire and air strikes to keep the area around Beirut International Airport, where the MNF was stationed, safe. Eventually both sides agreed to a ceasefire, but by then the damage to Reagan's Lebanon policy had been done. Facing opposition at home, Congress used the War Powers Act to put a time constraint on the Marines' presence, and Weinberger suggested a full withdrawal. The State Department still wanted an active military presence in a peacekeeping capacity, which led to paralysis for the troops in Beirut.[15]

On October 23, 1983, less than two months after Nunn became the ranking member on the SASC, another truck full of explosives drove through the barriers in front of a four-story building housing the 1st Battalion 8th Marines of Battalion Landing Team 1/8, commanded by Lt. Col. Larry Gerlach. The explosion had the power of 21,000 pounds of TNT. The building collapsed, killing 241 American service members: 220 Marines, 18 sailors, and 3 soldiers. It was the largest single-day loss for U.S. military since the Tet Offensive and the largest for the Marines since the battle of Iwo Jima in World War II. One of those killed was the surgeon, John Hudson, who'd contacted our office about not wanting to fulfill his Berry Plan commitment. Now our office mourned his death, as well as that of other brave servicemen.

Back then, suicide bombings were still a novel idea, and security at the base had been lax. Hezbollah was behind this attack as well, and it succeeded. Within four months of the bombing, Reagan pulled all of our remaining troops out of Lebanon.[16]

The nation was stunned. How could this have happened? Chairman Tower decided that the SASC would need to do an investigation and conduct public hearings. Despite the tragic loss of life, the Marines were on the hot seat, and lots of questions were raised about locating them all in one vulnerable building in an open area with little physical protection.

I got a call from Lt. Col. Jim Jones, the Marine liaison in the Senate, with whom I had developed a productive relationship. He asked, "Arnold, would you be interested in reading the cables that are coming into HQ about what really happened?"

My immediate reaction was, "Of course!" The USMC channel would have unvarnished information that would be valuable to our investigation. I could bring information to the table others probably wouldn't have. It was on a weekend. I went over to the HQMC at the Navy Annex, up the hill from the Pentagon, across the street from Arlington National Cemetery. Jim set me up in the commandant's conference room and had a stack of cables for me to read. Only one other person was there: Maj. Gen. Matt Caulfield, who was working on Gen. P. X. Kelley's upcoming testimony before the Senate and House Armed Services Committees. The cables were focused on what happened and the actions taken to take care of the dead and wounded and provide additional security for those who remained. There was little detail in terms of the "why" and the "who," nor was there any assessment of why the security posture had been so inadequate. But the information would help me write up questions for the hearings and clear up some of the misunderstandings out there. Initial reports are always inaccurate and incomplete. Leaders should be wary of reaching conclusions or making statements or decisions based on them.

I was pleased with the info I'd gathered and was about to head back to the Hill when Jim came in and said the commandant wanted to see me. I knew

General Kelley from his days as the first head of the Rapid Deployment Joint Task Force, the predecessor of U.S. Central Command, so I didn't think anything of it. But when I walked into his office, just about every general from the headquarters was there. Kelley had gathered them to go over his upcoming testimony. He launched into his plan to defend the Corps. He insinuated that no one could have known of this threat, and even if they had, the Marines on the ground had not taken proper precautions.

I was stunned. This may not have been his intent, but it certainly sounded to me like he was going to blame his subordinates. This wouldn't be well-received, but I figured he'd have to find that out the hard way.

Unfortunately for me, he wanted to get people's reaction to his testimony, and I was the first guy he called on. I had two options: sugarcoat it or tell him what I really thought. I chose the latter. I said the committee reaction would be negative and its members would chastise him. No one else spoke up, except the commandant, who was displeased with my comments. He went through all the reasons why I was wrong. Once he finished dressing me down, the other generals jumped in and provided the amen chorus. Not even Jones rose to my defense.

I went back to my office to write up what I'd learned, expecting Nunn to be pleased with my exclusive information. First thing Monday I went and summarized the cables for him. Then I mentioned my being berated at the meeting with the commandant. Big mistake! Nunn was furious. He considered my advice to Kelley a serious breach of the separation of powers and a conflict of interest with my duties on the committee. I was to have no more involvement in the Beirut matter. I could not attend any of the committee proceedings and could not share any of the information with anyone. He then called Chairman Tower and let him know what had happened. Nunn also told me that he would have to think about my future as his staff director.

In more than ten years of working for him, I had never seen him this angry. When I got back to my committee office, Tower's staff director, Jim McGovern, met me. He said neither he nor Tower were concerned, and they wanted to know if there was any information they should be alerted to. I told him I was under direct orders to stay out of the matter. McGovern had underestimated Senator Nunn's fury at me. Then he asked the question I was dreading: "What's going to happen next?"

And all I could answer was, "It's up to the senator." I told Lieutenant Colonel Jones what happened, and he said, "If it's any consolation, I agree with your assessment of General Kelley's testimony." It wasn't, though, when my career and reputation were up in the air.

Kelley testified before both the House and Senate Armed Services Committees and was extremely combative in both settings. Just as I'd predicted, his testimony was roundly criticized. This also was little consolation, since I was still in the doghouse. Over the course of the week, Nunn consulted with his fellow senators and others. He decided that while I'd crossed a red line, it was not a career-terminating offense. But he warned me clearly that if I ever did anything like that again, it would be immediate curtains. He had no issue with using my contacts to get inside information, but he drew the line at giving advice to executive branch personnel testifying before our committee. Of course, I never let this happen again. At least not without securing his explicit permission first.

～

One of our committee's vital areas of emphasis was the North Atlantic Treaty Organization. NATO was founded in 1949 to try and keep the peace in Europe, particularly considering the aggressive posturing of the Soviet Union. Each of the original twelve member countries pledged to come to the aid of the others if their security was challenged. The U.S. commitment resulted in more than a quarter of a million troops stationed in Europe for most of the Cold War, a massive expense in terms of manpower, equipment, and personnel.

Nunn was considered one of the most influential leaders on NATO matters throughout his twenty-four-year Senate career. He authored three major reports on the alliance and drafted and passed major legislation to both strengthen NATO and challenge our allies to do more. His efforts led to a fundamental shift in the U.S. military posture to better deal with the Soviet Union and Warsaw Pact adversaries. In the event of an invasion across the Fulda Gap, the intra-German border region that was the putative main route of attack, we pledged to have ten full divisions in Europe within ten days to help block the incursion. Nunn recognized that while the U.S. presence on the European continent was sizeable, the nature of the threat had changed substantially. The Soviets had developed the capability to invade rapidly, while NATO forces were maldeployed and unprepared. He also considered NATO's tactical nuclear posture, designed to offset the Warsaw Pact's conventional superiority, not credible, since the delivery vehicles had such a short range they would explode over the very populations we were trying to defend.

The head of the Center for Strategic and International Studies and future ambassador to NATO, Dr. David Abshire, sparked Nunn's interest in this key alliance in the early 1970s. Nunn was also a strong supporter of the parliamentary body that supported NATO, the North Atlantic Assembly, and always met with fellow parliamentarians on their visits to Washington and his trips to their countries. Nunn met Manfred Wörner early in his career, and Wörner later became German defense minister and ultimately NATO secretary general. Their two decades of friendship helped ensure they could work together to resolve tough issues in a responsible way.

The relationship with Michael Heseltine, defense minister of the United Kingdom, was different. On one of his trips to Washington, Heseltine met with Nunn in his Dirksen office to complain about a provision Nunn was pushing to force NATO allies to spend more on their own defense.[17] At the time, Democrats were the minority in the Senate and there was a Republican president. Heseltine was both critical and condescending. At one point he taunted Nunn, "You are just a backbencher." In the UK's parliamentary system, the prime minister's party controls both the legislative and the executive branches, thus there's never a need to challenge the executive. Nunn retorted, "Minister Heseltine, the colonies' revolution against the Crown led to the creation of three separate but equal branches of the United States government. According to our Constitution, Congress has a leading role in defense and foreign policy decisions, not to mention the power of the purse. I have over fifty votes for my NATO spending amendment, and in the United States, the majority rules."

It was a diplomatic put-down. Heseltine later resigned his post in a bitter dispute with Prime Minister Margaret Thatcher; he clearly did not have much regard for those in authority in his own country, either.

When Nunn penned his first report in 1974, NATO was celebrating its twenty-fifth anniversary. The alliance had expanded to fifteen countries but was marred by concern about its future, especially since U.S. domestic support for it was starting to wane. Senate majority leader Mike Mansfield annually sponsored an amendment to withdraw U.S. troops from Europe, and it was getting harder to defeat him.

Nunn pointed out that the United States continued to have major security interests in Europe, aside from just the long, deep historical and cultural ties. His fourteen-page report was replete with statistics, analyses, charts, and hard-hitting recommendations for fundamental changes to the political, military, and economic approach by both the United States and our allies. He advocated restructuring the hair-trigger nuclear alert system, improving conventional capabilities, decreasing support costs, deploying fighting units farther forward, improving burden sharing, and challenging the Pentagon's position that everything was just dandy as it was, thank you. As with his other endeavors, he involved independent civilian and military experts such as Lt. Gen. James Hollingsworth. "Holly" was a legendary Army war fighter whose knowledge of tactics and capabilities provided the basis of many of Nunn's recommendations. The senator credited his longtime friend Secretary of Defense Jim Schlesinger for allowing Hollingsworth to author a study outside of Pentagon circles. Dr. Jeff Record of our staff, Dr. Phil Karber, and Dr. Joe Braddock were other experts who were always engaged with our work on NATO.[18]

Nunn was a strong proponent of the concept of defensive alliances. He recognized that the United States needed international support on both the military and diplomatic fronts, even though this did not always translate to support back home in Georgia.

After he published one of his reports, we got a letter from a farmer who'd heard Nunn talking about NATO and its importance. He asked, "Senator Nunn, how do you grow one of them there 'natos'? Sounds like it would make a good crop." Nunn's accent would occasionally run afoul of other constituents. He once got a postcard from a Georgia schoolteacher who challenged his pronunciation of the word "nuclear," which came out "nucula." She wrote, "Sen. Nunn, a *nucula* is a shell fish. You are trying to say the word *nuclear*, which is a weapon."

But he never changed the way he said it. Not one syllable.

11

THE BATTLE CONTINUES

1985–87: Washington, DC

The beginning of 1985 ushered in a new chairman. Barry Goldwater's two years as chair were some of the most consequential in the Senate Armed Services Committee's (SASC) history and included such historic legislation as the Goldwater-Nichols Act and the Defense Acquisition Improvement Act and the creation of Special Operations Command. Goldwater and Nunn led us through the most fundamental changes in the power structure since the National Security Act of 1947 that created the Department of Defense.

By the 1980s, even though the services were under a single department, they were still anything but unified or joint. Numerous operational setbacks were attributed to service parochialism, from the botched Iranian hostage rescue to the seizure of USS *Pueblo* and the Beirut barracks bombing, the *Mayaguez* incident, and the ultimately successful but still flawed Grenada and Panama operations. The problems included noninteroperable communications and equipment, lack of realistic unified strategy, imbalance between readiness and modernization, and continued domination of decision making by the services. But leaders at all levels were locked into the status quo. Secretary Weinberger took the idea of further unification as a criticism of his management and a threat to his budget, but even worse was the thought of congressional "meddling" in an area he felt was an executive prerogative.

By the mid-1980s calls for reform came strictly from outside: Congress, the National Security Council, led by former SASC staffers Bud McFarlane and Mike Donley, and the independent Packard Commission, led by Rhett Dawson, the former SASC staff director.

In 1986, led by Goldwater and Nunn in the Senate and Les Aspin, Bill Nichols, and Ike Skelton in the House, Congress completed years of investigations. Fundamental reform was required. But there was no consensus on how to solve ten major problems: serious imbalance between service and joint interests; inadequate professional military advice on joint matters; poor qualifications of those serving in joint billets; insufficient authority for combatant commanders; confused and cumbersome operational chains of command; ineffective strategic planning; poor supervision and control of defense agencies and field activities;

confusion on service secretaries' roles; duplication in military department head-quarters; and congressional micromanagement. We needed a comprehensive reorganization of the chain of command and the interaction among the services.[1]

Chairman Tower had begun efforts at reform back in the early 1980s, but it wasn't until Goldwater took over that the work really began. Goldwater and Nunn began with choosing Jim Locher as the lead staffer, along with Rick Finn from the majority and Jeff Smith from the minority. Goldwater's staff director, Jim McGovern, had strong ties to the Navy and was skeptical of reform—he'd all but derailed previous efforts—so Nunn and Goldwater thought it best to have Locher, Finn, and Smith report directly to the senators. That meant Jim and I weren't in the chain of command. I agreed because it was the only way to ensure that the process moved forward. I would function as a "stealth staffer." I would even complain from time to time, just to keep up appearances, that the reform staff ignored our chain of command.

I can outline our legislation as follows. First, we needed to strengthen civilian control by incorporating into law that everything in the Department of Defense is subject to the "authority, direction and control of the Secretary of Defense." The service chiefs and their staffs were also subject to the "authority, direction and control of the Secretary of the service," who in turn were under the secretary of defense.

Second, we improved the quality and timeliness of advice by making the chairman of the Joint Chiefs the senior military adviser to the president. The joint staff was also put under the chairman and the position of vice chairman was created.

Third, we intended to strengthen and streamline the chain of command from the president to the secretary of defense to the war-fighting combatant commanders. The COCOM was given authority to streamline the layers below him. The COCOM's direct reporting relationship to the civilian leader of the Pentagon made it clear that neither the service chiefs nor the chairman were in the operational chain. Instead, the service chiefs and secretaries had to focus on their responsibilities to organize, train, equip, mobilize, and supply in support of the combatant commanders.

Fourth, we increased emphasis on the formulation of strategy and contingency planning. The chairman was required to develop a military strategy to support the national strategy, to assess the budget decisions of the departments in support of that strategy, and to be involved in setting joint requirements. Contingency plans, previously exclusive to each combatant commander, had to be reviewed by senior civilians to ensure they were current and consistent.

Lastly, we intensified the development of joint doctrine, training, and personnel by making joint service more career-enhancing. The new law made it almost impossible to get promoted to general or flag officer without a tour in a multiservice organization. The law mandated that major professional military training colleges focus on joint doctrine and operations.

There were many other provisions to this landmark act. But to pass it, Goldwater and Nunn fought every single senior civilian and military leader, from Weinberger to one of the most hostile opponents, the Department of the Navy. From my early days as a staffer, I knew that the Pentagon always overreacted to reform efforts. So we included fake provisions in our proposal to keep them diverted in their response. One was to get rid of the Joint Chiefs of Staff entirely. We obviously had no desire to actually do this, but while the Pentagon was busy pummeling our straw man, we were gathering votes for the real elements of change, like unifying the Joint Chiefs through a more powerful chairman and vice chairman. Then we'd "reluctantly" back away from those extreme positions, making the Pentagon believe they were winning major concessions. This tactic was especially useful with the Navy and Marine Corps. Through these creative means, Nunn and Goldwater were able to marshal the SASC behind strengthened civilian control, streamlining and empowering the combatant commands, improving military advice to decision makers, and making joint operations more effective.

As a lead-up to the committee vote, Nunn and Goldwater gave a series of Senate floor speeches to highlight the problems they were trying to solve. The Pentagon finally understood that they were dealing with formidable foes, and they changed strategy from frontal attack to divide and conquer. They set their sights on the committee to try to persuade at least nine of the nineteen members to vote against the measures, which would make them look more radical than they actually were and thus fare poorly on the Senate floor. Their motto became "Ten to nine." Well, after the committee finished its marathon markup sessions, I reported back to the Navy-Marine liaison office, "You got what you wanted. The vote was ten to nine: ten Republicans for it and nine Democrats for it." When the legislation was debated in the Senate, it sailed through on an overwhelming bipartisan vote of 95–0.[2] President Reagan signed the final bill on October 1, 1986, despite initial veto threats from his administration. Until the very end, the services kept insisting that these reforms would eviscerate our national security.[3]

Even after the bill's passage, Senator Nunn said it would take up to ten years to be fully embraced and implemented by a department that had so zealously opposed it. And he was right, but over the years, everyone from Dick Cheney to Joint Chiefs chairmen Gen. John Shalikashvili and Gen. Colin Powell to current-day leaders has praised Goldwater-Nichols. To ensure that senior decision makers understand its importance, in 1987 we instituted a series of questions for each nominee coming before the SASC about his or her views on Goldwater-Nichols. These questions continue to be asked today.

Nunn had also been a proponent of improving our special operations capabilities ever since his first exposure to them in the investigation of the Desert One crash. Nunn felt a unified Special Operations Command was the way forward. The House had pushed for a separate command, but it never got off the ground due to opposition from the Pentagon.

Nunn and Cohen were determined to fix this. They attached it as a rider to the annual National Defense Authorization Act, which tells the Pentagon how it can spend the money appropriated by Congress. The legislation created the assistant secretary of defense for special operations and low-intensity conflict, which would become the unified Special Operations Command, and it included special acquisition provisions for Major Force Program 11 so they could buy specialty equipment. Again the Pentagon argued that the legislation was unneeded, but the performance of our specials ops forces proves that Congress was right on this one as well.

Goldwater-Nichols dramatically improved the operational chain of command, but the management chain of command also had major flaws. During Reagan's presidency, there were widespread reports of mismanagement, with $435 being spent on a hammer, $640 on a toilet seat, and $7,622 for a coffeemaker.[4] In 1985, Reagan formed the President's Blue Ribbon Commission on Defense Management, chaired by David Packard.

Its final report, given in June the following year, concluded that the overruns weren't due to corruption or abuse, but to the acquisition bureaucracy. It advocated reductions in rules, regulations, and review processes. It also advised recruiting civilians with experience in managing highly complex technical areas to head the military acquisition system. It recommended the creation of an acquisition czar, today the undersecretary of defense for acquisition, technology, and logistics, and established the framework for today's acquisition system. Each service got its own acquisition executives, reducing the service chiefs' roles in the process.[5] The commission's recommendations were taken up in Title IX of the National Defense Authorization Act for fiscal year 1987, also known as the Defense Acquisition Improvement Act of 1986.

But success was only partial. Thirty years later, the Packard reforms are in need of major revisions. The promise of the Packard Commission was never fully met. Today the Pentagon spends more than $400 billion on goods and services, supplies, and equipment, and the result can be summed up as "spend more, take longer, and get less." The system is still plagued with red tape that increases costs and causes delays.[6] We need to reinsert the service chiefs to both link and streamline the requirements, acquisition, and budget processes. The quality and experience of the acquisition workforce has suffered under the management of the civilian acquisition leaders. It's overdue for the military to manage their own personnel and reinstate the dual track, where military acquisition professionals have both operational and management tours as well as a tour outside the Pentagon in industry.

Thirty years later not all the elements of Goldwater-Nichols fit today's realities, either. We need to revisit the management of officers' careers. They're too rigid for those junior officers just starting. The joint requirements process is also too bureaucratic, paper-laden, and cumbersome. The chairman's role needs to be examined to ensure it still adheres to the military independence required by the act. It's time to take another look at the legislation and make appropriate adjustments. Again the Senate Armed Services Committee and the House Armed Services Committee are taking the lead pushing the needed reforms, but this time the Pentagon is more open to change.

〜

Each year, the committee worked long and hard to ensure that the annual defense authorization bill was passed into law, a tradition kept up since 1961. The process began each year with full committee hearings in January, then the subcommittees would conduct detailed reviews in March and April. The staff prepared draft markups of the bill, with its hundreds of pages authorizing thousands of individual programs. Typically, it's the largest bill considered each year, with more than five hundred pages of bill language and another several hundred (if not a thousand) pages of the report. That meant six-day workweeks—with half days on Sundays—from about March to the August recess for us staffers.

In May and June, the committee would spend several weeks behind closed doors making individual decisions on programs and funding. The SASC would report the bill and the explanatory report so it was placed on the Senate calendar and would be deliberated prior to the July 4 recess. Then we prepared for the hundreds of amendments we would surely get during the several weeks of Senate floor consideration. I always looked forward to the Senate floor debate because it gave our senators a chance to showcase their expertise and for the SASC to demonstrate the thoroughness of our bipartisan decisions. The fact that the committee position prevailed more than 95 percent of the time was concrete proof.

Once the Senate approved the bill as amended, it headed off to conference with the House Armed Services Committee, so any differences between the House and Senate bills could be smoothed over. Even though they followed a similar process, there were always thousands of differences in budget lines and language. But they had to be identical for a conference report to become law. First subcommittees met and worked out their differences and reported back to the full conference, which would then work out the remaining disagreements. For those provisions that could not be agreed on, the two chairs and ranking members met to reach a final compromise.

I disliked the painstaking conference process. We had no control over the other body, and reaching agreements was hard enough when we had to accommodate both the House and the Pentagon. The entire process was supposed to be completed by the time the appropriations bill rolled around, typically September.

On top of the conference process, the bill then had to be approved by the president. Several times, I had to deal with our defense bill being vetoed. For example, in August of 1988 President Reagan vetoed it because he thought it was too weak on his Strategic Defense Initiative. Specifically, House Armed Services Committee Chairman Les Aspin said he "took the stars out of Star Wars." It only cut Reagan's Star Wars program from $4.9 billion to $4.1 billion, but the defense supporters had their sound bite and were up in arms to save Star Wars, and they convinced Reagan to veto the bill. It was more of a symbolic veto—to help boost candidate George H. W. Bush in the presidential race—so we quickly made a few changes and sent it back to Reagan to sign into law.[7]

∽

At 3,510 feet in elevation, in some of the most desolate terrain imaginable, the Khyber Pass—the legendary route from Pakistan into Afghanistan—cuts through the Spin Ghar Mountains. Powerful armies throughout history, from Alexander the Great's to Genghis Khan's, have used this route to expand empires. It was also a major supply route for our forces in Afghanistan starting in 2001.

It had been just as critical when we were supplying the Afghan Mujahideen to fight the Soviets. In 1984, Nunn wanted a firsthand assessment of how U.S. support was working, as well as an assessment of the insurgents' capabilities and shortfalls, so we went there. After a visit to the command barracks of the famous Khyber Rifles, we took the dusty, winding climb to the pass. Looking from Pakistan to the ragged cliffs of Afghanistan, I felt an overwhelming sense of foreboding, knowing the history of the various invading armies that had marched into a country nicknamed the "graveyard of empires."

Earlier in Peshawar, we'd visited the bare-bones camps where Afghan citizens, forced from their country by the invasion, had found refuge. The faces of the refugees reflected the hardships of their day-to-day lives. We then had a separate session with some of the anti-Soviet fighters. Their miens were completely different from those of the refugees. The Mujahideen, "holy warriors," in traditional white robes and headgear, had fierce eyes. Their leader would shout a chant and as everyone replied in unison, voices booming, I thought, *Boy am I glad we're on the same side.*

Before our visit to Peshawar and the Khyber Pass, we'd met the head of Pakistani intelligence, Lieutenant General Akhtar Abdur Rahman, and President Muhammad Zia-ul-Haq. Zia had built a close relationship with the United States. He granted us access and helped provide supplies to those fighting the Soviets, and in return the United States provided funding and intelligence and looked the other way when it came to human rights abuses. Zia had led his country through the fastest economic growth in Pakistan's history, and he had accelerated its nuclear weapons program. Conspiracy theories still surround his death in a plane crash. Notwithstanding opinions about his legacy, it's clear that without his personal involvement, the Mujahideen would not have been able to drive the communists out of Afghanistan, since our support was funneled through his country.

One night, the president hosted a dinner for us. Sticking to custom, the men dined with Zia while his wife, Begum Shafiq Zia, hosted the senators' wives. After dinner, everyone joined up for the entertainment, which included traditional dancers in colorful costumes and melodious sitar music.

As a member of both the Armed Services and Intelligence Committees, Nunn had to take a position on U.S. support of the freedom fighters. The Mujahideen were in direct conflict with the Soviets, who had invaded their country. After our trip, Nunn went down to the White House to make a special report to the president on insights from both Pakistani and Afghan leaders. As to whether to arm the rebels with Stinger missiles, Nunn had decided they were necessary to counter the Soviets' Mi-24 attack helicopters. Yes, these lethal—but light and easy to operate—weapons might get in the wrong hands, but Nunn believed the Soviets presented the bigger threat and had to be defeated at all costs.

He successfully made his case both in the Senate and the White House. The Mujahideen got their Stingers, and it proved to be a turning point. After more than 350 of their aircraft and helicopters were shot down, Soviet leaders decided the cost was too high to keep fighting. Mikhail Gorbachev's accession in 1985 changed Moscow's outlook, and they started withdrawing in mid-1987. The war was both costly in terms of lives lost and money spent, and it was hugely unpopular in Russia, where the families of drafted troops killed in action were causing problems even in the tightly controlled totalitarian state. Brezhnev should have studied the lessons we'd learned from the Vietnam War.

The United States had tried to push the Pakistanis to ensure that the missiles wouldn't fall into the wrong hands—particularly those of the Iranians—but unfortunately that's exactly where some of them ended up. Zia did not fully support the U.S. position, especially our support of Iraq and Saudi Arabia during the Iran-Iraq War. He had a long-standing friendship with Iran, so he played both sides during the 1980s. He supported the United States in Afghanistan and Saudi Arabia in helping Iraq, but he also secretly sent some of the Stingers to Iran, and he helped transfer weapons between China and Iran. Of course, Zia did not reveal these intentions during his meetings with our delegation, and he ended up with everything *he* wanted.[8]

Popular culture credits Congressman Charlie Wilson as the champion of the brave Mujahideen fighters, and he was. But Senator Nunn's quiet support and our committee's funding were vital to the success of this policy. At the end of each year, I would get a call from the CIA's budget man, Leo Hazlewood, asking for a large transfer of funds from the DOD to CIA for covert operations. As we supported this year after year, it reinforced the joint jurisdiction the SASC had on intelligence matters. We had access to highly classified information on all the CIA's activities around the world. I was always pleased when someone from the executive branch came to the committee because it meant we could leverage something in return. In this case, funding covert operations in exchange for information sharing was a good quid pro quo. The SASC retains this jurisdiction today, but in the past decade or so it has not been as aggressive in exercising it. Because of this, there are now many essentially military operations that are run by the CIA (under Title 50 of the U.S. Code), not under the traditional military chain of command (under Title 10).

From Islamabad, we headed to the Republic of India, the second most populous country in the world. One highlight was our meeting in New Delhi with Rajiv Gandhi, who had taken over as prime minister after the assassination of his mother, Indira. Rajiv was leading India in a different direction than his mother, who'd been close to the USSR. He wanted to improve relations with the United States, and our delegation wanted to ask him how we could work together to further this. While we'd studied his background and interests, we were unprepared for what would unfold. Gandhi was a pilot, and we had John Glenn, world famous fighter jock and astronaut, in our delegation. All Gandhi wanted to discuss was flying—which planes they'd flown, questions about space flight, and their love of private airplanes—while the rest of our delegation sat on the sidelines. While we may not have covered all the talking points the staff had painstakingly prepared, if the goal was to improve relations, we were definitely successful. Unfortunately, in 1991 Gandhi, like his mother, was assassinated.

⌣

Though Jimmy Carter had done his best to ease tensions with the Soviet Union, the invasion of Afghanistan put a huge strain on the relationship. Reagan denounced the Soviet Union as an "evil empire" at the same time he was taking steps to modernize our nuclear stockpile. In 1983, when the Soviets shot down a Korean Airlines flight, NATO increased the number of missiles in Europe, and the Soviets walked out of arms control negotiations. The Cold War was heading toward a new deep freeze. Then, in 1985, Mikhail Gorbachev was elected general secretary of the Communist Party, and Reagan found a negotiating partner.[9] With his country in economic free fall, Gorbachev recognized the need for reform. He introduced glasnost and perestroika to make Russia more open and democratic, and he renewed a dialogue with the United States.

About six months after Gorbachev came into power, we headed east to meet with this new, revolutionary ruler. As we prepared for the unprecedented meeting between a Soviet leader and a Senate delegation, there was no way anyone could predict the outcome. The delegation was led by Robert Byrd and Strom Thurmond, the two senior members of their parties, Senators Nunn and Warner from the Armed Services Committee, Claiborne Pell from the Foreign Relations Committee, and Senators Dennis DeConcini, Paul Sarbanes, and George Mitchell as well.

I'd been to Moscow with Nunn before and knew that the KGB, the Soviet intelligence service, would go through our luggage and bug our rooms. So I reprised a disinformation campaign I had used on a previous trip: I had put a bogus map of NATO forces, their locations and capabilities, in my suitcase. We figured it would drive the KGB crazy trying to figure out why our fake map didn't match any of their intelligence. This time I had the Pentagon draw up a phony contingency plan for the U.S. reinforcement of the Korean peninsula, and I hope it drove them crazy again.[10]

The senators met to go over the plan of action: what each would ask and say. We worked with Dick Combs, deputy chief of mission and senior State Department official in the ambassador's absence. Dick was a career foreign service officer and another of those stellar individuals who devoted his life to the diplomatic corps.[11] Our focus that day was Gorbachev: would he be different from his predecessors? In previous meetings, Nunn and I had found Soviet leaders predictable. They worked from lengthy talking points, or set speeches, that covered any subject that could be raised, and they never deviated from the party line. These meetings were unproductive and boring, since we always knew what they would say. I usually advised that someone from the U.S. delegation say something completely off the wall just to see if it would throw them off. Since no one ever did, my theory went untested.

But it was clear from the outset that Gorbachev was different, both in personality and substance. He urged our delegation to focus on real issues instead of reading from talking points. For the most part, we obliged, except for our two most senior members, Byrd and Thurmond. Byrd had spent a considerable amount of time preparing his remarks, even practicing them with Nunn, so he wasn't inclined to throw that hard work away. He went ahead with his twenty-minute diatribe. Even worse, though, was Thurmond. The man who'd parachuted into

Normandy on D-day with the famed 82nd Airborne was now recounting how the United States had saved Russia and the rest of Europe from the Nazis and that the Soviet Union should be grateful. Gorbachev listened patiently, and when it came his turn, he thanked Thurmond for his service and talked about his own father's role in combat in World War II, the millions of Russian casualties, and his commitment to doing everything he could to avoid another conflict in the future.

The rest of the senators stuck to the issues and by the end we were all stunned by how open-minded Gorbachev was. After the meeting, we spent hours with Dick preparing the cables that were to go back to our most senior officials. But everyone was so curious about the new leader that the administration invited the senators to the White House to personally brief the president. I was even asked to come out to the CIA to brief the analysts on my firsthand impressions of Gorbachev for their country leader profiles.

⌒

Just as 1980 had been a shock to the Democratic majority, 1986 was a shock to Republicans. Many of those elected on Reagan's coattails in 1980 were voted out. The SASC staff went through a major upheaval as the majority and minority flipped back. For me, the physical change was that I moved to the staff director's office off the main hearing room in Russell 212. I now worked in the same office and at the same desk as its legendary chairman, Senator Richard Russell.

In six years of Republican rule, the professional staff had grown considerably, which gave us a major space problem. Senator Tower had refused to move to the new Hart Office Building and the lure of much more office space than in the Russell or Dirksen buildings. But he preferred the historic location. Personally, I'm glad we stayed, but we did have more butts than chairs and no place to expand. So one of my first tasks became organizing a total renovation of the committee space, including converting a corridor into our main entrance, still in use today. I also made office space out of stairwells and converted to modular furniture and cubicles. These renovations were met by fierce opposition from the architect of the Capitol, George White. So I got a former staffer to draw up plans and ran them past Senator Nunn. He got his close friend, Wendell Ford, chairman of the Rules Committee, to provide funding. By then, there was enough support to override White, who then decided to approve the plans, and the work was soon underway. So while the committee was holding strategy hearings and modernizing rules and procedures, workers were breaking down sixteen-inch-thick brick walls, tearing up floors, and putting in ceilings and lighting.

Nunn left most of the decisions up to me, that is until construction inadvertently drained the swimming pool in the Senators-only gym down below. Another senator approached him about this, and he came looking for me. I explained that we were building a small kitchen for the staffers, which required new plumbing. To install it, the workers had to temporarily drain the pool. Nunn was having none of that and told us to stop, but fortunately they'd already finished and the pool was being refilled.

I wanted the entrance to the committee to reflect its importance, so I had the flags of all the services, with battle streamers, erected in the reception area. We created a library behind the reception room for meetings and to house our laws and procedures. Twenty years later, these renovations remain unchanged.

We also implemented formal procedures for hearings to ensure proper coordination with the minority. I remembered from my time in the loyal opposition that we didn't always know what the committee was up to, which I didn't want the new minority to have to endure. Hearing notices now required signatures from both sides of the aisle, as well as mine as staff director. We also put in place written procedures for handling classified materials. And even though the Senate didn't require it, we set down rules on stock ownership and financial considerations to avoid even the perception of conflicts of interest.

$$\backsim$$

One immutable fact of my entire time in the Senate was the services' parochial approach to their major weapons systems. In 1986, the Air Force began developing the next-generation fighter plane, the F-22 Raptor. This would replace the F-16 Fighting Falcon and the F-15 Eagle. From the beginning, the F-22 program was public. But unbeknownst to the public—and even to most of Congress—the Air Force had begun work on a different fighter in the late 1970s. Due to the stealth technology it incorporated, the program was highly classified. The F-117 Nighthawk made its maiden flight in secret in 1981. By the time the F-22 was getting off the ground, the F-117 was already operational.

Nighthawk was conceived under the supervision of the brilliant Dr. William Perry, a mathematician and engineer who was director of defense research and engineering at the time. The contract was awarded to Lockheed and, due to its importance and sensitivity, the research, design, and ultimately construction commenced within its secretive Advanced Development Projects division. Also known as Skunk Works, this division had produced some of the most advanced aircraft of their times, such as the U-2 and SR-71 spy planes. Perry and the engineers at Lockheed, led by Kelly Johnson (and later Ben Rich), turned the concept into reality. Perry kept tight control to avoid the requirements creep and cost escalation that plague most major programs.

One of Nunn's concerns was that the F-117 couldn't carry guided weaponry. Due to its revolutionary shape and the need to avoid external mounting of weapons, which would have negated the low radar cross-section, payload considerations had become secondary. Nunn pushed to have internal weapons carriage and cockpit electronics for the latest smart weapons. Col. Paul Kaminski, the program manager, shared this concern, and he spearheaded the effort to rectify this deficiency. The remarkable success of the Nighthawk in the early hours of operation Desert Storm vindicated this decision. The F-117 used stealth to evade Iraqi air defenses, and its smart bombs hit critical command and communications nodes with a stunning accuracy previously unseen in air warfare.

Senator Nunn also opposed the Air Force's decision to stop production of the fighter before its full requirement was reached. There was concern in some USAF circles that once the stealth fighter became public, it could reduce support for the F-22, the fighter community's sacred cow, even though the Nighthawk was primarily a ground attack aircraft. The Air Force wanted to forgo the last two squadrons to protect the F-22. But Nunn, convinced of the program's value, kept it alive by putting it in the classified annex of the annual defense bill. He enlisted the support of the House and the appropriations committees. This was difficult considering so few in Congress were briefed on the program, so it couldn't be included in the normal bill and accompanying report. Because I was concerned that the Pentagon would ignore our guidance, I designed a way to incorporate the classified annex into the statutory bill. The bill language had a phrase that the classified annex was "incorporated by reference" and had the effect of law, and in it we outlined the direction to procure the original objective, the last two squadrons.

In testimony before the committee after Desert Storm on the conduct of the war, multiple witnesses testified that had these additional squadrons not been present, there would not have been enough Nighthawks to sustain operations throughout the conflict.

One final initiative that grew out of the Nighthawk program was information sharing. Many of our combatant commanders, the generals and admirals who commanded forces around the world, were unaware of the F-117. Given its revolutionary nature, this capability could have greatly impacted their operational planning. We directed the Joint Chiefs to create a special section to ensure that our commanders had access to information about highly classified and sensitive programs. This became the Special Actions and Operations Directorate (J38).

When the stealth fighter became public, it shocked the aviation world. Looking back, the fact that it remained a secret for more than a decade, well after it became operational, is remarkable. I often wonder if such a feat could be accomplished today, but I use this example when I hear complaints that "Congress can't keep a secret."

And the additional squadrons did *not* jeopardize the F-22. After reviewing two proposals for the F-22, one from Lockheed and the other from

Boeing-McDonnell Douglas, Don Rice, secretary of the Air Force, awarded the contract to Lockheed Martin, who produced a magnificent fighter until Secretary of Defense Robert Gates prematurely terminated the program in 2009.

~~

One of the strong relationships Nunn fostered as chairman was with David Boren, the chairman of the Senate Select Committee on Intelligence. Nunn was the second-most senior member on the SSCI behind Boren, and his staff director George Tenet and I worked closely together. We also enjoyed an excellent relationship with the Appropriations Committee chairman, Senator Byrd, and Dick D'Amato, his staffer who covered intelligence programs.

A little-remembered fact on the Hill is that the Armed Services Committee drafted the legislation that created the Select Committee on Intelligence in 1976. Before that, the SASC had sole jurisdiction over all defense and intelligence matters. SASC was so protective of its role that when it passed Senate Resolution 400 to create the SSCI, the latter had full jurisdiction only over the CIA; jurisdiction over all the other national and tactical intelligence programs remained with the parent committee. The resolution also required SSCI authorization bills to come through the SASC before reaching the Senate floor. Nunn and I always ensured that we worked with the SSCI staff and senators to exercise our jurisdiction in a firm but collegial way.

As leading members of the SSCI, Nunn and Boren were the only two Democrats who'd supported the covert program to arm the Nicaraguan Contras until Congress finally blocked the program. To get around the law that precluded support to the Contras, members of the Reagan administration engaged in what came to be known as the Iran-Contra Affair. As presidential scandals go, this one was particularly disturbing. There were several parts of this controversy that made it troubling: selling arms to Iran, an arms-for-hostages deal, and financing Nicaraguan rebel groups, all contrary to law, policy, and U.S. interests.

In 1985, the Reagan administration began selling weapons to Iran—the same country that held sixty-six Americans hostage for 444 days in 1979, was linked to the Marine Corps barracks bombing of 1983, and was on the State Department's sponsors of terrorism list. He felt compelled to help the American hostages whom Iranian-backed terrorists were holding in Lebanon. His staff knew his dedication to bringing them home and took a "whatever means necessary" approach. But sales to Iran had been illegal since 1979; the administration was consorting with our sworn enemy. The executive is also supposed to give Congress advance notice on covert operations, which Reagan also ignored. He had ordered his CIA director, William Casey, not to tell us about the arms sales, again contrary to law. On the Intelligence Committee, Nunn referred to Casey as "Mr. Mumbles" because

Briefing my infantry platoon in the Que Son Mountains on an upcoming operation.

Serving hot chow to my Marines one of the very few times it was available to us in the field.

My platoon firing the 60-mm mortars prior to an assault on a fortified position.

The USMC "high and tight" haircut is mandatory even in combat. Gunnery Sergeant Martinez gives me a regulation haircut in the mountains using a C-rat box as the barber chair during a break in the action.

Lima Company commander Capt. J. K. Van Riper with Company Gunnery Sergeant Martinez in the rice paddies and lowlands near LZ Ross with the Que Son Mountains in the background.

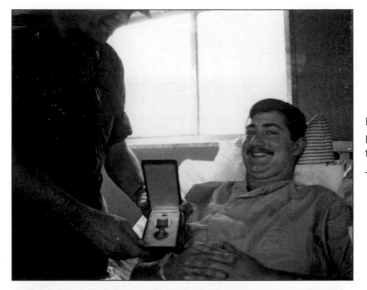

Receiving my purple heart in the hospital in January 1970.

Family picture taken on the steps of my childhood home, 854 Orange Terrace, Macon, GA, when I returned from Vietnam in September 1970. Top left to right: Anthony, my mother, Annina, and my father, Angelo. Second row left to right: Frank, Mary Angela, and me. Bottom row left to right: Vincent, Michael, and Trudie.

On one of my first days in 1973 as an intern with Sen. Sam Nunn in an outfit that I bought at the PX after my tailor-made Hong Kong suits had fallen apart. I wish Jan hadn't made me throw out that classic jacket and tie.

Getting in the limousine with my beautiful bride, Jan, after our wedding ceremony at the Navy Chapel, Nebraska Avenue, Washington, DC, on February 23, 1974.

Jan and I enjoy our Cheez Whiz, peanut butter, and cold duck on our honeymoon at Seven Springs Ski Resort in Seven Springs, PA. Doesn't get much better than that!

The Senate delegation photo on our visit to China in 1979. Bottom middle is Chinese premier Deng Xiaoping. Top of the third row: me and Capt. John McCain, USN.

My family with Sen. Barry Goldwater, then chairman of the SASC at a picnic in the Virginia countryside in 1987.

Chairman Nunn, me, Pat Tucker, and Senator Warner in a serious discussion during a SASC hearing.

The members of the SASC in the 101st Congress, 1990, in our formal hearing room in Russell 212. Seated left to right: Sens. Jeff Bingaman, Ted Kennedy, Carl Levin, Jim Exon, Chairman Sam Nunn, Ranking Member John Warner, Strom Thurmond, Bill Cohen, and John McCain. Standing left to right: Sens. Robert Byrd, Dick Shelby, Tim Wirth, Al Gore, John Glenn, Alan Dixon, me, Pat Tucker, Sens. Malcolm Wallop, Slade Gorton, Trent Lott, and Dan Coats.

Before I deployed for Operation Desert Shield in early December 1990, my children surprised me with a heartfelt goodbye.

Then a colonel, I deployed with the 2nd Marine Division in Operation Desert Shield to the deserts of Saudi Arabia in December 1990, where we linked up with the 1st Marine Division for an intelligence assessment.

As staff director of the SASC during our visit to the combat zone during Operation Desert Storm, I wrote a heartfelt message on one of the 2,000-pound bombs that would be dropped from a B-52.

Gen. Norman Schwarzkopf, United States Army, commander of the U.S. Central Command during Operation Desert Shield–Desert Storm, testifying before the Senate Armed Services Committee in 1993 on gays in the military. To my right: Chairman Nunn, Gen. Norman Schwarzkopf, and Rick DeBobes, committee counsel.

Visiting with the chairman of the Joint Chiefs of Staff Gen. Colin Powell as he was completing his second two-year tour as chairman in September 1993.

President Clinton, Senator Nunn, Senator Thurmond, Les Brownlee, and I in the Oval Office when President Clinton signed the Defense Authorization Bill in 1996 on the occasion of Senator Nunn's final defense bill. This was our twenty-third consecutive defense bill signed into law.

I was director of the Marine Corps Reserve when President Bush met with all of us Reserve chiefs to discuss mobilization of the Guard and Reserve six days after 9/11.

Jan and I stand with President Bush at a ceremony in his honor at Marine Barracks 8th and I.

Standing at attention at the historic Marine Barracks, 8th and I, Washington, DC, on the occasion of my retirement in October 2003 after thirty-five years of service. Then supreme allied commander Europe Gen. Jim Jones, USMC, presided at the ceremony.

SASC chairman Sen. John Warner and former SASC staff directors attended my retirement ceremony at Marine Barracks 8th and I. Left to right: Dick Reynard, Frank Sullivan, Bud McFarlane, Ed Braswell, John Warner, me, Judy Ainsley, Les Brownlee, Carl Smith, and Rhett Dawson.

With my daughters at my retirement ceremony, Meghan on the left and Julie on the right.

Ringing the opening bell at the New York Stock Exchange on October 13, 2006, when we took SAIC public. The initial public offering team, left to right: Stuart Davis, Bill Roper, Ken Dahlberg, Larry Prior, me, and Mark Sopp.

As executive vice president, I introduced Gov. Tim Kaine at the ceremony when SAIC's headquarters moved from La Jolla, California, to McLean, Virginia.

Hosting secretary of defense Leon Panetta in my role as chairman of his Reserve Forces Policy Board. The board serves the secretary of defense as an independent adviser on National Guard and Reserve policy.

Standing with my sons, 2nd Lt. Dan Punaro, newly commissioned in the U.S. Army, and Maj. Joe Punaro, USMC, at Fort Benning following Dan's graduation from Officer Candidate School in 2013.

Secretary of Defense Ash Carter welcoming me to his personal office in the Pentagon. I had the privilege of serving on his transition team and helping him through his Senate confirmation process in early 2015.

Sen. John McCain, chairman of the Senate Armed Services Committee, and I discuss defense reform prior to my testimony before the committee in 2015.

Family photo in fall 2015. Seated left to right: Jan with grandson Jack and granddaughter Colbie; Laura, my daughter-in-law, with daughter Reese; Meghan with son Bryce; Julie with daughter Logan. Standing from left to right: my son-in-law, Sean, Dan, me, Joe, and my son-in-law Matt.

whenever we would ask a question he didn't want to answer, he mumbled through his response in a completely unintelligible way.

When the story broke, Reagan came out on the defensive, claiming that he hadn't broken any laws and was acting in the best interests of the United States. Still, he took a lot of heat over the arms-for-hostages link, which directly contradicted his campaign promise never to negotiate with terrorists.

Two weeks later, another scandal erupted when the Nicaraguan Contras link was revealed. Some of the money from the Iranian arms sales was being diverted through a Swiss bank account and winding up the hands of Nicaraguan rebels, a direct violation of the law. The Sandinistas had overthrown the dictatorial Somoza regime in 1979, which turned Nicaragua into an ally of the Soviet Union. Since the Reagan Doctrine called for containing communism, he supported the right-leaning rebel groups based in Honduras. In 1982, Congress specifically banned aiding the Contras through the Boland Amendment and strengthened the restrictions in 1984. Reagan said he was unaware that the profits from the arms sales were going to the Contras.[12] The administration pointed the finger at two individuals in the National Security Council, one of whom brought me back to my days at TBS: now Lt. Col. Oliver North.

Nunn already had a negative view of North, based on a meeting with him earlier about funding the Contras, a position Nunn supported. After giving a detailed presentation about the reasons for funding, North got in Nunn's face with an emotional diatribe about helping the Contras now to prevent American blood from being spilled in a future conflict. Nunn had left that meeting with a firm impression that North had very poor judgment.

Ollie now became the focus of the joint Iran-Contra investigating committee. Senator Nunn, who had a full plate as chairman of the Armed Services Committee and Permanent Subcommittee on Investigations (PSI), as well as with the SSCI and the Small Business Committee, reluctantly joined this one as well at the insistence of the majority leader, Senator Byrd. Nunn, a Contra supporter, knew this Iran-Contra committee would take valuable time away from his own chairmanships. Both parties and both bodies put some of their strongest, most capable, and most well-known members on the committee, with Daniel Inouye and Warren Rudman serving as chair and vice chair, along with George Mitchell, David Boren, and Howell Heflin joining Nunn. On the House side, Representatives Dick Cheney and Les Aspin, both future secretaries of defense, were appointed. The investigation of the Iran-Contra Affair ran from January to August 1987, with the hearing phase starting in May.

Each member of the joint committee was allowed one staffer to support their work, so I suggested Jeff Smith, our general counsel, who was also Nunn's designee to the Intelligence Committee. Jeff was familiar with both Intelligence

Committee matters and SASC issues, and he obviously worked well with the senator. Due to the workload, we also put Eleanor Hill, staff director of the PSI, on Iran-Contra. You would be hard-pressed to find two more capable individuals to work on such a high-profile assignment.

From the outset, Nunn had concerns with how the committee was approaching the hearing phase. From his experience on PSI, backed up by Jeff and Eleanor's advice, he knew the best way to build a case was from the ground up; start with the plankton and work up to the whales. The committee leadership thought otherwise and felt they should hear from the most senior people first, such as national security adviser Bud McFarlane, his successor John Poindexter, and North, before the groundwork was set. Nunn was also concerned that the committee considered granting North immunity before they knew what information he would give. All the special prosecutors opposed this move, but they were overruled by the committee leadership. Nunn was also unnerved that Rudman and the committee's main focus seemed to be proving Reagan's involvement, or lack thereof, in the affair, rather than taking the time to conduct a full, comprehensive investigation. The committee set arbitrary deadlines and rushed the hearings, and preparing witnesses became a secondary concern. Nunn believed the entire approach was poorly handled, from both an investigatory and legal standpoint. While the Senate side remained mostly bipartisan, our House counterparts were always at each other's throats.

Nunn also disagreed with the committee's approach to North's testimony. The leadership had decided that instead of senators, the lawyers would lead the questioning. There are many differences between a congressional hearing and a trial, a point easily seen by senators' lines of questioning as opposed to those of prosecutors. Hearings don't require the burden of proof, and there is no judge or jury to appeal to. Nunn's modus operandi was to start off friendly and get the witness to venture out on a limb, then pound him on the contradictions in his testimony. If this was done right, witnesses would hang themselves. The counsel's approach was the opposite, and the effect was antagonizing. Having the prosecutors lead the questioning, instead of Nunn, Mitchell, Rudman, and Cohen, was a bizarre mistake. The problem was even worse because we were dealing with North, a charismatic guy who looked impeccable in uniform. I told Nunn, Cohen, and Rudman that these long-haired lawyers wouldn't stand a chance against North. But Rudman, as vice chairman, was still firm that the lawyers should take the lead. Arthur Liman, lead attorney for the Senate, and John Nields, lead for the House, were no match for either North or his attorney, Brendan Sullivan.

Unfortunately, my prediction was on the mark. While Ollie's emotional appeal failed as a policy argument, the media and the public ate it up, especially in contrast to the lawyers' aggressive badgering. North was painted as an American hero, not the "ends justify the means" loose cannon we'd seen in Nunn's office earlier.

The hearings showed that Reagan didn't know about the affair, but the real indictment was that he didn't understand what was going on in his own office. Having NSC officials running shell games like these highlighted major White House mismanagement. Overall, fourteen people were convicted on cover-up charges. But North's conviction was overturned, and when President Bush came into office, he issued pardons to six individuals involved with the affair, including McFarlane and Weinberger.[13] North went on to a successful business career in the security field and became a popular speaker and television narrator, but he failed in a later run for the Senate. The lesson, I guess, is that charisma goes a long way, but not all the way.

∽

JAN

Throughout the years Arnold and I have always worked as a team. While we each had our primary responsibilities, we always valued each other's opinion. Just as his job made it possible for me to stay home, mine made it possible for him to pursue his career, for he knew everything else would be taken care of.

Not working in an office made it possible to pursue other interests in the community, schools, and church. I served as age group coordinator for our local soccer program, recruiting coaches and organizing team drafts, rosters, schedules, and end-of-season tournaments. I always volunteered at the schools in various capacities, from the PTA to classroom assistance to organizing fundraisers. One of the fundraisers we did was an auction at St. John's School. Arnold took a Congressional Club cookbook around to senators' offices to have it signed. We had signatures from Ted Kennedy, Robert Byrd, John Glenn, Howard Baker, Bob Dole, and of course, Sam Nunn. That cookbook sold at the auction for several hundred dollars.

∽

ARNOLD

Our children all loved sports. Over the years they participated in T-ball, soccer, football, basketball, field hockey, lacrosse, and track, starting when each was about five. When I had some time away from work, we'd play "horse" with the basketball hoop I put up, or kick soccer balls, or play on the swing set with slide, swings, and jungle bars.

The work-life balance for me was unfortunately skewed to the office rather than the home side. With the bottomless pit of Senate activities and Reserve duty at least once a month, I was used to the 24/7 pace customary then among my peers. I did spend as much time as I could on the weekends at their games or sports practices. The kids were often on travel teams, which meant driving to distant locations, or else at home games nonstop on Saturdays and Sundays. They earned multiple varsity letters and awards. Julie played field hockey at George-town. Meghan played field hockey and Dan played lacrosse at Mary Washington. Jan and I were glad they played sports in college so we could continue our tradition of cheering them on from the sidelines.

At McLean High, Julie played on the same soccer team as Jen Robb, daughter of Sen. Chuck Robb. He was on the Armed Services Committee at the time, and we would both sneak away from work to watch our kids play. During one particular match, the referees were blatantly prejudiced against McLean, and the game went to penalty kicks at the end. McLean scored the final goal for the win. But even though the ref at the goal line called it for us, the ref on the other side, after being "lobbied" by the opposition, called "no goal." I got up and shared a few choice words with the referees and was kindly invited by the school leaders to leave the premises. I protested, "Senator Robb actually started all the commotion," but they didn't buy my blatant attempt to pass the buck.

Washington is replete with social functions. These are essential see-and-be-seen events for staffers in the legislative and executive branches. The gears turn on social networks. Cultivating them not only greatly aids one's career path—as climbing the ladder often depends not on what you know, but who—but it's also necessary to accomplish the job at hand. For example, military officers and senior defense civilians should attend nonpolitical congressional events because it allows them to interact with the lawmakers who control their budgets. It's harder to cut a line item when you can visualize a friendly face that goes with it!

⌒

JAN

When Congress adjourned in August, Arnold always got a week off. For many years we went to Virginia Beach for a family vacation. Bob and Susie O'Donnell, two lifelong friends, kindly let us stay at their home while they went to the Outer Banks for their own vacation. We took care of their dog and overlapped our stays a few days on each end to spend time with them and their three boys.

Arnold went out of his way to arrange special excursions while we were there. We rode on helicopters and landing craft, shot guns on a cruiser at sea, rode the elevator on an aircraft carrier, loaded the 16" guns on a battleship, and rode Amtracs out of the well deck of an amphibious ship. He was able to provide the family with these exciting and educational experiences through his military connections.

Amidst summer camps and hectic schedules, it was nice to have that one week at the ocean to relax together. Although Arnold's never been a sun-and-sand kind of guy, he still trekked out to the beach with us each day, body-surfed with the kids, and enjoyed a break from the Capitol. I really did love being there with the family, watching dolphins offshore and hearing the Navy jets flying overhead. Two very different sights and sounds, but both to me meaning freedom.

While the kids were growing up, we took advantage of all DC had to offer, including the Children's Museum and the Air and Space Museum, two favorites. We also attended most of the presidential inaugurations. Arnold could usually arrange choice seats, as he was almost always working during such events.

Every so often, when the Senate wasn't in session, I'd take the kids and often their cousins, too, to visit him at work. They loved to sit around the large mahogany conference table in the committee office and talk with serious voices into the microphones, as if they were senators. And every year, we made sure to attend the ice cream social hosted by the Dairy Association, to enjoy sundaes and root beer floats. DC's a great place to raise a family!

∽

ARNOLD

In the 1980s, the USA—the Union of South Africa—was in turmoil. Whites in South Africa held all the power, while the majority black Africans had no representation and were classified based on their race. Riots, protests, and confrontations were common, as was South Africa's increasing international isolation. Since the beginnings of apartheid in the 1960s, militant groups had plotted to overthrow the Pretoria government. In Southwest Africa (present-day Namibia), South Africa was fighting the South West African People's Organization (SWAPO). When Angola gained its independence from Portugal in 1975, it created a power vacuum that allowed SWAPO to thrive. Making matters worse, the USSR and Cuba were sending aid, weapons, and advisers, and Cuba even sent troops to the Marxist-leaning government of Angola. South Africa wanted to keep SWAPO away from its northern border, so it conducted many counterinsurgency operations within Southwest Africa and Angola. By the 1980s, the war had turned from a counterinsurgency to a dangerous showdown between South Africa, Angola, and Cuba, and by extension the United States and the Soviet Union.[14] Our interest in the fight was governed by the containment strategy: we wanted to prevent the Soviets from gaining a foothold in this key part of Africa.

Congress overrode a presidential veto in 1986 to impose sanctions on South Africa, demanding that prime minister P. W. Botha make serious reforms before these sanctions could be lifted. The goals were to end apartheid and create a democratic, multiparty system, immediately release Nelson Mandela and all other political prisoners, and end the military aggression against its neighbors. The Senate bill passed 78–21 with many Republicans voting against the president.[15] The sanctions had little effect on Botha; in fact, he clamped down harder on anti-apartheid groups and media coverage of protests. Then, in 1988, Congress tried to pass a new round of much tougher sanctions, including stopping all trade between the United States and South Africa. That bill failed to muster a veto-proof majority and never made it to the Senate floor. Many argued that the first sanctions package had done little to end apartheid and had actually hurt the people it was trying to help.[16]

In 1988, Nunn and Boren teamed up again to get a firsthand look at the situation there, and Tenet and I accompanied them. Before heading to South Africa, we stopped in Kenya and Zaire. Our first stop was Nairobi, where President Daniel arap Moi had just succeeded Kenya's first independently elected president, Jomo Kenyatta. Moi was a potential ally, and the United States hoped to develop a closer relationship with his country for a foothold in troublesome East Africa. The highlight of that leg was a safari ride through the Maasai Mara National Reserve and a visit to a typical tribal village. It was important for us to see firsthand how tribal communities still dominated this part of the world and how few of our Western comforts, like electricity and running water, even existed. I was much more grateful and appreciative of our way of life back home.

From Kenya we headed to Zaire (today the Democratic Republic of the Congo). Zaire was supporting our effort to help Jonas Savimbi, leader of the National Union for the Total Independence of Angola (UNITA), which was fighting the Angolan government. When we landed, I was struck by the poverty in the capital, Kinshasa. The roads were racked with potholes, buildings were in disrepair, beasts of burden were pulling carts of supplies that elsewhere would be transported by trucks, and the citizens at roadside stands buying basic necessities wore dirty, tattered clothes. Our embassy told us to avoid the local beverages and drink only the bottled water we brought with us. The economy was so rocky they wouldn't even accept their own currency at our hotel; we had to pay with American dollars. All the while, Zaire's president, Mobutu Sese Seko, was raking in billions from rampant corruption. But in him, Ronald Reagan saw an ally to fight the spread of communism in Africa.[17]

The two senators had been invited to go out on Mobutu's barge for a working dinner on the Congo River. George and I had heard in advance that these dinners typically lasted hours and hours, so we begged the senators to let us stay behind to "get some work done." True to the rumors, the senators reported that they did spend long hours on the barge, but that it was productive in our efforts to get approval to continue our covert operations.

After seeing the disturbing poverty of Zaire, we were excited to explore beautiful South Africa. We started with meetings in Pretoria, then took a short drive to Johannesburg to board the famous Blue Train to Cape Town, with a side trip to Durban to meet the Zulu leader, Mangosuthu Buthelezi, and a secret side trip to link up with the leader of the insurgency, Savimbi. Our trip was like a roller coaster: we alternated between meetings with legendary figures such as Nobel Prize winner Desmond Tutu and anti-apartheid activist Albertina Sisulu, then visiting the site of the 1976 Soweto Uprising, which reminded us just how pervasive racial oppression still was. We met with the country team at the embassy in Pretoria in preparation for our government meetings. We underscored our request to visit Nelson Mandela in prison (which we were still denied), to keep up pressure to end apartheid, and also ensure South Africa's continuing support for the guerrilla campaign of General Savimbi against the Angolan forces.

Finally, we met with President Botha, the "big crocodile." An avid supporter of racial oppression, he continued to lead South Africa down a road of isolation. The senators pressed him to stop demonizing the nonviolent moderates, create equal representation in the government, eliminate detentions without charges, and ease the regulations that kept nonwhites out of the business world. They reiterated their disappointment in being denied the opportunity to visit Mandela, and Nunn expressed his frustration at the denial of permission for Albertina Sisulu to travel to Georgia to receive an award. To drive their points harder, they told Botha that Congress was ready to impose even more sanctions. Botha was unmoved. He was committed to preserving the status quo. Looks were aimed like daggers, voices raised, insults hurled every which way, and any pretense of cordiality devolved into verbal brawls. In twenty-four years in government, this was the most contentious encounter I ever witnessed.

Later, while George and I were waiting for the senators to finish another meeting in Pretoria, we ran into one of George's colleagues from Georgetown. He casually asked us how the meeting with Botha had gone. Our Army escort, Lt. Col. Bo Bludworth, quipped, "He certainly seemed well-fed." What we didn't realize was that this guy was a reporter. The headline in the country's largest newspaper the next day was "Senators Call President Botha Fat." We were actually on the Blue Train when we saw the headline. George and Bo and I took straws to determine who would tell the senators. They wouldn't appreciate these headlines. We were all in the café car when they came in, and I had the task of telling them about our undiplomatic incident. Before I could rat out my colleague, their stoic faces broke and they burst out in laughter. They'd seen the headlines already, but wanted to put us through the wringer first, just for fun. We learned later that the whole time we'd been shadowed by South African intelligence. I can only guess at how they reported the senators' reactions.

While I am sure there may have been exceptions in history, the dictators and strongmen I met on our travels did not merit our confidence in them. This was true for the ruthless Mobutu of Zaire, the oppressive Zia of Pakistan, and Manuel Noriega of Panama, and it is just as true today. Dictators cannot and should not be trusted.

After visiting Cape Town and the Cape of Good Hope, we boarded a plane back to the States. I was glad to be heading home, where President-elect George H. W. Bush was about to take the reins. As we wrapped up eight years of a defense buildup and both positive and negative developments, from Iran-Contra to the Gorbachev era, we thought we'd seen it all. But we could not have imagined the tumult the next years would bring, from committing more than half a million troops to the Middle East to the fall of the Berlin Wall. President Bush's one-term presidency would prove to be as consequential as any.

BATTLES LOST AND WON

1987–97: Washington, DC

In the 1980s, even though we had a new, reformist leader in Gorbachev, and he and Reagan had both publicly committed to arms control and nuclear reductions, the United States was still worried about the threat of a Soviet nuclear strike. In particular, we were worried about our communications systems and their survivability in the event of such an attack. So the Air Force came up with the Military Strategic and Tactical Relay, or Milstar satellite, to create a "global, secure, nuclear-survivable, space-based communication system."[1]

We knew this was an important program both strategically and tactically, but by 1990 the costs were out of control and some of the requirements were relics from the depths of the Cold War. So we tried to work with the Pentagon to impose some common sense and reduce the cost. Our efforts were rebuffed, so I told the SASC staff that in order to get the Pentagon's attention, we would have to kill the Milstar program. Both the professional staff and the chairman of the Strategic Subcommittee, Jim Exon from Nebraska—home of Strategic Air Command—were reluctant. I convinced them the best way to save the program was to kill it. I also knew the Pentagon's assistant secretary of defense for command, control, communications, and intelligence, Duane Andrews, could be counted on to work out a compromise.

After the committee markup that voted to strip Milstar's funding, Lockheed (which built the platform) lobbyist Dick Cook came knocking on my door. Dick couldn't believe we would just yank our support. He warned me that Lockheed, along with the Pentagon, would pull out all the stops to fight the chairman on the Senate floor to reinstate the program. I knew how weak our position was, but I told Dick, "I welcome that fight! I might add that this committee does not lose votes on the floor. Do what you need to, but realize that we'll be forced to expose all the cost and technical issues with your program. And once you lose that vote, we won't have to budge in conference with the House." Cook called me back the next day and said they'd decided not to fight the chairman on the floor and to work with us in conference on a compromise. I breathed a sigh of relief; my bluff had worked.

Then, when I met with Rudy deLeon, the House staff director, to go over preliminary issues for that year's conference committee, I ran into trouble with my grand plan. To my surprise, Rudy praised the Senate's decision to kill Milstar, as the House had had the same concerns we did. I was stunned. I'd planned on the House being the big champion for the program. So I had to sheepishly tell Rudy, "Our intention was never to kill it . . . so the SASC is going to recede to you in a compromise on Milstar, and we're going to need you to make a concession to us so we don't look bad." In the end, we reached a compromise, and at the Pentagon Duane was able to dial back the costs. What would have been a $40 billion satellite program went operational for $800 million each and had an operational life of more than ten years.[2]

～

Battleships had long been the capital ships of the Navy, yardsticks of national power, and favorites of both naval historians and armchair captains. Although superseded by aircraft carriers for force projection, USS *Iowa* (BB 61) was still in service as the lead ship of the final American battleship class. Her massive 16-inch/50-caliber guns could fire 2,700-pound shells twenty-three miles. I'd had firsthand experience of their devastating power, viewing the moonscapes the fire missions of USS *New Jersey* had left in Vietnam. *Iowa* had had a distinguished history in World War II and Korea and had carried President Roosevelt and the Joint Chiefs to the Tehran Conference. Decommissioned in 1958, she'd been reactivated in 1984 as part of Lehman's six-hundred-ship Navy, but she had not undergone the usual inspections due to the rush to get her to sea. In 1986, she failed her in-service review and the lead inspector recommended she be taken out of service. Navy leadership rejected the warning.[3]

On April 19, 1989, three hundred miles off Puerto Rico, an explosion tore through one of her main turrets during a firing exercise, killing forty-seven sailors. In a remarkable feat of damage control, the crew contained the fire in less than two hours and prevented her from sinking.[4]

While the nation mourned one of the worst accidents ever in peacetime, the Navy focused on blaming an individual sailor for the tragedy. The Naval Investigative Service, the service's detective force,[5] reported that Clayton Hartwig had just gotten out of a relationship with another (male) sailor and was suicidal. The latter, who'd survived the explosion, was allegedly the beneficiary of Hartwig's life insurance policy, which provided additional fuel for the conspiracy theory. The investigators also concluded that some of the debris found in the wreckage of the turret was part of a detonator.[6]

On the SASC, we were skeptical of this theory for several reasons. First, it was clear the Navy was going overboard to ensure no fault was found with the ship itself, specifically its huge guns. Second, her captain, Fred "Moose" Moosally, known to us from his service as the House liaison officer, told us behind the scenes he wasn't convinced. We heard similar doubts from Adm. Bud Flanagan, who had strong ties to the Hill and was noted for being a straight shooter.

After many years of working with the Pentagon, we knew they didn't always get it right. Our inclination to conduct an outside investigation was confirmed after we asked the Navy to dig deeper and Adm. Bud Edney, vice chief of naval operations, flat-out refused. He stubbornly insisted that the NIS's conclusions were accurate. We knew then we had to find out if there was a broader problem with the battleship fleet, the gunpowder, or some other factor. It was our duty and obligation to ensure the safety of the nation's sailors. Even though we respected Edney, there was just too much smoke not to find out where the fire really was. So, after our staff determined that the General Accounting Office (now the Government Accountability Office), with Sandia National Laboratories, had the necessary expertise, Nunn and Warner asked them to conduct an independent investigation.

The exhaustive GAO and Sandia reviews agreed with the Navy that the powder itself was stable, but concluded that the explosion was probably caused by an overram, a too-speedy mechanical loading of the bags of propellant powder into the chamber, which can fracture pellets and cause them to ignite.[7] Sandia pointed to inadequate training of gun crews as the underlying problem. They also found that the residues the NIS had identified as evidence of sabotage were commonly present after normal firings. The DOD disagreed with several of these conclusions, particularly in regard to inadequate training, but they grudgingly accepted many of the other findings. Still, it would take the Navy until October 1991 to apologize to Hartwig's survivors for wrongly accusing their son, since a scientific investigation found that he was not at fault nor was the powder used by *Iowa* defective. This enabled the other battleships to restart using their massive guns after revising the loading procedures.

⁓

In 1980 Saddam Hussein attacked Iran, marking the beginning of an eight-year war that left his regime owing billions to its Arab neighbors, principally Kuwait. Shortly afterward, Saddam demanded that these debts be forgiven, since he'd been protecting all of the Arabian Peninsula from Iranian aggression (a dubious proposition, since Iraq wanted to become the regional superpower). His lenders disagreed and insisted on repayment.

Meanwhile, ever since the United Kingdom had ended its protectorate over Kuwait in 1961, Iraqi Ba'athists had insisted that Kuwait was a province of Iraq. The dispute neared the breaking point in 1990, when Saddam accused Kuwait and the United Arab Emirates of keeping oil prices low by increasing supply to hurt Iraq's revenues.

Along with its prickly interactions with its neighbors, Iraq's relations with the West were also deteriorating. Saddam accused the United States and Israel of encouraging Kuwait to sell more oil at the expense of Iraq's economy. President George H. W. Bush staged military exercises in the Persian Gulf to deter Hussein from invading Kuwait, while trying to improve economic and diplomatic relations. He even asked a delegation of senators, led by Robert Dole, to foster stronger ties during their visit to Iraq in April 1990.[8]

Bush's policy was unsuccessful, however, especially considering the infamous meeting between Ambassador April Glaspie and Hussein where she said the United States "has no opinion on the Arab-Arab conflicts, like your border disagreement with Kuwait," which he interpreted as a green light for invasion.[9] Saddam invaded on August 2, with a force of more than 100,000 troops backed by tanks, trucks, and helicopters. They subdued the small country in a matter of hours. President Bush made the decision to deploy troops to Saudi Arabia days later in Operation Desert Shield. The Armed Services Committee conducted extensive oversight hearings, and its leaders were included in the Senate deliberations and ongoing consultations with Pentagon and White House leaders, all culminating in a vote in January 1991 to authorize the use of military force to roll back the Iraqi occupation.

The 1st Marine Division, out of Camp Pendleton, California, were some of the first troops on the ground in Operation Desert Shield, beginning in August 1990. The initial deployments of U.S. ground, air, and naval forces totaled 100,000 troops. This show of force, coupled with economic sanctions and efforts to develop an international coalition, went on through September and October. The sentiment at that time in the foreign policy establishment was that economic sanctions over time would eventually make Saddam retreat.

Senator Nunn, exercising his usual diligence, wanted the committee to hear from military leaders and experts about the continuation of sanctions, the costs of a possible war (both in terms of expected casualties and dollars), and, ultimately, the probability of success. Vietnam still loomed in the rearview mirror. Nunn and others remained cautious about another Tonkin Resolution that would commit us to another long, costly conflict. While Nunn supported expelling Iraq from Kuwait, he wanted to ensure we tried every other way prior to pulling triggers.

When we met with Bush, national security adviser Brent Scowcroft, and other key leaders, Senator Nunn sensed that Bush needed to get back at Hussein for crossing his "line in the sand." The president didn't want to be viewed as indecisive. Nunn believed this push for war was personal rather than strategic and that the administration wasn't looking thoroughly at the implications of even a successful war. This was not the thoughtful Bush we'd met with when he was CIA director and hosted breakfast roundtables to discuss complex issues. The original intent was to deploy forces in a defensive mode in Saudi Arabia, but wait at least several months for our sanctions to work. But during the fall of 1990, Bush decided, without briefing Congress or the public on his rationale, to double our troop presence and shift from a primarily defensive to an offensive position. In mid-October, our troop presence had grown to 200,000, and Bush decided to increase it to more than 400,000 by adding the rotation (or replacement) force to the total. This far exceeded anything necessary to defend Saudi Arabia, and Bush now owed Congress an explanation and justification for what appeared to be an inevitable march to war.

The hearings started on November 27, 1990, and lasted four days. They included such witnesses as former chairmen of the Joint Chiefs of Staff Adm. William Crowe and Gen. David Jones, Dr. Henry Kissinger, Vietnam hero James Webb, Richard Perle—a policy expert from the Reagan administration—and Dr. Edward Luttwak, a noted strategist. Most testified that if the objective was to get Iraq out of Kuwait, the administration should let sanctions work. There were also worries about whether Bush could maintain nearly half a million troops in the region and still keep the international coalition together. In early December, Secretary of Defense Dick Cheney and Gen. Colin Powell, chairman of the Joint Chiefs of Staff, testified. They spoke in favor of an attack, worried that we would lose the window of opportunity to beat back Iraq. Cheney argued, "While we wait for sanctions to work, Saddam Hussein continues to obliterate any trace of Kuwait and her people. While we wait, he continues to dig in in Kuwait, to send more forces south, to deploy and mobilize additional manpower, to dig more formidable fortifications . . . he continues to see if he can acquire more weapons of mass destruction. And while we wait, he continues to hold hundreds of Americans hostage."[10]

Another factor that made Nunn doubt the wisdom of an attack was that the experts were quoting casualty rates in the thousands, with the Marine Corps assuming a casualty rate of 50 percent. Everyone, from the military to the intelligence community to outside experts, thought it would be a long, drawn-out conflict, with the Corps taking the brunt. Nunn was hearing unofficially from senior leaders, from Chairman Powell, to the commander of our forces in the region Gen. Norman Schwarzkopf, to the commandant of the Marine Corps, Gen. Al Gray, that we needed to give the sanctions more time. They all feared Iwo Jima–like body counts.

In December 1990 I was mobilized and deployed to Saudi Arabia. I would go over with the headquarters elements of the 2nd Marine Division from Camp Lejeune, North Carolina. I was excited to deploy; that was why I'd stayed in the Reserves. I also got to see my old company commander, now Col. Jim Van Riper, chief of staff of the 2nd Marine Division. He conducted a personal seabag inspection to ensure all my gear was properly included according to the landing party manual. The next day, I was on another charter aircraft, heading toward combat once again. But this time, I knew many of the folks on board, from Maj. Gen. Bill Keys, commanding the 2nd Division, Brig. Gen. Chuck Krulak, the commanding general of the 2nd Force Service Support Element, and Col. Ron Richard, the operations officer of the division.

When we landed in Saudi Arabia, we helo'd right from the commercial airfield to a remote site in the desert—1st Marine Division HQ—for an intelligence briefing from the commanders, who had firsthand knowledge gathered over months. The briefing was all about the difficulties the Marines would face when they tried to break through positions ringed by artillery and tanks, fire trenches, and reinforced concrete equivalents of the Normandy hedgerows. I met personally with the CG of the 1st MarDiv, Maj. Gen. Mike Myatt, and his deputy, Brig. Gen. Tom Draude, as well as the 1st MarDiv ops officer, Col. Jerry Humble. All three underscored the difficulties associated with their tactical assignments under Schwarzkopf's plan. I wished I had some way to get this information back to the committee, but I knew that would not be possible or appropriate. Then, just as quickly as I'd been called up and sent to the sandbox, word came I was going back to DC. The commandant wanted my firsthand report.

I landed in Washington just in time for the holidays, on December 22, 1990. I checked in with HQMC and gave General Gray my firsthand impressions of both the operational plan and the novel way the USMC had collapsed the component level command and war-fighting HQ into the same organization.[11] I confirmed what the division commanders and the intelligence assessments said: we would face tens of thousands of U.S. casualties. "Get this information to the chairman," Gray commanded. I did, and this reinforced Nunn's commitment to letting sanctions continue to work before hazarding such devastating losses.

At that point it was clear that I was a back-channel messenger with firsthand knowledge. This was an advantage, in my view, of being able to wear the combat uniform of a U.S. Marine in the field one day and work directly for the U.S. Senate in a coat and tie the next. And this time there was no conflict.

President Bush officially asked Congress to authorize the use of force on January 8. Nunn worked with majority leader George Mitchell, Sen. David Boren, chairman of the Intelligence Committee, and Sen. Claiborne Pell, chairman of the Foreign Relations Committee, on a resolution to postpone the war and keep the sanctions in place longer.

The Senate then experienced one of the most serious debates I recall in my twenty-four years there. On January 12, Nunn, Mitchell, and the others pushed for a vote on their resolution for additional time. It was defeated, 46–53. The next vote would be on a resolution, sponsored by John Warner, to authorize the use of force.

Nunn was torn between uniting the country behind the war and heeding the cautions he'd received from the generals. Being good vote counters, we knew the position to keep sanctions in place would fail. I felt strongly that, therefore, everyone should unite behind the resolution authorizing the president to use force. I urged Nunn to vote for the authorization, to show the troops the country was behind their actions. He was inclined to, but it would put many of his colleagues who'd voted for sanctions in a difficult position if he, as chairman of the SASC, changed his vote. So he voted against. The authorization still passed 52–47.[12]

To this day Senator Nunn considers this one of his biggest regrets, not because his "no" vote swayed the outcome, since clearly it didn't, but because he should have shown our enemies we were united and reassured our troops we were behind them. I was disappointed with his choice, too. Nunn's gut said *vote for the war*, and I should have pushed him harder. To his credit, he's acknowledged his mistake in an interview with Nolan Walters published in *The Macon Telegraph*, stating, "I would like to go back and change my vote, and I knew this right after I did it."[13]

Despite the close vote, with the congressional authorization President Bush officially took the nation to war on January 16, 1991, beginning Operation Desert Storm. In the end, and with the help of Security Council sanctions and a coalition air and ground war, the Iraqis were forced out of Kuwait in one of the fastest and most successful military operations in history.[14] Their defenses collapsed and allowed our troops to roll in and avoid the huge casualties we'd feared. (The military had sent 30,000 to 40,000 body bags over to the Persian Gulf.) Nunn conducted hearings after the war, as well, to allow the military to showcase the successes of the operation. The committee also required the Pentagon to conduct a major lessons learned study, again to underscore what went right and what went wrong (very little). The postwar hearings and the study indicated that some of the major factors that contributed to our success were those Nunn and I had worked on during the 1970s and '80s, such as Goldwater-Nichols' strengthening of the joint forces approach and the role of the combatant commanders, the sale of AWACS to Saudi Arabia, and the procurement of additional stealth fighters, with their Nunn-dictated precision weapons, that made such a difference in the air campaign.

∽

About the same time Chief of Naval Operations Frank Kelso was apologizing to the Hartwig family, Navy men and Marines were on their way to the annual Tailhook Symposium in Las Vegas. Each year since 1956 the Tailhook Association, a fraternal organization, had held a reunion for sea-based aviators to meet, exchange ideas, and discuss successes and failures. (The symposium took its name from the device that halts an aircraft on the carrier deck. The "tailhook" catches a wire that jerks the plane to a forced stop and thus distinguishes naval aviators—"tail-hookers"—from land-based pilots.) While most guests applauded the opportunity to network and meet with high-ranking officers, others reported a darker side to the September 1991 gathering. The weekend had traditionally been a venue for rowdiness and frat-style partying, but this one reached a new low. As many as eighty-three women and seven men, civilians and officers, reported they'd been sexually assaulted. The most egregious was the "gauntlet": about two hundred aviators waited in the third floor hallway of the hotel and grabbed and groped any woman deemed attractive who walked past. Making a disgraceful situation worse was the fact that many senior officers likely knew of the misconduct but turned a blind eye, displaying a "boys will be boys" mentality.[15]

When word got out, in part thanks to the bravery of Lt. Paula Coughlin, many pilots stonewalled; they closed ranks and refused to comply with the investigation. As with *Iowa*, the Navy's inquiry was both incomplete and incorrect. Rear Adm. Duvall Williams concluded that the poor behavior was only by junior enlisted personnel and no senior officers were culpable. Assistant Secretary of the Navy Barbara Pope rejected this conclusion and demanded that Secretary of the Navy Larry Garrett bring in the DOD inspector general. Garrett agreed and the investigation was led by DOD Assistant Inspector General Derek Vander Schaaf. When we heard that the legendary head of the House Surveys and Investigations Committee was heading the investigation, we knew no stone would go unturned. Vander Schaaf had been such a thorn in the DOD's side in his House days that they'd hired him just to get him off their backs. He produced a massive, hard-hitting report that ultimately resulted in fourteen flag officers being sanctioned and more than three hundred Navy and Marine aviators punished, a far cry from Admiral Williams' conclusion that only junior personnel were the culprits. Williams himself resigned.

When the adverse conduct initially came to the attention of the SASC, Senators Nunn and Warner conferred with the chair and ranking member of the Personnel Subcommittee, Senators Glenn and McCain, both former naval aviators. Both were adamant that the committee not process any nominations for promotion until we had concrete evidence of either the innocence or guilt of each nominee who had attended the event. In particular, they would not consider any flag or general promotions until all the investigations were completed. We dubbed it the Tailhook Era, as it took more than seven years—from 1991 to 1998—for all those who attended to be considered at their normal promotion points.

While the Navy took internal action against many attendees whose names were never submitted to the Senate, of the 35,000 service nominations processed by the committee in this time frame, the Senate did not confirm eight because of their involvement in Tailhook (even though they had been approved by a service promotion board). Several of these were controversial; they were well-known and respected and the sea service did not consider their behavior egregious enough to warrant removal from the promotion lists. Some of the committee's decisions were perceived from the outside as a witch hunt since the committee continued the scrutiny long after the public and Pentagon had lost interest. One of the most high-profile cases before the SASC was Cdr. Robert Stumpf's promotion to captain. Turned down during the chairmanship of Senator Thurmond in 1995, Stumpf resigned due to what he saw as an unjust decision. In 2002, the Bush administration overturned the decision by authorizing the Board of Correction of Naval Records to amend Stumpf's file so that it showed he retired as a captain.[16] The committee's decision in 1995 on Stumpf was a close call, based more on his decision to fly a military aircraft to the Tailhook convention (which was not permitted) than any behavior at the convention. The Bush administration's decision was made a decade after the event, when concerns about inappropriate behavior had long faded.

Today, the U.S. military is still plagued by sexual misconduct. The Pentagon estimates there were more than 20,000 cases of sexual assault in 2014, with more than 85 percent of those cases going unreported. Most women and men don't report because they fear retaliation; about two-thirds of women who had reported sexual assault faced some kind of social or professional punishment for doing so.[17] While the SASC did its best to show that such misbehavior would not be tolerated, it is clear there's much more that needs to be done to change the culture in the military. In the quarter century since Tailhook, the military chain of command has not sufficiently held people accountable for unacceptable behavior and has not created the climate to ensure victims can report unacceptable behavior without fear of retaliation or being ignored. In 2013 and 2014, Congress passed a comprehensive set of measures to pressure the Pentagon to make the adjustments that should have been made after Tailhook. We won't know for a number of years if these will be successful.

᠆᠊ᠥ

Even though the inspector general cleared him of wrongdoing, Adm. Frank Kelso was never really able to shake the criticism after Tailhook. Kelso had attended the convention but said he hadn't witnessed any misconduct, even though he'd been on a patio adjoining one of the party rooms.[18] Several senators, led by Barbara Boxer and including all seven women then in the Senate, called for his rank to be reduced when he retired in 1994, as had been the case with several other admirals involved. They felt justice had not been served. At that time, all three- and four-star ranks had to be confirmed to retirement by the Senate, as they were actually only temporary ranks. Nunn had always felt an individual's entire career record should be considered in making this determination, and he and I had worked closely with Kelso since he was a captain working submarine issues. To help his case, Nunn brought in Secretary of Defense Bill Perry, Navy Secretary John Dalton, and Chairman of the Joint Chiefs Gen. John Shalikashvili to testify on Kelso's behalf.

Kelso was approved by the committee on a 20–2 vote (only the committee's sole woman, Sen. Kay Bailey Hutchison, along with Senator Byrd, voted against him), but he faced fierce opposition on the Senate floor, where the yes vote was a much closer 54–43.[19] Still, he prevailed, helped by Nunn's statement that "While the Navy tradition is for the captain to go down with the ship, this ship went down three years ago and now everyone wants to row Adm. Kelso out to where the ship sank and drown him with it." Kelso did end up retiring two months before his four-year tour was up, and his replacement, Adm. Mike Boorda, served an even shorter and more tragic tour.

Boorda faced the task of restoring the Navy's tarnished reputation after Tailhook and after a widespread Naval Academy cheating scandal in which two dozen midshipmen were expelled. I'd personally worked for Boorda wearing my Reserve hat in 1993, when I was commander of Joint Task Force Provide Promise (Forward) in the former Yugoslavia. When Boorda visited us for Thanksgiving dinner, I went out to meet his plane at the NATO airport in my camouflaged utilities with the sleeves rolled up and without a field jacket (though it was freezing and everyone else was in Arctic weather gear).[20] Even though I was shivering when I met Boorda, I did stand out from the crowd. Another time I was called down to his headquarters in Naples, Italy, to brief a congressional delegation that happened to include senators and key staff from the SASC. It was a different feeling sitting at the same table with admirals and senators as a colonel and not as the staff director. As a subordinate officer, I had to follow the lead of my boss and could not exercise the independence and the ability to challenge the Pentagon I enjoyed in my Hill role.

I was back in my staff director's chair when Boorda's nomination to be Chief of Naval Operations came to the committee. He and I had some chuckles as we sat at the long table in my office, as the roles were now reversed. I was in charge and he needed my assistance to get through the confirmation process. Boorda was the first former enlisted sailor ever to become CNO, and he had a unique rapport with sailors. He worked hard to overcome the troubles he inherited. Unfortunately, he also ran into some of his own. In 1996 a *Newsweek* reporter told him he was investigating whether he'd actually earned the "V" device he wore on two of his Vietnam medals. In Boorda's defense, the CNO during that period, Adm. Bud Zumwalt, had said those who served in Vietnamese waters were entitled to the devices. But Col. David Hackworth (Ret.), a disreputable media darling, pushed *Newsweek* to write that Boorda was wearing medals to which he was not entitled. Tragically, Boorda, not willing to further hurt the Navy's good name, committed suicide.[21]

The fact that Hackworth, a decorated combat veteran but one who'd broken numerous laws and regulations and who had himself inadvertently worn decorations to which he was not entitled, was given credibility on this issue is a sad commentary that there are always some media outlets willing to attack those in high position in government, no matter the facts.

~

Most military people understand the classification system: for official use only, confidential, secret, and top secret. Less well-known is the level above top secret: sensitive compartmented information, which restricts access to only those cleared for the specific compartment. These special access programs can run the gamut from operational and intelligence to procurement and research and development.

Senator Nunn and I began to worry about proper oversight of highly classified programs when he became chairman in 1987, as some of these programs were only disclosed to the chairman and ranking member and the two staff directors. The big problem I saw was that everything was done verbally; the department did not provide any of the written budget justification materials required of every other program. And with so few members and staffers cleared, there was not enough time or resources to do proper oversight. There was no annual record of problems with the programs and no real way for Congress to address concerns or provide direction.

During one such briefing on a highly classified special access program, the DOD briefer said they needed more than $100 million for something they couldn't tell us about. I immediately replied, "That's not gonna happen."

The briefer retorted, "We don't need your approval anyway." At that point I kindly reminded him that when we mark up the DOD bill, we don't use their submitted bill, we begin from scratch, which means that every program starts with zero unless we add in funds for it, including this highly restricted one. The briefer returned to the Pentagon and came back with the quintessential government solution: "We can tell you about the program if you allow DOD to administer a polygraph on you and Senator Nunn."

I told him, "The Senate sets its own procedures for dealing with classified material, and we are not going to let a separate branch of government tell us who can and who can't be briefed. We are not going to subject legislative branch personnel to executive-branch-run polygraphs or adjudications processes." I had talked to experts on Senator Nunn's Permanent Subcommittee on Investigations who told me that polygraphs are inadmissible in court due to their unreliability and that they can be used by adjudicators to draw arbitrary conclusions. I refused to turn over congressional oversight power to faceless DOD bureaucrats who could unilaterally decide who was and was not briefed into their programs, which they expected us to fund.

In response, we drafted up a provision for the 1992 NDAA that governed how special access programs would be reported on and justified. We permitted the Pentagon to waive a very small handful of incredibly sensitive programs from the reporting requirement, but they would still have to brief us on them in a sensitive compartmented information facility—an extremely secure, eavesdrop-proof room. We also included a provision that Congress's decisions on these programs would have the same force of law as any other program. An added advantage of seeing all the Pentagon's special access programs was that we required a special section of the joint staff to be read in so that combatant commanders knew of these capabilities. This had been a problem with the F-117: it was so stealthy that a number of the COCOMs hadn't known about it, even after it was operational.

These provisions govern how Congress and the DOD deal with special access programs to this day. The executive branch learned a powerful lesson: don't mess with Congress's constitutional roles of oversight and the power of the purse.

∽

One of the provisions of the Goldwater-Nichols Act was changing the chairman of the Joint Chiefs of Staff's tour from one four-year term to two two-year terms.[22] This gave a new president the opportunity to select a new chairman, since in reality it was next to impossible to replace a senior military officer prior to the completion of his tour. This option came into play with Colin Powell, the first chairman affected by the new law. Powell was chairman during the Gulf War and was widely popular, so it seemed unthinkable he wouldn't be tapped for a second term. Nunn and I had had the good fortune to work with him from early in his career, and we entertained no doubts about his ability.

But there was a hiccup. The problem stemmed from Bob Woodward's book *The Commanders*. Examining the Bush administration's actions in Panama and in the Gulf War, Woodward revealed insights that could only have come directly from Secretary Cheney or General Powell. The book was published in 1991, which meant Cheney, Powell, or both had talked to a reporter in the middle of the process of making a decision to go to war. This concerned a number of senators on the committee, notably Senator Warner and other senior Republicans, primarily because the account Powell gave Woodward was different than what he gave the committee. Based on a number of requests from senators, Nunn added several questions about Woodward's book to Powell's advanced policy questions. When we received his answers to the APQs, the members weren't satisfied, so they brought it up in his confirmation hearing. Still unsatisfied, Nunn asked me to let Powell know he would need to come in for an additional closed hearing.

I didn't consider this unusual, so I called up Col. Paul Kelly, USMC, Powell's legislative liaison, to let him know. Kelly told me he didn't think Powell would agree. I asked him to make sure, since it was highly unusual for a military official to refuse such a request. He called a bit later and confirmed that Powell would not answer any more questions on the Woodward book.

This would not be well-received. I told Kelly I would need to go advise both Nunn and Warner. I then told Pat Tucker, the minority staff director, and he had the same reaction: *Uh-oh.* We told Nunn and Warner together, and after checking with several of the senators who'd registered concerns, they authorized me to call Kelly back to inform Powell that we would not vote on his confirmation for a second term until he agreed to answer the committee's questions. His term was set to expire on September 30, the Monday after his hearing.

Over that weekend, there were nonstop calls back and forth between the Pentagon and Chairman Nunn, with an escalation in rank with each call. Nunn was getting calls from everyone from Defense Secretary Cheney to National Security Adviser Brent Scowcroft. It came down to who would blink. They were insisting Powell would not and should not have to answer the SASC's additional questions; the SASC needed to just confirm him and move on. Nunn was adamant that the nominee needed to explain why he had cooperated with a journalist and provided contradictory information to what he'd told the SASC. Kelly kept calling me, incredulous we would let Powell's tenure conclude on such a negative note.

About midmorning on Monday, September 30, Nunn got what sounded like the final call from Scowcroft. "Senator you need to understand General Powell is perfectly comfortable with letting his tour expire at midnight tonight, and going home. The nation will no longer have a chairman of the Joint Chiefs of Staff."

Without missing a beat, Nunn retorted, "That's why we have a vice chairman."

That's when the executive fully understood that we would not yield. Within the hour, Kelly called to say Powell was willing to come in.

The closed session was well attended, and essentially the concerned senators took Powell to the woodshed for what they considered his poor judgment. But no adverse information about him came out during this session or, to my knowledge, since. The SASC approved his nomination and sent it to the Senate floor, where it was voted on right away. And we still had a couple of hours to spare before his term expired. It was never about his qualifications or leadership abilities; he remains one of our most accomplished military and civilian leaders and belongs in the unique pantheon of five-stars, like Dwight Eisenhower, Omar Bradley, and George Marshall. But the executive branch learned, once more, that it could not infringe on the legislative branch's constitutional responsibilities.

They just seem to need reminding once in a while.

↩

Since before the birth of our country women have served in the military, but previously as cooks, nurses, and laundresses. During the Civil War, they continued in these support roles but also served as spies, and between two and four hundred (that we know of) even disguised themselves as men to be able to fight. In World War II, they took up the call to defend their country. Hundreds of thousands served with distinction, including my mother-in-law, as a Navy nurse, and my mother, as an Army dietitian. Many performed the jobs of today's civil servants and contractors, as they riveted, welded, stitched, and assembled weapons for the arsenal of democracy. In 1948, however, Congress passed a law that limited women to no more than 2 percent of the armed forces. While this was repealed in 1967, it took almost a quarter of a century for women to serve in previously prohibited occupational specialties.[23]

Finally, in 1991, Congress authorized women to fly combat missions after witnessing their success on the front lines during the Gulf War, when 35,000 women served. By this point in time, their percentage had grown from 2 to 11 percent.[24] The initial pressure came from Ted Kennedy, a leading liberal, and Bill Roth, a leading conservative. When Kennedy first pushed to lift the ban in the committee markup, the opposition was led by Senators Glenn and McCain, the chairman and ranking member on the SASC Personnel Subcommittee. They believed that the proper studies had not been conducted and this was more about political correctness than military requirements. They were joined by Nunn and Warner, and the SASC voted the provision down.

Kennedy took his and Roth's proposal to the floor to add it to the defense bill. After debate, Glenn and McCain moved to table (kill) the amendment. Nunn and Warner supported the tabling motion, but they were trounced with sixty-nine votes to lift the ban and only thirty to table the amendment and keep the ban. The committee rarely lost on the Senate floor, but clearly the defense leaders were not in sync with the sentiments of the day.

The amendment gave the military the discretion to lift the ban on women flying combat missions, but it did not outright *force* the services to open the positions, nor did it open infantry combat roles to women. Glenn and McCain offered their own proposal, which allowed the secretary of defense to grant exclusions to combat roles on a trial basis. That provision passed with huge bipartisan support.[25]

The 1992 Authorization Act also established a fifteen-member presidential commission to study which roles should be opened to women, including those involving ground combat, and the effects on readiness. The commission was bitterly divided on some issues, concluding that women should be allowed to serve on warships but not in ground combat. Two years after the initial legislation passed, Secretary Les Aspin accepted the commission's suggestions and agreed to open up combat aviation jobs (permitted under the Kennedy amendment) and asked Congress to lift the ban on women serving on combat ships. The Navy was especially eager for these changes to help polish its reputation after Tailhook. By 1993 there was more support in the Senate, including from Nunn, Warner, Glenn, and McCain after they had seen the detailed assessments and studies. In the 1994 Authorization Act, Congress finally included provisions that allowed women to serve on combat ships and in aviation.[26]

Without question, Congress, including our committee, was slow in recognizing women's potential. Due to my own experiences, I did not support in 1991 permitting women in infantry units due to the raw physical strength required to hump all the weapons and gear in difficult terrain for months on end and the degradation in unit cohesion (essential for combat effectiveness) that I believed would inevitably occur with mixing of the sexes. Infantry units are composed of eighteen- and nineteen-year-old males. Elements that intensify teenage hormones did not belong in the foxhole. I was still open-minded on women in other roles, however. In 1997, as commanding general of the 4th Marine Division, I allowed women to serve in positions that were prohibited in the active Corps (though I don't believe it was contrary to any policies in the Reserves). For example, in our artillery regiment, we had a sizeable tonnage of heavy machinery, trucks, and self-propelled howitzers that required skilled mechanics. We had female Marines who worked for long-haul trucking and construction companies. They were excellent mechanics, much better than any of the males. Had we deployed, I intended for these highly qualified women to accompany us to war.

This is another issue where the committee didn't do as much as it should have to push solutions to issues on which the Pentagon had their collective head in the sand. In 2015, military women still face closed-off jobs and promotion tracks, sexual assault, and retaliation. It's been more than twenty years since Tailhook and since women were first allowed to fly combat aircraft. In 2013, following the direction of Secretary of Defense Leon Panetta and with more than a decade of wartime experience with women on the front lines, the combat exclusion policy for all military occupational specialties was lifted, including in infantry units and special operations forces, with a 2016 deadline to implement the changes. But since it takes more than fifteen years of service to become a qualified first sergeant or battalion commander, it will be that long before we have a large number of women in these leadership roles. The military first needs a sizeable number of women to volunteer for these roles and be qualified, without lowering the standards, to accumulate a pool from which to promote. But they have and are excelling in every phase of military life.

⟿

This wasn't the only socially charged issue the SASC faced during the 1990s. Even more controversial was the question of lifting the ban on gays and lesbians so they could serve openly in the military. Homosexual service members had had a difficult history in the U.S. military, from exclusion to discharge and discrimination to denial of benefits. Antisodomy laws or unfit-for-service mandates kept them from the ranks if they admitted or demonstrated same-sex desires. In 1981, the Pentagon issued Directive 1332.14, which stated, "Homosexuality is incompatible with military service." Potential recruits were required to answer a question on the recruiting form as to whether they were homosexual. If they said yes, they were precluded from serving. If they lied and said no and their orientation was discovered later, they were dishonorably discharged.

But with the gay rights movement gaining traction in the late 1980s and early 1990s, the Defense Department was facing pushback against this policy.[27] The issue was first brought to the Senate's attention by Sen. Howard Metzenbaum, who proposed an amendment to the fiscal year 1993 National Defense Authorization Act in the fall of 1992, about the same time presidential candidate Bill Clinton had surfaced gay rights in his campaign. Metzenbaum's goal was to flag the issue for the Senate and the SASC, not to force a vote on his amendment. His strategy worked, because Nunn promised a hearing.

On the campaign trail, Clinton promised to repeal the ban as soon as he was elected. Senator Nunn discussed the issue with him several times back then. I remember one such meeting at Pamela Harriman's Georgetown home.[28] At this meeting, Nunn conveyed to Clinton his concerns on lifting the ban, namely that it would be opposed by the military, it would be a very unpopular position in the South, and the Bush camp would take advantage of it. Clinton assured Nunn that he didn't consider it a major issue and that it would not be a highly publicized position in his campaign.

Despite Nunn's concern, the Bush campaign didn't pick up on it. They were trying to avoid divisive issues after Pat Buchanan's "Culture War" speech at the Republican National Convention, which had underscored the lack of tolerance in a wing of the Republican Party at that time.

We met with Clinton again at the New York Hilton, this time along with Les Aspin, chairman of the House Armed Services Committee, to discuss some other issues, after which the three would head down to a press conference so Clinton could announce he had the support of the two leading Democrats on defense. Nunn again brought up the gay ban, and this time he asked me to chime in as a former infantry platoon commander. I walked Clinton through the typical day in the life of a rifle platoon to express the concerns military personnel would have about the inclusion of openly homosexual individuals in combat situations, and he seemed to acknowledge my points. I provided graphic details of life in a foxhole: the lack of privacy and sanitation, the trust that had to exist among all members, and the problems sexual tensions would create. I told him, "The combination of all those factors would render a platoon or company-sized unit in harm's way less effective. I worry that the essential bond in combat—that you fight for the guy on your right and the guy on your left—would snap." Hillary was also at the meeting, standing to the side. If looks could kill, hers were sharper than any bayonet I'd ever fixed. But again, the candidate assured us he wasn't going to push it, so our minds were more at ease. Nunn and I knew the military would not support a change, and we hoped the issue would fade away.

This rosy picture was shattered after the election, when Clinton made a strong statement in support of repealing the ban. Just to show how divisive the issue was in the South, it cost Sen. Wyche Fowler his seat. The Georgia election had gone into a runoff because Fowler only received 49.5 percent of the vote, half a percent less than needed for a win. Fowler was fairly liberal, with his base of support in Atlanta, but he was pinned down in "no-man's land" under heavy fire after Clinton's announcement. He lost the religious vote because he refused to say he would oppose the newly elected President, and he lost the gay and liberal vote because he also wouldn't say he would support Clinton. Fowler knew he was a sure goner if he came out in favor of lifting the ban. The backlash pushed lots of previous Fowler votes to his Republican opponent, who won the runoff (he publicly opposed the proposal).

Neither the Congress nor the administration was prepared for the pitched battle that Clinton's new secretary of defense, Les Aspin, declared in the first weeks after the inauguration. Aspin started a firestorm when he said on *Face the Nation* that Clinton should consider a compromise on his position and wait for the proper studies to be conducted and get input from the Hill before acting. The White House immediately rebuked him with a strong statement that they were going right ahead with the change. Naturally, Senate Republicans exploded and said they would pass an amendment blocking the move on the first available piece of legislation (which happened to be the Family and Medical Leave Act, which had strong bipartisan support and would pass easily).

Jeff Smith, who'd previously served as SASC general counsel and would become the CIA general counsel under Clinton, had authored a white paper during the transition period (after the election and before the inauguration) that quoted Senate majority leader George Mitchell to the effect that there were fewer than thirty votes in the Senate for the president's plan. The strong Republican opposition and the weak vote count, which had leaked, caused a number of White House meetings with the president, vice president, and other senior personnel with Nunn and Mitchell. Nunn also met with his committee members and asked for their views so he would know where they all stood. A majority on the Democratic side opposed the president, which also came out at a White House meeting in the Roosevelt Room with the president. Nunn, as usual, outlined the pros and cons of the issue, then Kennedy expressed his strong support for the president. Dick Shelby then expressed his opposition. The strongest dissent came from Senator Byrd, who spoke for almost forty minutes about the historical evils of homosexuality and concluded that when it came down to it, "I will take my guidance from the good Lord, not from the president." With overwhelming Republican opposition and the Democratic caucus split, Mitchell's count of thirty votes seemed optimistic.

With Clinton witnessing the backlash and realizing he didn't have enough support in either the House or Senate, he agreed to maintain the status quo for six months while the military and Congress conducted reviews. Republicans still offered their amendment, but Nunn and Mitchell countered with a second-degree that required the Senate to conduct hearings on the issue. But in the meantime, no gay service member could be discharged unless he or she openly said they were gay, in which case they would be moved from active duty to the standby reserve. With the mandate from the Nunn-Mitchell approach, we began the committee's review.

When we began designing the hearings, we met with key individuals representing all sides of the issue, including organizations supporting gay rights. We wanted a balanced approach and to ensure that all witnesses would be treated respectfully. We refused to have provocative witnesses from either side. Some would say the initial hearings were dull, as we heard from scholars and analysts who approached the issues from a detached, objective perspective. In addition to hearings in the committee room, we arranged for the staff to visit scores of military bases around the country and meet with thousands of military personnel and families. All interviews were confidential. In the course of them, many homosexuals on active duty met privately with us to share information about their lives, careers, and what needed to be changed to make them more secure in serving their country. Had they come out to their seniors as they did to us, they would have been discharged, but we made sure there were never any leaks.

In the interviews I conducted, I was impressed with the dedication, professionalism, and passion for service these men and women demonstrated. I was also impressed with the patriotism, professionalism, and passion of those who opposed gays serving openly because they believed it would harm effectiveness on the battlefield (the same concerns I'd voiced to Clinton a year earlier). As we compiled the results, it was becoming clear that lifting the ban was strongly opposed by all age groups and all ranks in the uniformed military. "Sir, I don't want to be forced to room with a homosexual any more than I would want to be forced to room with a female soldier," was a common sentiment at the NCO level.

The senators also decided to hold field hearings. I scheduled these at the Norfolk Naval Base, Fort Bragg, and Camp Lejeune, North Carolina. At Norfolk several gay sailors courageously volunteered to go public, though it would result in their removal from active duty. The senators visited various ships, and Nunn and Warner toured a submarine to see firsthand the close quarters and living conditions. On board subs, three sailors would often share one bunk, with one sleeping and the other two on watch; this was called "hot racking." Occasionally up to six sailors had to share one mattress under the torpedo tubes. A photo of Nunn and Warner looking over this situation ended up on the front pages of more than 350 daily newspapers, including the *Washington Post* and the *New York Times*. That one shot probably did more to underscore the lack of privacy in the military than anything else.

The field hearings concluded with a light moment. Senator Thurmond was more than ninety years old at the time and nearly deaf, but he refused to wear hearing aids. So when two sailors were testifying, the following exchange took place:

Senator Thurmond: "What did you say you were?"

The witnesses responded, "Senator, we are homosexuals."

"You're what?"

"Homosexuals, sir."

"Don't we have a cure for that?"

"Senator, this is not a disease and there is no cure."

"Well, if we had one would you take it?"

At this point, the other senators could no longer stifle their smirks. Ted Kennedy was laughing so hard he almost fell out of his chair. Nunn salvaged the situation by thanking the witnesses for their honorable service and their courage in testifying, ending with, "Please don't take any comments made here as disrespectful in any way."

After these, we had several more field hearings slated, but the rights groups thought it was hurting their case more than it was helping and asked us not to conduct any more. The hearings showed the challenges for the military in their daily lives and were tilting public opinion against lifting the ban. We consulted with the proponents on the committee, such as Kennedy, and decided to forgo the rest.

One of the most impactful hearings back in our Senate spaces was with Gen. Norman Schwarzkopf. He'd also been in charge of personnel policy as a one-star. Schwarzkopf was strongly opposed to gays serving openly. He felt it would degrade unit cohesion in ground combat units, the backbone of the Army. Unit cohesion describes the ability of a unit to operate as one with all members together in close quarters and without distraction. Another outspoken opponent was Navy Command Master Chief David Borne, a black senior sailor from the carrier USS *America*. He took head-on the suggestion that bias against homosexuals was like racial discrimination and that the military had eliminated the latter and could tolerate gays the same way. Borne said, "The gay rights movement is piggybacking off of a just and right cause to justify a lifestyle behavior." A Marine colonel, Fred Peck, who'd been a press spokesman in the operations in Somalia and was well-known to the public because of his many appearances on national media, was also opposed, but for a different reason than most of the other witnesses. His own son was gay and he was concerned he would be harmed if he joined the service. This didn't speak well of our military, but we didn't push witnesses one way or the other and told Peck he didn't have to mention this. But he still went ahead.

At this point in the process it was becoming clear that a large majority of military personnel mirrored the majority in the Senate, opposed to the president's position. The opposition was from all ranks and all ages, from the military service chiefs to the most junior enlisted.

Despite our personal views, Senator Nunn and I knew it was important to reach a bipartisan consensus that could be supported by the military, the Congress, and the president. We also wanted an improvement over the current ban, with the entrapping recruiting questions and intrusive investigations of active-duty members. Our staff and our senators worked closely with leaders in the Pentagon and with key Republican senators such as Dan Coats and John Warner. The compromise was that recruiters would no longer ask about sexual orientation and the military would no longer investigate suspected homosexuals. Nor would their colleagues have to turn anyone in if they happened to find out. This became known as "don't ask, don't tell." While it wasn't the monumental change gay rights groups and the president were hoping for, it was a significant improvement over the full-on ban. At that point, that was as far as the military and its supporters in Congress were willing to go.

I believe that in 1993, "don't ask, don't tell" was the appropriate approach. In the legislative business, you either have the votes or you don't. And the votes were just not there for the president's position. Seventeen years later, in 2010, circumstances were different when President Barack Obama took the next step and allowed gays and lesbians to serve openly. The chairman of the Joint Chiefs,

Adm. Mike Mullen, led the military in favor of the position, as their views, along with those of the public, had also changed. Even with this support, the Pentagon conducted another review and put in place a deliberate and phased approach to implementation once "don't ask, don't tell" was repealed. While there was still opposition, this time the votes were there and I was a public supporter, along with Senator Nunn, of lifting the ban.

Those who suggest we could have gotten the same outcome in 1993 are out of touch with the realities of that time. Back then, I agreed with the majority. As a senior leader in the Corps, I was convinced that open service would hurt our readiness and perhaps cost lives. I also did not have a problem with discharging openly gay service members prior to "don't ask, don't tell." They knew the rules; they broke the rules. You can't turn a blind eye to disobedience. We made the right call in 1993 and we made the right call in 2010. Today gays and lesbians are serving openly with little or no impact on operations. This is due primarily to the significant changes in both public opinion and especially in the military at all levels, who accepted the change as they would not have before.

ᠸ᠆ᢒ

In October 1995 Nunn decided not to seek a fifth term, though all agreed he would have been re-elected in a landslide. He wanted to pursue other interests. A number of his Senate colleagues, such as Bill Cohen, David Boren, Bennett Johnston, Lawton Chiles, and Warren Rudman, had also decided to retire, and this probably influenced him as well. These men had consistently placed the country's interests ahead of party politics and had commanded the influence to sway important votes. They were the moderate center of the Senate, but it was slowly eroding away beneath us. With their departure (along with a few other key senators in the following years) went any ability of getting real work done. Nunn's retirement on January 2, 1997, would open the door for me to explore new opportunities as well.

13

THE CORPORATIONS

1997–2010: Washington, DC

After twenty-four years working with Senator Nunn, I was disappointed when he announced he would not be seeking re-election. I'd never considered leaving the Senate while he was still in office. It would have been like abandoning my comrades under fire. I'd had opportunities to leave before but just couldn't bring myself to retreat from the fight. I relished the ability to take on entrenched interests and make much-needed reforms. There's no other job out there that can match the influence of working for a senator like Nunn, and there's more power in the Senate than in most high-level Pentagon positions.

I'd long ago decided not to accept or even look for a private-sector job while I was still on the Senate payroll. It would have been legal to do so, and that's what the majority of staffers do. But my senator had a perfect record on ethics issues throughout his entire career and I didn't want to be the bozo to mess that up. I knew this meant I might not have an income for a number of months, but Nunn's example had rubbed off, and I wanted to end my government career on a high note. While I thought seriously about a senior Pentagon position, our family finances were severely strained after twenty-four years of government service and four kids to put through college. The private sector was the right move.

But where would I aim? I didn't want to go into lobbying, though that was a popular career choice for former staffers. I wasn't thrilled by the idea of using my connections to ask for things to be done for a private company or a special interest. I was more comfortable on the "deciding" side of an issue, rather than the "asking" side. I'd never had a negative view of lobbyists—they're seldom the grubby sleazemeisters they're often portrayed as—but I knew myself well enough to realize I wouldn't be happy. Besides, I wanted to try my hand at the business world; the profits and losses aspect and being free from governmental red tape sounded like a new challenge. Since I didn't have a business degree or previous commercial experience, this might be a stretch, but perhaps I could find a company willing to let me learn.

Over the years, I'd had the good fortune to meet and work with many titans of the defense and aerospace industry, along with other businesses that had sought Nunn's engagement. These included Ted Turner at CNN; Norm Augustine, CEO of Lockheed-Martin; Jack Welch, CEO of General Electric; and Bev Dolan, CEO of Textron. I always paid close attention whenever they met with Senator Nunn. I was intrigued with the way they approached and analyzed issues and took decisive action, the exact opposite of the government. Bureaucrats have no appreciation for the value of time and too often take a cavalier attitude toward spending tax money. They drag out decisions and reviews ad nauseam. I'd always enjoyed making fast decisions based on hard data and informed analysis.

While I didn't start my job hunt until after I officially left the Senate, I began my transition earlier. I handed over the reins of minority staff director to David Lyles, who would be the staff director for Sen. Carl Levin. I moved out of the director's office, my home for the past fourteen years, and into one of the cubicles. I always worked a full day during the last few months of Nunn's final term, but David was officially running things, as smoothly as I could have hoped.

January 3, 1997, was the first time since I went into the Corps back in '68 that I had no assigned location to report to. There was no morning muster. I no longer had the morning's intel reports, the National Intelligence Daily, or the Pentagon Early Bird at my fingertips. There was no staff to answer questions from, no assignments, and no office, not even a desk. I couldn't call up the Pentagon and put solutions in motion or get the military liaison officers to set up trips or cut red tape. I'd prepared for this for more than a year, so there were few withdrawal pains, but boy was I glad not to suffer through that commute anymore. In 1973 driving the twelve miles from my home in McLean to the Capitol had taken twenty-five minutes. By 1997, it took almost an hour.

Before we left, I remember observing to Nunn that I was worried what would become of the committee and the Senate without us. The senator wisely intoned, putting his hand on my shoulder, "Arnold, no one is irreplaceable."

⌒

I had one other caveat for a new job: it had to be a ten-minute drive or less from home and it could only require right turns. So I drew a circle on a map and identified the businesses that fit my requirements. The list wasn't long. It included the CIA (but I wanted to avoid the government), the Farm Credit Bureau Administration (another government nonstarter), the MITRE Corporation, a federally funded research and development center (quasi-government), and two for-profit companies, Braddock Dunn & McDonald (BDM) and Science Applications International Corporation (SAIC). Lifting the no-left-turns restriction would have put six more companies in the running, but I decided to focus on the first set to start with.

I went to Norm Augustine for advice, not because I wanted to work for Lockheed but because I wanted to understand the key considerations for seeking and accepting a job in the business world. One of Norm's recommendations was to discount the base salary and focus more on overall compensation and bonuses, especially stock options and stock grants (great advice that paid off).

But despite experience, strategy, and advice, days became weeks and I wasn't hearing back from anyone. But in the middle of February, I finally got a call from a former colleague, Duane Andrews, who asked if I might be interested in working at SAIC.

"We'd like to explore a senior position for you here," Duane said. There were two attractive elements right off the bat: I knew Duane well from our time on the Hill working intelligence issues and when he was the assistant secretary of defense for command, control, communications, and intelligence. SAIC had a great relationship with the Pentagon, and the office was at Tysons Corner, which fit nicely within my magic circle. I told Duane sure, I'd be happy to come in and talk.

Science Applications International Corporation was one of the country's most prestigious consulting companies. It had been involved in defense and intelligence matters since Dr. Robert Beyster founded the company in 1969. SAIC specialized in information technology and systems integration, which is a fancy way of saying it provided the technical expertise not found in government that keeps weapons systems working, business processes producing, and computers computing.

In our initial meeting in a fourteen-story tower at Tysons Corner, I told Duane I was interested in learning the business first and staying away from government affairs or lobbying. He was agreeable and recommended I fly out to meet with the senior leaders, including Dr. Beyster, at the headquarters in San Diego. I was always willing to go to San Diego, with its perfect weather. My first interview was with retired admiral Bill Owens, the company's number two, whom I knew from his time as vice chairman of the Joint Chiefs. That went smoothly. I then met with Jim Idell, who had a small office overlooking La Jolla Cove and the Pacific. For him, casual Fridays were every day. His long ponytail would never meet Marine standards, but despite our differing hairstyles, he was an astute businessman and one of Dr. B's most trusted colleagues. Jim was focused on increasing government business, and we hit it off right away. My third interview in this gauntlet included Joe Walkush, a board member and financial guru. He was one of the company's most respected leaders, and we became good friends.

The next stop was Dr. Beyster himself. Tall, thin, with large glasses, he sat at a small desk in a small office on the top floor of his nondescript three-story building in downtown La Jolla. His entire office was filled with stacks of papers and notebooks; he took copious notes to keep track of all the actions he tasked his employees with. He peppered me with questions about Washington and, in particular, the Defense Nuclear Agency. He was a nuclear physicist himself.[1]

Unfortunately, I came out with a comment about the "nuclear nuts" who worked there. Beyster quickly retorted, "I was one of those 'nuts,' you know, Arnold." I tried to recover with, "Uh, you understand, I meant 'nuts' in the most positive way." Trying to look smarter than I am, I'd brought along to the interview *Nuclear Weapons Effects*, a textbook that included a little plastic calculator in a back pocket you could use to estimate fallout from different sized warheads. Hoping to impress him, I pulled out the device—which I had no idea how to use—and said proudly, "I always have my calculator with me. You never know when you might need to predict fallout patterns." I started playing with the dials as if I knew what I was doing. Beyster said dryly, "You know, you're holding that upside down."

He had me totally figured out. Just as I was thinking, *Boy have I flunked this interview*, he said, "So, what are you going to be doing for us?" With Jim Idell's words still ringing in my ears, I replied confidently, "Growing our revenues and profits with more government contracts." I'd aced that question, at least. This was the engine of the business world, especially for an employee-owned corporation such as SAIC.

I called Duane immediately after and told him everything that happened, and he said, "Congratulations, you're in! When can you start?" We'd never discussed the specifics of my duties or compensation, and I wanted one more outside opinion before I made a commitment. I was able to get an appointment with the current secretary of defense, Bill Perry, whom I'd first met in 1977 when he was the director of defense research and engineering. I recalled that he'd served on SAIC's board of directors, and I wanted to get his thoughts on the company. Perry had nothing but good things to say. He said SAIC wasn't just strong at the leadership levels, but also at the second and third tiers of management. Since it was a technology-based firm, it was definitely in a sweet spot to secure more work. I called Duane and asked to start on March 2, exactly two months after leaving the Senate.

∽

My title was senior vice president of business development. My first shock was when Duane told me on my first day I had to meet a development goal of obtaining $250 million in new contracts . . . in my first year. This goal would be raised each year. This had not come up during any of my interviews or compensation discussions. But I thought, *I have lots of experience hitting targets. It'll be different, but I can handle this.* The first step was to know where the government spent its contractor dollars. Then I would determine which opportunities matched up with our capabilities, particularly in areas where we had existing work. Next, we would submit bids tied to exact specifications, then wait to see which contract the government ended up picking.

Over the years, I learned from Duane and my other colleagues, and I climbed the corporate ladder. Positions I held during my thirteen years with the company included head of corporate development and marketing, general manager of SAIC's Washington operations, sector manager, deputy president of the federal business segment, and finally executive vice president in charge of business development, government relations, worldwide communications, and support operations, which included facilities and real estate at 450 locations worldwide, crisis and risk management, classified and physical security, and a long list of tasks under the title "CLJO," crummy little jobs officer. Try fitting that on a business card!

Just as at the Senate, I rose from being a mid-level employee to a key participant in all major decisions. The company had $3 billion in annual revenues when I started and $10 billion when I left. When SAIC made the decision to move from an employee-owned company to a publicly traded for-profit in 2006, I was out there with the CEO and CFO for the initial public offering road show pitching our stock to potential investors.[2] I woke up every morning looking forward to going to work. I was glad my superiors valued me based on performance and results, not on my title, my time in grade, or by playing it safe.

⌒

When I started at the high-rise in Tysons, Duane took me around to meet with all the SAIC business leaders. One of the first was Allen Herskowitz, who ran the company's substantial intelligence-related business. After my time with the Armed Services and Intelligence Committees, I thought I knew a thing or two about the subject. I went in there with my Rolodex of names, rolling off stories of George Tenet and John Deutch, when Herskowitz stopped me midsentence. "I know who you are. You killed my largest program." Not missing a beat, I responded, "And now I'm here to get it back for you."

Herskowitz told me SAIC had been a key contractor on the Continuity of Government program, a program that ensured that our leadership would be able to survive and operate after a major WMD attack, such as a nuclear exchange. Nunn and I had found significant problems with the program: cost overruns, poor management, and an unrealistic operating concept. So we convinced the White House to make serious cuts and establish an oversight regime.[3] In those cuts, SAIC lost a major contract (as staffers, we rarely focused on the contractors in these types of situations). Of course, I was really in no position to restore Herskowitz's contract. But once I learned about his other intel contracts, I put together a program to ensure they continued to grow.

Later in my SAIC career, I became involved with the Special Projects Committee, an internal, independent review group that ensured our classified activities were conducted, managed, and reviewed to meet the strict government and business requirements.[4] When SAIC's Board of Directors created the Classified Business Operations Committee in 2008, I recruited George Tenet, former CIA director, and Gen. Doug Brown, former commander of Special Operation Command, to instill confidence in our internal governance and review.

When I became executive vice president for support operations, those responsible for oversight of our classified programs reported directly to me. We worked with the Defense Security Service to ensure that everyone who was in contact with classified materials had the proper training and followed regulations. Everything was done by the book because I knew the government doesn't necessarily apply common sense in this arena; their way was the right way and the only way. If we failed an inspection or mishandled secrets, our contract would be in jeopardy, which could cost millions. I was fortunate to have a former Secret Service professional, Steve Colo, in charge of both our classified and physical security. He was not only respected in the field, but he was also a strong leader. Choosing capable subordinates and letting them do their jobs is essential in the business world.

As head of business development, I had several large proposal centers, run by Roger Gruben. SAIC had a reputation as a "proposal machine" for the sheer volume we submitted. For example, when we bid to replace the Coast Guard's aging ships, the Deepwater Program, we submitted nearly sixty five-inch binders, essentially one page per $100,000 task for this multibillion-dollar program. The company had to bid more than $30 billion a year and win more than $1 billion a month just to break even, much less grow. I brought in several operations research analysts who had retired from the DOD to look over our process, so we knew what we were submitting, what we were winning, and where bids were in the pipeline. They also modeled what we'd need to do to meet our revenue goals. While I'd never attended business school, I'd learned early on in the Senate the importance of accurate data and that you can't manage what you can't measure.

$\backsim$

One unique part of my job was leading the crisis management team. Our responsibilities included anything from resurrecting a troubled government program to addressing natural disasters that threatened employees and facilities. The most challenging, hands down, was Hurricane Katrina in 2005, which affected a number of our facilities in the Gulf of Mexico.

Before the storm hit, Duane and I were monitoring its path. We had a growing suspicion that FEMA was underestimating the danger. At this point, I had retired from the Reserves, but I was familiar with the New Orleans area and stayed in touch with some of my Marine colleagues. When they told me they were moving their command post from New Orleans to Baton Rouge, my antennae went up. We needed to start the evacuation.

We went to CEO Ken Dahlberg and recommended pulling all our employees out. He agreed. This was huge, considering that SAIC's profits are based on time sold, meaning hours billed, physically on site and working. We were fortunate to have such a strong and caring leader.

We activated our crisis management center—essentially a military-esque war room—and had SAIC representatives from each of the line organizations that might be affected, along with corporate representatives that might be required for support, such as finance, housing, insurance, communications, contracts, human resources, and legal. I had the authority to make decisions and coordinate action. Our number one priority was the safety of our personnel and their families, followed by supporting our customers. We had a contract to run the major IT system for Entergy, the power source for most of the Gulf, and another with a major backup data center for the federal government in Mississippi. As the storm unfolded, the threat, and possible scale of the damage, got steadily scarier.

My first task was to account for all our people. We put a sophisticated system in place to find everyone, including where we'd relocated them. We accounted for all hands in under a week. By comparison, some of the major defense contractors in the area weren't able to account for theirs for more than thirty days. We conducted the equivalent of musters, with team leaders responsible for finding their members from interns up the line to top business leaders. For the more difficult cases, we had special-operations-trained personnel from the Fort Bragg area (who'd done security operations for us in war zones) cruising the gulf in rubber raiding craft, using GPS to find our outliers. We also authorized cash disbursements, since the banks and ATMs were out of service. I authorized our special ops personnel to carry weapons so they could keep themselves and our other employees safe (we had the required permits). A few of our folks stayed on site to run the systems essential to Entergy and the government, so we loaded up trucks with food, water, clothing, generators, and water pumps, and the special ops guys delivered them despite floods and high winds. At all times we made sure we had lines of communication open between all of our key sites, using satellite phones, the only dependable comms at the time.

Our response was made easier due to the steady hand of my chief of staff, Col. Glenn "Smoke" Burgess, USMC (Ret.). His airdrop of the Marine Corps birthday cake hadn't gone so well, but he kept everything on track during a chaotic period in New Orleans.

Ken had given us a simple mission order, or what we call commander's intent: People First. Through this philosophy, we were able to both protect our employees and satisfy our customers' needs. It ran as smoothly as the best military operations, partly because most of the team had *been* military.

More than 1,800 people died as a result of Katrina, which caused more than $100 billion in property damage. Amidst the suffering, we took consolation that our employees and families were safe, as were our customers. SAIC spent millions of dollars to ensure this, and while our insurance did cover some of the costs, when one of our own was in danger, there was never any hesitation.

~

In another situation, I enjoyed a similar level of support from Ken. That incident began when several low-level employees from Florida, supporting an Air Force Europe health care contract, sent privacy-protected data in the open. This was not only a violation of all our internal procedures, but a huge contract violation. Once we realized the problems this breach could cause, we immediately notified our customer, the Tricare Management Agency. We initiated forensics to learn what data might have been compromised, and we learned that health records for more than 850,000 active-duty military, retirees, and their families were threatened.

This was potentially damaging, not only to SAIC's reputation but also to our revenues, as this was a lucrative contract. But Dahlberg fully agreed with me that we should do the right thing. First, I wrote a personal letter to the more than 850,000 of those potentially affected, letting them know what SAIC was prepared to do to ensure their data was still secure and that we'd do everything in our power to fix any problems they ran into because of our mistake. We hired Kroll, a risk-consulting firm, to run a call center to help the affected people. There was an escalatory process; if someone was unsatisfied with the results of the initial call, he or she would go up the chain until they eventually reached me. Of the tens of thousands that called in, I personally spoke to about five. A year afterward, to my knowledge, no one's medical data or finances had actually been compromised because of our employees' mistake.

Those employees were fired immediately and that office was shut down following the breach. We conducted a major review of all our IT systems and put in improvements to reduce the potential for similar issues in the future. We took pains to contact every stakeholder, and the associations that represent military families, to let them know what had happened and how we were fixing it. We were candid with the media. It cost us tens of millions. But the Pentagon later adopted our response as their standard operating procedures for similar types of events. Though we had screwed up, our response set the gold standard for addressing data breaches and is followed to this day.

✑

Just as I had with Nunn and the Senate, I planned to stay with SAIC as long as Ken Dahlberg did, because one's boss has a huge impact on one's daily life. I started under a fantastic boss, Duane, and finished up SAIC under another. Ken was completing a five-year tour as CEO, so I had just a little while to go before I would leave as well. But I had one final major project: moving our headquarters from San Diego to McLean, Virginia. We'd been getting ready for several years. I'd already renovated the top floors of our fourteen-story tower in McLean; we were just waiting for the board's approval. Prior to the move, we did our research. We wanted to ensure that the new location was business-friendly, and at the time Virginia offered the best package. The move happened in September of 2009. A new CEO came on board, and Ken remained as the board chairman.

My decision to leave was reinforced by a request from Secretary of Defense Bob Gates to chair a major study for the Defense Business Board on the Pentagon's massive overhead and come up with world-class business practices to reduce it. Given my previous toil in this vineyard under Cohen and Rumsfeld, I jumped at the opportunity. But it would be awkward to work for the DBB attacking overhead while on the payroll of a major defense corporation. And my concerns for the unconstrained costs of the all-volunteer force were still growing, as was my concern for the inefficiencies of the DOD's acquisition system. I wanted to speak out more forcefully about these needed reforms, but a full-time job with a defense contractor wasn't the platform for it.

More or less at the same time, I was being recruited for a top position at a Fortune 20 company, but the job included lobbying and I still had no interest in that. So I decided to see if I could make it as a small businessman. I formed the Punaro Group to provide consulting and analytical services to corporations. On May 1, 2010, I left SAIC and pushed out on my own, with no government or corporate safety net, for the first time.

But first we need to turn the coin over and examine the obverse: an alternate role that I also took on now and then, here and there, throughout the years. I wore a suit and tie and a carefully pressed shirt (both front and back, Jan) on Capitol Hill and in the business world. In the field, I had the face and wore the uniform of the citizen Marine.

14

CITIZEN MARINE

1972–2003

All through my time with Senator Nunn, I'd maintained my links with the Corps. During the 1970s and '80s, with the nation enjoying a relative calm in our foreign relations, Reserve life was uneventful, composed of routine training, attending schools, teaching courses with the Law of War unit, and unit maneuvers and staff assignments. My own assignments were interesting and rewarding, but, I would have to say, not especially exciting. I was promoted when the usual time came, along with most of my peers. The 1990s, however, ushered in a more challenging era.

Desert Shield was my first combat deployment since Vietnam, although I'd deployed overseas several times during my annual training. Three years after the Gulf War, in 1993, I was deployed to another period of extended active duty. This time, as a colonel, I would command Joint Task Force Provide Promise (Forward) in Zagreb, Croatia. We were providing life-saving supplies to starving Bosnians threatened by Serbian forces as part of the UN peacekeeping forces keeping the warring parties separate in the former Yugoslavia. Part of my command was a full field hospital staffed by Air Force medical personnel. Concerned about security, I implemented standard USMC procedures and walked my perimeter several times a night, as I had a quarter-century before in the Que Son Mountains. This was a novel approach for the Air Force special police manning our positions. They weren't used to maintaining full-up twenty-four-hour watches. The previous commander, an Army colonel, had neither required the watches nor checked his positions. I had the USAF fortify their too-exposed bunkers and checked their weapons qualifications and general orders.

Previous commanders of the Joint Task Force had let other basics deteriorate, along with security. We didn't have heat in the enlisted tents—in the dead of winter with temperatures below freezing every night—adequate lighting in the heads, or hot water in the showers. Our entire operation was one large tent city, dependent on huge diesel generators for power. When I decided to test the backup generators, they were broken. I turned off the heat in the officers' tents until it was fixed in the enlisted tents. Until we had hot water for all personnel, only cold water was made available for the officers. It didn't take long for a laundry list of overdue maintenance items to get fixed.

A couple weeks into my tour, I was inspecting our lines around 1:00 a.m. when a heavy snow began to fall, those big, heavy, wet flakes that stick. It was piling up both on the ground and on our general purpose tents, and I could see trouble brewing. I woke up the lieutenant with the Red Horse unit (Air Force engineers) and asked him to calculate how much this snow would weigh if it kept up and how much the tents could bear before they collapsed. He concluded that at the current rate our entire city could collapse within a couple hours.

I immediately woke up the Air Force commander and roused the camp. Of course, we had zero snow-removal equipment. We jury-rigged rakes out of broom handles and plywood ripped from packing boxes to pull the snow off the tents, makeshift shovels to put it on hospital litters, and had neurosurgeons, cardiologists, nurses, and orderlies carry litterfuls of the snow off our compound.

As it turned out, this was one of the worst storms in Balkan history. When all was said and done, Yugoslavia lay buried in more than fifty-five inches, with most of the country shut down. All around us, other forces' steel buildings (not to mention tents) collapsed under the weight. No civilian hospitals in the region were open. Just ours. And thank goodness, because the UN commander, French General Jean Cot, suffered a heart attack and the only place he could get emergency treatment was our field hospital. Our snow-clearing prowess and Cot's gratitude made it all the way to the Joint Chiefs. They sent a one-star commander from the European Command—Brig. Gen. Jim Jones, a welcome visitor—to inspect what we called "Operation Snow Shovel."

My eyebrows rose when Jim said to me prior to landing, "It can't be that bad." He got a firsthand view when the wings of his plane anchored themselves in twelve-foot-high white mounds on either side of the runway. I was quite proud that our unit was able to continue the mission, and I developed a new respect for my medical personnel and their leaders, Colonel Jennings and Chief Nemerow.

I was completing my Marine career in an operational assignment, and for a grunt this is the peak. On my flight back to the States in December of 1993, I was thinking how fortunate I'd been to serve in uniform for more than twenty-five years. I was in the zone for consideration by the brigadier general promotion board. But since only about 1 percent of colonels are selected, I was planning to retire. While I felt my record was competitive, I didn't expect to make stars. Actually, I'd been pleasantly surprised to make colonel.

So I was astonished when I returned to Washington—trading the wobbly planks I'd used as a desk in the Balkans for the massive, ornate SASC staff director's desk—to get a call from the commandant, Gen. Carl Mundy. I assumed it was about a nomination, since that was the most common reason he called us.

I was right, it was. Mundy boomed, "Congratulations, Arnold, you've been selected for promotion to brigadier general. Your nomination has cleared all the normal internal reviews and will be announced by the White House and sent to the Senate tomorrow."

I was shocked. The Corps had treated my nomination with the same radio silence as all the others. I got the same silent treatment from the committee's general counsel, Andy Effron, because I couldn't be involved with any part of the committee's consideration of my nomination. It would be processed like any other service member's, and they would neither cut corners nor grant any special treatment.[1]

So for several months I was "pending." Then, during a committee meeting, Chairman Nunn mentioned that "Arnold's list" was up for approval, along with a long list of other routine nominations. The committee members subjected me to some good-natured ribbing, suggesting holds and further investigations. Jokes notwithstanding, they approved the list, and the Senate confirmed me a few days later. While I'd handled thousands of confirmations for others, I had nothing to do with my own. Every officer from the rank of major to general requires Senate confirmation. Each year, the SASC considers tens of thousands. Most of them are on long, consolidated lists so the SASC can consider, for example, those being promoted from lieutenant colonel to colonel all at once. For those, my desk was always the final stop in the review process before they were put on the calendar. While I was in the loop for hundreds of thousands of these, my own was handled by the committee counsels. I was confident of one fact: political connections were not involved. The process is sacrosanct in the Marine Corps; I know from my own service on promotion boards that anyone flagged as a namedropping "VIP" is immediately thrown out. Each candidate for promotion is judged exclusively on his or her performance.

I almost didn't have a promotion ceremony because I didn't see the point. It only happened because Col. Terry Paul convinced me to do it. "Arnold, you'll never regret having a ceremony. Years later, you'll be glad you did." We held it in the Russell Senate Caucus Room to take advantage of the commandant and the Marine Drum and Bugle Corps being there for the annual USMC birthday celebration.

I felt honored that so many senior personnel from the executive branch and the Senate joined my family and relatives. I was blessed to have my company commander and fellow platoon commander from Vietnam, J. K. Van Riper and Eric Chase, present, as well as a number of those who'd served with me in Yugoslavia. With speeches from Secretary of the Navy John Dalton, Senators Thurmond, Warner, and Nunn, and comments from former secretary of defense Jim Schlesinger and soon-to-be-CIA head George Tenet, the event did run a little long. But it was a special thrill for my dad to join Jan and the kids to pin on my stars.

In the end, Terry Paul was right. Whenever you can, celebrate your life, and let those you love toast it with you. You'll always be glad you did.

⌒

My first assignment as a general was as deputy commander of Marine Reserve Forces, headquartered in New Orleans. I flew down to the Big Easy at my own expense, as required of drilling Reservists. Typically, a Reserve headquarters is collocated on an active-duty base, such as Camp Lejeune or Camp Pendleton. This leads to a closer integration between the active and reserve components. But the former chairman of the House Armed Services Committee, Eddie Hébert, had forced the Navy and Marines to locate their headquarters in an old dockside warehouse in a run-down part of town. It was the only Reserve component not headquartered on an active installation or close to a major active headquarters. I pushed for relocation, but I couldn't make the Pentagon see that it made more operational sense.

On one of my first days in the office, I was trying to impress my colleagues. I saw a sergeant making his way through all the Marines in the office toward my door. As he came within earshot, I picked up my phone and, speaking loudly so all could hear, snapped out, "Tell Senator Nunn I'll have it solved this morning. Tell General Mundy I'll have my recommendation to him this afternoon, and tell General Powell I'm busy, but will get back to him in a couple of days." As the sergeant reached my door, I popped the phone down smartly. "Sergeant, what can I do for you today?"

"Sir," he replied, "I'm here to hook up your phone." Great first impression . . . and I'm sure he enjoyed retelling that story.

My boss was Maj. Gen. Jim Livingston, a Medal of Honor recipient from the Vietnam War. Deputy commander was a new position, so my duties weren't clear, but I tried to help in those areas where my knowledge of budgets and Pentagon decision making were appropriate. Livingston was a hands-on leader and in constant touch with his subordinate commands: the 4th Marine Division, the 4th Marine Aircraft Wing, and the 4th Force Service Support Group. I got the impression in my ten years as a general working with the New Orleans headquarters that the HQ staff was mediocre at best. They were what we called Active Reserves: Reservists who served on permanent active duty, but only in key Reserve locations. When promotion boards considered them, they were compared neither to traditional drilling Reservists nor to active-duty officers, but competed just among themselves. There are some outstanding performers, but compared as a whole to either active staffs or the drilling Reservists they support, they don't have either the operational currency or varied assignments that are necessary to be top performers. Both as a general and as the chairman of the Commission on the Guard and Reserves, I often recommended that they be replaced with active-duty inspector-instructors, temporarily assigned to the Reserves, who would bring current operational experience. While I had support from at least one commandant and one Marine Forces Reserve commander, the AR protective society stonewalled any change. To this day, we still don't have either the optimal location for the HQ or the optimal support staff.

I was fortunate to get my first command as a general in less than a year: the Marine Corps Mobilization Command. At the time it was named the Marine Corps Reserve Support Command, in Kansas City, Missouri. The MCRSC was responsible for managing individual mobilization augmentees and their units, running the individual ready reserve of more than 60,000 Marines and maintaining all reserve records. MCRSC also had a civilian section that wrote code and maintained many of the information technology systems that managed personnel and pay. The command was about half Marine and half civilians. The latter had worked there for many years and were a real strength for their expertise and dedication.

Back in my SASC days, I'd worked with Brig. Gen. Mike Downs to relocate MCRSC. During my visit then, the command was in several run-down civilian rented facilities in an economically deprived area. The Air Force was closing the Richards-Gebaur Air Force Base, and MCRSC was scrambling to get better facilities, pitted against other Corps and Navy interests for the space. In my committee role, I helped MCRSC gain those facilities and build a new HQ building, but when I finally got there I joked, "If I knew I was going to be the commander here someday, I would have built myself a bigger office."

I commanded this staff for two years. While there was a lot of paperwork, the command also had serious management responsibilities, and I tried to get out to Kansas City at least one week out of every six. The tour at MCRSC flew by. It was one of the most enjoyable and rewarding assignments of my military career. But as its end neared, I learned I was next going to command the 4th Marine Division.

This was a truly big deal. The 4th had distinguished itself in World War II battles in the Pacific—including Iwo Jima—and now as a Reserve division had more than 20,000 Marines and sailors in units in more than 125 cities around the country. As a Reserve general, I considered my major responsibility to be ensuring the division was organized, trained, and equipped for the war-fighting missions it had in the combatant commanders' contingency plans. While in theory the 4th Division could operate as it did in World War II, it was highly unlikely. I didn't have the 365-days-a-year, 25-years-plus of operational experience to command a division in combat and I was realistic about my proper role.

I took command in a ceremony at Camp Pendleton. The division's overall warfighting readiness was C-4, "not ready for war." My initial commander's intent was to improve this as rapidly as possible. I instituted a tracking system to measure the key categories that determine, under the Pentagon's readiness rating, to what degree a unit is combat-ready. These measurements are pretty much the same ones used today and include the required number of personnel for each unit, whether they're trained in their military occupational specialty (MOS), whether the individuals have the proper training both in their individual skills and whether the unit has been trained in its own mission-essential task lists, whether units have the proper equipment, and finally to what degree that equipment is combat-ready. Finally, personnel have to meet the medical and dental readiness standards for deployment. I listed all the units so each commander could see both how his unit met the required standards and how he fared against the others.

I modeled my approach on one used by Maj. Gen. Jim Jones when he was commanding general of the 2nd Marine Division. Every quarter, I met with my major commanders and subordinates and, using the SORTS reporting system where everyone reported his status, I assessed the division's readiness and rated every unit. I would list what I called "readiness killers" so each unit could easily focus on what improvements were needed. Over three years, we were able to get up to the highest level of combat-readiness, C-1, which not even all active-duty divisions were able to achieve. This required getting everyone's individual gear, and ensuring everyone got his rifle and pistol qualifications and that the machine-gun and tank crews fully qualified on their weapons. Units went through the same combined arms training exercise at Twentynine Palms as the active units, doing exercises with active units and volunteering for special assignments. Achieving a C-1 rating was both difficult and rare for a Reserve division, and my troops were justly proud when they realized what they'd accomplished.

⤳

In 2001 my old friend Jim Jones, now commandant, asked me to take a two-star billet at Quantico as director of Reserve affairs (normally filled by a full-time active-duty general), part of the Manpower and Reserve Affairs organization. I was in charge of Reserve policy, manpower, and budgets at headquarters. I occupied the billet as a drilling Reservist, since I had extensive experience with personnel policies and issues. I had the advantage of knowing all the key players in the Pentagon and on the Hill and while I kept my full-time job (by then I was working at SAIC), I spent considerable time in this new role as well.

I recognized immediately that there was little in this area that I could influence from a desk in Quantico. So, I set up a forward office in the Pentagon to work issues directly. At the time the assistant secretary of the Navy for manpower and Reserve affairs was Billy Navas, and his deputy for Reserves was Harvey Barnum, two colleagues I'd worked with for years, which made my job much easier. Years before, I'd recommended that the management and administration of Reserve general officers be moved from MCRSC to HQMC and be managed by Reserve Affairs in coordination with the active-duty general officer management that was also at Quantico in manpower and Reserve affairs. So I was again in the business of supporting all of our Reserve generals.

Two other unfinished items I wanted to complete were to lock in the Marine for Life program and to get approval for integrating active personnel into the war-fighting table of organization for the 4th Marine Division. Marine for Life was a program I designed to help Marines leaving active duty, whether they had served four, fourteen, or twenty-four years, to transition back into their communities of choice. They were linked with a Reservist who had developed a network of housing, education, and job support and also would keep them informed on the goings-on of the Corps. Our DIs had always said, "You're a Marine for life," and I wanted to put that slogan into practice. I also wanted to include as many of the active-duty inspector-instructors on the war-fighting table of organization as possible, as an integral part of the unit they supported each day. Prior to integration, when the Reserve unit was called up, the inspector-instructor stayed behind and ran the vacant drill unit. In my view, that was a job for the community-based Reservists. This integration paid off when the 4th Division was mobilized for Iraq and Afghanistan. Both required fighting the bureaucracy at Quantico and at HQMC, since the projects were paperwork-intensive processes with many layers of bureaucrats who had to sign off, and bureaucrats hate change.

I had expected this to be a relatively uneventful tour. Boy, was I wrong! Soon I would be part of the largest mobilization of the Guard and Reserve in half a century.[2]

September 11, 2001. I was in the Pentagon, in my office on the fourth floor. There was no hint in those early hours this day would be different from any other. I was in my Charlie uniform and tanker jacket. I had to be at the Army Navy Club by 0830 for the quarterly meeting of the Reserve Forces Policy Board. We were being briefed by Army Secretary Thomas White and the undersecretary of defense for personnel and readiness, David Chu. Also attending the RFPB meeting would be Lt. Gen. Dennis McCarthy, commander, Marine Forces Reserve. He and I had worked together for years, as we had both policy and operational control of the 39,600 drilling Reservists, the 60,000 members of the Individual

Ready Reserve, the 5,500 active-duty Marines serving with the Reserves, and the 2,600 Reservists on full-time active duty with the Reserves.

White had just completed his briefing and Chu was starting his when someone interrupted, yelling, "Turn on the TV!" We watched breaking news of the attacks in New York. Within minutes, someone else rushed in, shouting, "They've hit the Pentagon; the Pentagon!" I personally did not hear the explosion, but this man had, and had seen the smoke billowing from the west face. From Army-Navy, where we were all sitting, to where Flight 77 crashed was a five-minute drive by car. We all rushed outside and saw billowing black smoke. Since all the senior leaders of the Reserves and many active leaders were present at the meeting, everyone headed back immediately to his Pentagon office. McCarthy's military cell wasn't working, but I had my business phone. I called our Reserve fighter unit at Andrews Air Force Base and ordered them, with McCarthy's nod, to get airborne immediately to protect the capital's airspace. McCarthy and I decided to head out to my civilian office in Tysons Corner, about thirty minutes away, since SAIC had functioning communications and most military systems were out of operation.

On September 17 I got a first glimpse of the magnitude of what was expected of us in a meeting with President Bush, Secretary Rumsfeld, Deputy National Security Adviser Stephen Hadley, and Undersecretary Chu, when Bush asked to meet in the Pentagon with the heads of the seven Reserve components. He told us he was calling up the Reserves. I was impressed with his knowledge of Reserve matters. But then, he'd been a governor and commander of the Texas National Guard and had flown F-102s in the Air Guard himself. He charged us with making sure we kept the families and employers informed and to make sure our personnel had all the necessary training. Bush was all business, and his impatience showed when he snapped at Rumsfeld, "What's next? Let's get on with it" during some dead time in the meeting (our portion was done and they were arranging for the news media to come in). Rumsfeld filled the gap by saying to Bush, "General Punaro, in his civilian role on the Defense Business Board, was helping us get more bang for the buck by bringing world-class business practices to DOD." I saw a quizzical look on the president's face, so I quickly added, "Unlike the other Reserve chiefs, Mr. President, I'm not on full-time active duty at this point."

Then the media came in and Bush moved on to his statement about Osama Bin Laden "wanted dead or alive." He then had his picture taken with us. As we shook hands afterward, the president asked me, "How's that work going reforming the Pentagon?" Since Don Rumsfeld was standing right next to us, all I could find to say was, "Sir, you'll need to ask the Secretary." This was another great impression on a member of the Bush family. The first occurred several years earlier, when Senator Nunn persuaded the Pentagon to have a stealth air show and bring all the amazing programs to a hangar at Andrews Air Force Base, but keep it all under wraps. The displays included the B-2 bomber. As National Security Adviser Brent Scowcroft and I were climbing down from its cockpit after looking at its massive internal bomb bays, Secretary of the Air Force Don Rice brought over President George H. W. Bush to where we were standing under the wing. I was speechless until I blurted out, as Bush looked up in the bomb bays, "Mr. President, it's a big sucker." What a persuasive justification for a $2 billion plane.

There were lots of meetings with the senior policymakers and the Reserve chiefs about the call-up. The commandant decided to mobilize me as well. Within a month of the attacks, we went to war with Afghanistan. Less than two years later, we went to war with Iraq. And our folks responded. At one point in the Iraq War, more than 40 percent of the forces on the ground were Guard and Reserve. Every single battalion of the 4th Marine Division deployed at one point or another during those two wars. I was confident that the years we spent improving their readiness contributed to their success on the battlefield.

⤳

I retired on October 1, 2003, with more than a decade as a general officer, well beyond the normal guidelines. I left the Corps in the same chaotic fashion as I'd joined; the week of my planned retirement ceremony at Marine Barracks 8th and I, Hurricane Isabel hit Washington and we had to reschedule. General Jones, now supreme allied commander Europe, was the presiding officer. As I spoke, I thought back to my first day at Quantico thirty-five years before, when a drill instructor screamed at me, "You are *too stupid* to ever be a second lieutenant!" He'd said I would never amount to anything in the Corps. *I sure proved him wrong*, I thought, as senators, service secretaries, four- and three-star generals, and CEOs looked on. But what meant more to me was that my family was there, including my dad, who'd fought in World War II.

I concluded my speech with a reflection on Cpl. Roy L. Hammonds, the Marine who'd rushed out to help after I was shot, who had sacrificed his life for mine. "I stand here today deeply honored by this ceremony, but realizing that no one achieves any success on his own. Whatever any of us do is made possible by the Corporal Hammondses throughout our services, who choose danger over safety, who put their fellow serviceman first and their own personal welfare second. These good Marines, these good soldiers, these good sailors, these good airmen, and these good coastguardsmen. Let each and every one of us here make that same choice. And each and every day help a soldier, sailor, airman, or Marine and his or her family, by providing a strong military and one that will be ready thirty-three years from now. This is our day-to-day challenge and fight."

15

THE OUTSIDE INFLUENCERS

1997–Present: Washington, DC

When I taught a graduate course for ten years at Georgetown University, I emphasized that national security decision making was influenced by three major factors: people, processes, and institutions. After studying history, James Madison and the other founders designed checks and balances to create tension among the three branches of government so that no single branch could dominate. Though not always as consciously designed, processes within other governmental institutions, both civilian and military, create similar tensions as factions joust for jurisdiction, resources, power, and publicity. In Congress, Democrats and Republicans compete, particularly if the parties split control of the House and Senate. Committees such as Armed Services and Foreign Relations butt heads over jurisdiction and policy. Within the executive branch, departments and agencies such as the Department of Defense and State Department fight among and with one another for finite resources and policy dominance. This induces our institutions to act in ways that may appear self-defeating—or, at the very least, strange—to outsiders. For many governmental organizations, your next higher headquarters is your biggest enemy, until you get promoted into it.

Analyzing foreign and defense policy through the prism of bureaucratic politics explains more about why the United States chooses certain policies over others than the casual observer might think. Of course, individuals matter too. Forceful personalities can mean the difference between a policy becoming a reality or simply being edited out of the memo to the boss.

Most of the time, however, the bureaucracy is too large and entrenched for one person to move it alone. It functions in accordance with Newton's First Law, staying at rest unless some powerful external force intervenes. On the whole, I think fortunately, Washington is webbed with such outside forces. One is the think tanks. Some examples are the Center for Strategic and International Studies or the Center for a New American Security, which offer nonpartisan policy analyses. Also, institutions such as the American Enterprise Institute or the Center for American Progress perform policy analyses with a partisan slant. Powerful advocacy groups such as the AARP or the National Guard Association lobby members of Congress. Finally, industries also use their lobbying organizations to promote (or rebut criticisms of) their products and services.[1]

Outside groups can provide political incentives by scoring votes—meaning that they'll keep track of anyone who votes against their position and use it against them in the next election—or by providing cover for long-needed but internally stymied legislative and policy change.

For example, in 1991, when military leaders began to contemplate an appropriate post–Cold War military, Secretary of Defense Cheney and Chairman of the Joint Chiefs General Powell—two men at the peak of their power within the defense establishment—recommended major reductions in the National Guard. Cheney and Powell had the facts, but the National Guard Association had the state governors. Wearing their citizen-soldier hats, its members overwhelmed Capitol Hill, lobbied all the members, and defeated the Cheney-Powell proposal.

It's not just associations and think tanks that can change policy, though. Other effective components of the policymaking process are government-sponsored boards and commissions. These are often made up of former policymakers and subject matter experts. When the legislative or executive branches want to examine a specific issue or are considering controversial legislation, Congress or the president will often sponsor a board, task force, or commission to delve deep and make specific recommendations. They can have immediate or long-term impacts on policy. Or none at all . . . their report might simply collect dust on a shelf. But many of the most dramatic changes in recent years have been the result of these commissions.

The Gates Commission recommended the abolishment of the draft and creation of the all-volunteer force and also predicted the problems we're grappling with today. Those problems—unsustainable costs due to antiquated personnel policies such as the military retirement, promotion, and compensation systems—required the creation of the Military Compensation and Retirement Modernization Commission in early 2013 to examine essential yet sensitive reforms.

Another example: In 1998, the Hart-Rudman Commission, on which I served as deputy executive director, was chaired by former senators Gary Hart and Warren Rudman. It noted that America was increasingly vulnerable to a terrorist attack and recommended the creation of a department responsible "for planning, coordinating, and integrating various U.S. government activities involved in homeland security."[2] That call went unheeded until the 9/11 Commission made a similar recommendation. That today's Department of Homeland Security came into being afterward seems akin to buying the fire truck after the house has burned to the ground.

Some associations, like the National Defense Industrial Association, which I chaired from 2013 to 2015, have as their principal purpose promoting a robust defense industrial base and working to foster a collaborative relationship with government so policymakers have access to reliable information.[3]

~~~

The Department of Defense is so large and complex that it has several permanently established task forces to provide continuous counsel to the leadership. These include the Defense Science Board and the Defense Policy Board. Some of our country's most notable scientists, engineers, and policy experts sit on these boards.

Another is the Defense Business Board, which had its origins in a reform task force set up by Secretary of Defense William Cohen and Deputy Secretary of Defense John Hamre.

I first met John in 1987 when I hired him from the Congressional Budget Office to be a staff member of the Armed Services Committee. Later, as the deputy secretary of defense, his job was to run the department on a day-to-day basis (the government equivalent of a corporation's chief operating officer). In 1997, he created a management council made up of the undersecretaries across the Office of the Secretary of Defense and the undersecretaries and vice chiefs of staff of the military departments to look at ways to improve business and management practices. It was a good idea, but because the task force was made up of government officials and military personnel who had little or no experience in the business world, it would have been hard for the group to identify or incorporate world-class business practices.

Secretary Cohen wanted an outside group to undertake an independent review of the issues. He was encouraged by his senior military assistant, then Lt. Gen. Jim Jones. In addition to me as chairman, this new Task Force on Defense Reform consisted of Michael Bayer of the Defense Science Board; David Chu, a former director in the Office of Program Analysis and Evaluation; Rhett Dawson, a former SASC staff director; Jim Locher, who was a key player in the Goldwater-Nichols Act and a noted expert on defense organizations; Gary "Kim" Wincup, a former HASC staff director and assistant secretary of the Army; and Dov Zakheim, who later became the DOD's comptroller under George W. Bush.

Our task force's remit was to identify organizational reforms, reductions in overhead, and streamlined business practices, with a special emphasis on the Office of the Secretary of Defense, the Defense agencies, the Joint Staff, and the military departments. After a yearlong investigation, we submitted our report to Secretary Cohen. We recommended reducing organizational bloat and management layers (such as principal deputies, deputy assistants, deputy directors, etc.), and focusing on core capabilities. Cohen was pleased with our report and said that our specific efficiency identifications were exactly what he was looking for.

Of course I responded, "Our recommendations aren't groundbreaking. In fact, they're generally the same ones made by a similar task force commissioned by President Eisenhower in 1956!"

Identifying the problems and devising solutions was the easy part. But Cohen found out, just as every SecDef after him, that implementing reforms is considerably harder.

A centerpiece of our report was our recommendation that the department create a Defense Business Board, made up of accomplished businesspeople, to advise the secretary on management practices. Cohen liked the idea and supported it in theory, but the proposal died a bureaucratic death and never became a reality during the Clinton administration. But like so many other proposals, its demise was not permanent.

Shortly after Donald Rumsfeld became secretary of defense, after George W. Bush's election, he asked me to come in one Saturday and brief him on the proposals from the defense reform task force. Don thought about things like a businessman and wore this distinction with the same pride as the military wears combat ribbons. He entered office on a crusade to bring the department into the modern age, to make the military smaller, more agile, and technologically sophisticated. Despite the common belief that the defense department is exclusively military, it includes roughly 1.4 million civilians and contractors. It's hard enough to effect change in any organization, let alone one as large and complex as the DOD. So in preparing for this meeting with Don, I wanted to focus some of my advocacy on the creation of a Defense Business Board that could bring ideas to the secretary's office that would never percolate up from under the twenty-eight layers of management in the department.

The secretary's suite occupies valuable Pentagon real estate along the outermost corridor on the third floor, overlooking a marina on the Potomac. Beyond the river lies the majestic National Mall, the Washington Monument, and the Jefferson Memorial. Don hadn't finished moving in when I walked in early on a cold, sunny Saturday morning in mid-January 2001. Half-empty cardboard boxes littered the room; we had to clear space at the conference table so we could sit. Dov Zakheim and Michael Bayer were there, as was Ray DuBois (a confidant who would become the deputy undersecretary for installations and environment and "Mayor of the Pentagon"), and Martin Hoffman, former secretary of the Army and Rumsfeld confidant.

Don's not much for extended chitchat, so I quickly began running through the proposals, underscoring how badly the decision process had deteriorated since his previous tour as SecDef in 1975. He listened intently, occasionally asking a question or nodding. I quickly got on a roll and was on high-speed transmit as I ran the gamut of how fouled up the Pentagon had become. Dov told me later, "After you left, Rumsfeld said he felt like curling up into the fetal position." Michael Bayer said the presentation reinforced Rumsfeld's instinct that fundamental reforms were long overdue throughout all elements of the department. "Don't just break the china, shatter it!"

Given his determination to reform and streamline, Rumsfeld was enthusiastic about the idea of a business board. It helped that some of his subordinates, such as Dov, were also proponents. Dov became the comptroller, responsible for the budget, and established the Defense Business Board in 2002. Initially, the board reported to the comptroller, but once it began to prove its worth, Rumsfeld demanded that it report directly to him and his deputy, Paul Wolfowitz, even though Paul was more policy oriented, with a PhD from the University of Chicago's famed political science department, and had little interest in the business aspects of the department. The board's first chairman was Lt. Gen. Gus Pagonis, USA (Ret.). Gus was in charge of logistics during Operation Desert Shield/Desert Storm and had gone on to oversee logistics for Sears Roebuck when he retired from active duty. Gus had a good working relationship with Don, a rarity for an active or retired senior military officer, given Don's well-known heavy-handed treatment of the brass.

The Defense Business Board received favorable attention from the secretary and was able to bypass the typical coordination and review process. This process sometimes includes a tortuous circuit through all twenty-eight layers in the bureaucracy. A proposal can be derailed at any point by an action officer signing "non-concur" on the policy memorandum, which stalls the process until the objecting office can work out a compromise with the one pushing the new policy. Sometimes an office will do this simply to forestall the creation of a new office that might result in competition for resources. It's a sad fact that such tactics are common within such a large organization.

The great strength of the Defense Business Board, like the science and policy boards, is that it provides independent, objective analysis. Over the years since its establishment, it has worked closely with the department's leadership to find areas where they want and need outside assistance, as opposed to simply creating solutions to problems the board thinks are important. The board works closely with the key stakeholders to identify a problem, gather the facts, and assess possible solutions. This collaboration increases the chance its recommendations will be accepted and implemented. While the Pentagon can be sensitive to criticism and defensive of its policies, it is also serious about finding ways to do things better. The military always does after-action reviews of training exercises and operations, and it summarizes and retains lessons learned so mistakes are not repeated. Men like Gus Pagonis and Michael Bayer, the first two chairs, were instrumental in ensuring the department viewed the board as an asset and not as an enemy.

In fact, it was such a valuable asset that we were given special assignments, such as examining controversial reforms to the national security personnel system. In 2003, the Bush administration, under the leadership of Wolfowitz and later his replacement, Gordon England, had persuaded Congress to replace the old Civil Service with a new pay-for-performance National Security Personnel System. Career civil servants resisted the reforms because the new regime resembled a private-sector workforce. But by 2009, it still was not fully implemented. So William "Bill" Lynn, President Obama's deputy secretary of defense, asked the board to examine both pay scales. Rudy deLeon was appointed as the task force chairman, and he presented the results to the full board in July 2009. Rudy's task force recommended that the DOD revamp, but not abolish, the National Security Personnel System because of its positive performance-management goals. But that recommendation went unheeded when President Obama signed the 2010 National Defense Authorization Act, which included a provision repealing the NSPS.

It is a privilege for me to be a plank owner of the Defense Business Board, having been associated with it continuously since its inception to the completion of my extended term in December 2013 and my reappointment to a new term in July 2015 by Secretary Ash Carter.

‌↬

In 2005, during some tough days for our active and reserve forces fighting in Iraq and Afghanistan, Congress established a Commission on the National Guard and Reserves "to recommend changes to ensure that the National Guard and other reserve components are organized, trained, equipped, compensated, and supported to best meet the needs of U.S. national security."[4] Though the Reserves were playing a larger role in major campaigns, the department still managed them with personnel policies dating from when they were a Cold War strategic reserve.

The 2005 National Defense Authorization Act established the commission; the executive branch and Congress would both pick the commissioners. Rumsfeld appointed me to chair it that January. Other members included former staff director Rhett Dawson; former secretary of the Navy Will Ball, an old Senate colleague; Les Brownlee, another Senate colleague and former secretary of the Army for George W. Bush; and James Sherrard, retired Air Force lieutenant general whose last assignment was chief of the Air Force Reserve, along with several others knowledgeable in Guard and Reserve matters. In all, there were twelve members, supported by thirty-two staff members. We met monthly, if not more often, in Crystal City, a collection of office buildings sandwiched between the Pentagon and Reagan National Airport on the Potomac.

We spent a lot of time simply figuring out how to best approach our enormous task. The issues were complex and contentious. The tension between the active and Reserve components had been building since long before Vietnam. So, as chair, the first thing I decided was that our investigation process would be completely open. We'd listen to everyone who wanted to be heard. This was one of the first commissions made up of individuals appointed by both the executive and legislative branches. Since congressional Democrats and Republicans had both appointed commissioners, I was concerned about how well such an ideologically diverse group would work together. We spent a lot of time getting to know one another, meeting for informal dinners the night before each meeting and traveling together on field visits.

Because each state has its own Guard units, we took a number of trips around the country to interview witnesses and collect data. One of our most important stops was San Diego because of its large presence of active-duty units and the size of California's National Guard, with its wide-ranging missions from disaster response to border security. This gave us access to many senior commanders. We made similar fact-finding trips across the country, and that, as anyone who's taken group trips can attest, always forces colleagues to spend a lot of time together.

The next obstacle was getting the commission up and running. I ran into a lot of problems with the Washington Headquarters Service, or WHS, the office charged with supporting the day-to-day operations of the Pentagon. We had to work with them to get our computers, support staff, and budget. But since the department viewed the commission as an outside entity forced on it by Congress, our relationship with some in the lower levels of WHS was prickly. Junior civil servants didn't want additional work.

We never did manage a great working relationship, but two things helped us get to a point where we could at least coexist. First, I leveraged my prior personal relationships with WHS directors Ray DuBois and Mike Donley to smooth any ruffled feathers. I'd worked with both on the Hill and at SAIC and we agreed on a lot of challenges confronting the department. Additionally, I'd been in a position to help them in my previous jobs. Mike had experienced a number of issues at the Reagan White House when Nunn had been helpful, like the AWACS sale to Saudi Arabia. I'd provided key help when Ray was the lead for Rumsfeld in getting his nominations confirmed in the early days of the George W. Bush administration. Both knew that my long-standing relationships with Armed Services Committee members could benefit their interests as well. Second, and more importantly, I hired a really solid support staff led by Tom Eldridge. He wasn't an expert on Guard and Reserve issues, but as a former prosecutor who had served as senior counsel for the Senate Committee on Homeland Security and Government Affairs report on Hurricane Katrina, he was highly organized, and he ensured we documented everything with authoritative sources. I remembered Russell Long's advice to neophyte Senator Nunn—"don't solve a problem before people know they have one"—so I wanted to identify the hard spots before offering solutions.

We issued our final report in January 2008, two and half years after being established. After 17 days of public hearings with 115 witnesses, 52 commission meetings, more than 850 interviews, and the detailed analysis of thousands of documents, our report contained 6 major conclusions and 95 recommendations supported by 163 findings. The department needed to sustain and preserve the Guard and the services' Reserves as an operational reserve. Significant changes, however, such as creating an integrated pay and personnel system, reducing the number of duty statuses, and elevating the National Guard Bureau chief to the four-star level, were necessary. Both the Congress and the department ultimately agreed with more than 95 percent of our recommendations. SASC Ranking Member John Warner praised our work on the Senate floor, saying, "The Commission has made profound and substantive recommendations for reforming the National Guard and Reserves."[5]

⌒

In addition to the formalized processes and procedures that task forces, boards, and commissions use to influence decision making, informal mechanisms also influence outcomes within the policymaking community. One is preparing political and military appointees for Senate confirmation. Military men and women plan for every contingency. One method they use is a meticulous focus on rehearsals. "Murder boards," as they are colloquially known, prepare nominees for questioning in front of the Senate Armed Services Committee. The goal is to ask nominees the toughest questions they could expect to get, questions that could kill their chances at appointment. Nominees can then see where their weaknesses lie and prepare the best responses ahead of time.

The Constitution assigns the Senate the power to approve or disapprove the president's choices for certain senior positions in the executive branch. Typically, the committee with jurisdiction for a particular department or agency will hold a hearing where the members question the nominee to determine his or her fitness for the job. Afterward, the committee votes either to forward the nomination to the full Senate for approval or in extremely rare cases votes down a nominee, making a full vote unnecessary. In recent years, the debate has taken place within the media as well. It can be grueling for nominees and their families to have journalists and various interest groups comb through their entire professional—and personal—lives, then put the results on display for the world to see. The Internet and social media have made this potentially traumatic experience happen faster and spread farther, on a virtual, worldwide stage.

From 1983 through 1996, when I worked directly for the Armed Services Committee, I handled roughly 15,000 military nominations and 25 to 50 civilian nominations each year. Upon leaving the Senate in 1997, I began helping the department by sitting on their murder boards, and in 2001 the department asked me to lead that effort. I enlisted several colleagues, Rudy deLeon, Rhett Dawson, and Kim Wincup, all former staff directors of the armed services committees, because they understand how the process works, how the committee goes after nominees, and the substantive issues. Each team member then assumes the role of one or two senators known for hardball questions. We run the sessions exactly like hearings, making opening statements like the committee chairman does, having the witnesses read opening statements, then taking turns asking the nominees questions. The most controversial nomination can turn out to be routine, or vice versa. Thus the number one rule is to expect the unexpected.

Sometimes the department may find it does not even want to proceed with a nomination after a run past the "murderers." For example, in 2011 President Obama nominated a former defense official to be the assistant secretary of defense for acquisition, but there were questions within the administration. Some evidence was uncovered after her nomination that she had embellished her resume by claiming to have a PhD and that she had exaggerated the scope of her responsibilities at several earlier points in her career. Even before this, there had been a general sense she was not yet qualified for a job at the assistant secretary level. The assistant secretary for legislative affairs identified these concerns and asked us to zero in on these discrepancies in the murder board. The White House personnel officer to the DOD prepared pointed questions on the inconsistencies in the nominee's record.

I gaveled the "hearing" to order, made an introductory statement, and then allowed the witness to do the same. After reading aloud a standard set of questions that each nominee is asked by the chairman, I came out guns blazing. "Ms. X, this may be an odd question to ask at a hearing, but could you state your age for the record?"

"I'm forty-eight."

"Okay, so if you're forty-eight, then you were born in 1963, correct."

"Yes."

"Well, I'm confused. On your resume, you state that from 1978 to 1982 you worked in NASA's Ames Research Center on the development of an explosive propulsion system. You were working on this at the age of fifteen?"

It was the most uncomfortable board we've ever done, but we were able to show that she didn't have credible answers to explain the inconsistencies. It was obvious to everyone in the room that there was a major problem with the resume.

We debriefed Ash Carter, then the undersecretary for acquisition, technology, and logistics, and the administration decided to withdraw the nomination.

Murder boards can also help prepare witnesses for a high-profile oversight hearing.[6] A prime example was the crucial testimony of Ambassador Ryan Crocker and Gen. David Petraeus on the progress of the Iraq surge in September 2007. This hearing captivated Washington's attention, much like Sen. William Fulbright's hearings on Vietnam. The 2008 presidential election was in full swing. Iraq was a major issue, and given how badly the war had been going, public interest in Petraeus's revamped counterinsurgency strategy was at a fever pitch. This hearing had what's known in the military as a high pucker factor.

The murder board convened in the SecDef's spacious E-ring conference room on a sticky, late summer Sunday afternoon. A number of staffers from the White House came over—an uncommon occurrence—and most everyone from the administration wore casual clothes. Not our team! We wore our sharpest suits to convey the formality of the scene they would face the next day. The White House knew Petraeus and Crocker's performance would make or break the administration's Iraq strategy. Normally, officials at their level come with an entourage of aides. But this was no ordinary board, so both men brought only a few close aides. Jeff Bergner, the assistant secretary of state for legislative affairs and a former staff director of the Senate Foreign Relations Committee, sat on our team as the resident expert on that committee, since it would be a combined hearing with Armed Services. Both men were already well prepared, but we grilled them for several hours until we felt as though they were ready, and their performance the next day validated the murder board concept. It was the definition of a home run.

Unfortunately, sometimes nominees, whether military or civilian, did not take this preparation process seriously enough. Gen. Gregory "Speedy" Martin, USAF, was nominated to become the first non-Navy commander of U.S. Pacific Command in 2004, but the Air Force decided that since he was a four-star general he could easily handle the rigors of a confirmation hearing. During his hearing, he was unable to answer questions about the Air Force Boeing scandal, where Darleen Druyun, the senior acquisition officer in the Air Force, had awarded a large contract in return for the promise of a high-paying job. Martin, who had been Druyun's military deputy at one point, and Sen. John McCain had an intense back and forth. As a result, McCain came out against his nomination. Before the day was over, Martin withdrew from consideration.

The boards aren't without lighter moments, though. In 2007, Adm. Mike Mullen was preparing for his hearing to become chairman of the Joint Chiefs. Since Sen. Hillary Clinton was in the midst of her campaign for the Democratic presidential nomination, I decided to go down a line of questioning, unleashed in a rapid-fire manner, that he couldn't possibly have prepared for, to throw him off his game.

"Have you ever had a female commanding officer?"

"No."

"Have you ever worked closely with a female of equivalent rank?"

"No."

"Would you have a problem taking orders from a female Commander in Chief?"

"Um, well, um—"

My questions were clearly unfair and would almost certainly never have been asked. But the point was to throw him off his game, to unsettle him, and so we had a chuckle. And it made the point well: *expect the unexpected.* As an aside, the only answer he could've given and still been confirmed was an unequivocal "No!"

Many nominees have told us that our grilling was worse than the actual hearing. That's music to my ears, because it means we've done our job by imparting lessons learned from many decades of experience.

Another important point is that nominees should never presume the outcome of the process. That means refraining from speaking or writing about the personnel and policy changes you *will* make once confirmed. In 1993, President Bill Clinton nominated Dr. Graham Allison, a distinguished academic from Harvard and author of *Essence of Decision*, the definitive account of the Cuban Missile Crisis, for a job in the Office of the Secretary of Defense. Before his hearing, Allison had begun working with the department as an unofficial adviser to Secretary of Defense Les Aspin and had involved himself in nuclear weapons and arms control policies in a way that was inappropriate for someone who had not been assigned an official position yet. Well, when word of that reached the committee, the Republicans were furious. This was partly because they disagreed with Allison's positions, but even some of the Democrats were put off by the nominee's presumption that they would confirm him. During his hearing, the senators asked him to explain his actions. Allison was apologetic and owned up to his error in judgment. This proved to be the right tack as ultimately he *was* confirmed, but as a result the department and our committee put together a series of guidelines on the type of work nominees could and could not do while awaiting confirmation.

Another important lesson is the 80/20 rule. That is, nominees should only speak about 20 percent of the time, letting the senators, who can be long-winded, talk the remaining 80 percent. The longer a nominee's answer, the greater the chance he or she will say something ill-advised. Stick to your talking points is what I always say. Since the confirmation process is also a venue for senators to get their own opinions on the record, this rule is a fairly easy one for a nominee to follow as long as he or she recognizes that many of the senators' questions aren't actually questions. Anybody who's ever tuned into a committee hearing on C-SPAN will know what I'm talking about.

Our third guiding principle for all nominees: don't make news. This means not arguing with or playing favorites with the senators. It also means not showing off how smart one is or advocating a policy that has not been previously announced by the White House. A nomination hearing isn't like an oversight hearing. The nominee's goal should be simply to answer the questions as briefly as possible and without making headlines, just to say something substantive to demonstrate a general knowledge of the issues, to convey a willingness to work with Congress, and to demonstrate the intellectual ability to perform the job.

Our expertise was really put to the test in 2013 with the nomination of former senator Chuck Hagel to be the twenty-fourth secretary of defense. From the moment his name was floated by the White House as a possible candidate, this one was anything but routine. In January 2013, I wrote him, "You are facing some issues that will be more difficult to deal with than the typical nominee. There is already an expectation that you will placate your critics and defuse the contentious issues during your courtesy calls and the hearing. If not, you will be labeled as doing poorly in your confirmation hearing and this will dog you post-confirmation. For this reason, you need to over-prepare."[7] Unlike typical SecDef nominees, who have historically received wide bipartisan support, Hagel's looked more like a federal judicial nomination. Interest groups such as the Emergency Committee for Israel ran attack ads on TV and in major newspapers. Senate Republicans, led by Sen. John Cornyn, filibustered the nomination (a first for a cabinet appointment).

Some media outlets such as *Foreign Policy* reported that Hagel had done several murder boards in preparation for his hearing. Our team only had the opportunity to run one, for about three hours, three days before the hearing. We'd certainly recommended more than one session; Robert Gates had participated in three. After our first, it was clear to all of us that Hagel needed another. He showed some confusion when I asked about the role of the chairman of the Joint Chiefs of Staff. His answers regarding Iran were muddled. But our recommendation was rebuffed and he continued to prepare on his own.

Although Hagel's ordeal was an anomaly for a cabinet-level appointment in terms of the vitriol, it is a vivid illustration of what I see as the gradual deterioration of the confirmation process. Part of this is due to the sheer growth of government. Today, the Senate is constitutionally responsible for providing advice and consent on approximately 1,200 positions in the executive and judicial branches. In 1960, top-level federal management positions totaled 196; by 2012, that number had ballooned to 522. Not surprisingly, the length of time the average nominee waits from nomination until confirmation has gone from just over two months during the Kennedy administration to over eight under George W. Bush.

The process has slowed at every step. Administrations have had a hard time recruiting top talent for key positions due to a burdensome public vetting process that many nominees, even qualified ones, prefer to avoid. First the FBI conducts a lengthy background investigation. Then the administration launches its own internal review prior to the president's decision. Some nominees prefer not to make the financial sacrifices required to conform to the ethics regulations, which often require the divestiture of holdings that relate to the position for which they are nominated, regardless of market conditions. The paperwork required has ballooned from ten or twelve pages to hundreds, including releasing years of prior tax returns.

Though the process has slowed for everyone, the Obama administration is the worst I've seen yet at filling vacancies in a timely manner. Key positions such as the Air Force assistant secretary for acquisition—responsible for billions of dollars in procurement—went vacant for six years. Even when the White House knew an appointee was leaving six to nine months in advance, it consistently waited months after the position was actually vacated before naming a replacement.

But the Senate isn't blameless, either, with its shorter workweeks and anonymous holds (essentially blocking a nominee from moving forward). Their reasons range from parochial concerns about DOD decisions that affect their home state to demanding the administration provide more information about scandals like the terrorist attack on the Benghazi consulate, which may have no relevance to the position being filled.

My top three recommendations for improving the nomination process, taken from a study I did on improving the acquisition system, include streamlining the process by reducing paperwork and using common procedures; minimizing financial disincentives, limiting recusals, allowing true blind trusts, and providing some incentives in adverse markets; and reassessing the post-government prohibitions.[8]

⤸

In August 2010, as the country struggled to claw its way out of the Great Recession and the national debt soared, Secretary of Defense Robert Gates announced major reductions to the Pentagon's massive overhead, which accounts for roughly 40 percent of the department's budget. The $195 billion spent on noncombat-related functions is roughly equal to the annual GDP of Ireland. As a longtime Washington hand, Gates not only knew the ax was coming, but that the department, after a decade of exponential growth and with the wars in Iraq and Afghanistan nearing their inevitable conclusion, would be the biggest target for cuts.

In late 2009, I led a Defense Business Board task force to identify inefficiencies and recommend where we could save the most bucks. Given my previous experiences, I shouldn't have been optimistic about our chances for reform, but I felt that budget pressures might provide an incentive not present before, and Gates's bureaucracy-busting style might prevail where others had failed. When we finished our six-month investigation, we reported sadly that the problems we'd discovered in 1997 had grown worse and even more entrenched, if that was possible. The Office of the Secretary of Defense had ballooned to more than 5,000 people. When you added the combatant commands, Joint Staff, and defense agencies, they totaled 250,000 and cost more than $116 billion a year. The offices with folks in the rear with the gear continued to grow bigger and spend more. Novelist Rita Mae Brown must have foreseen the Pentagon's bureaucracy when she quipped, in her novel *Sudden Death*, that insanity was doing the same thing over and over and expecting a different result.

Secretary Gates was just as determined as his predecessors to make the fundamental reforms everyone knew were needed, but like his predecessors, he left office before he was able to implement the biggest and most challenging, such as acquisition reform, bureaucratic creep, and the skyrocketing costs of the all-volunteer force.

⌐⌐

One of the DOD's lesser-known but still important entities is the Reserve Forces Policy Board. I served on it as a Marine Reserve two-star general from 1999 to 2003. The RFPB is one of the oldest advisory committees in the Pentagon. In 1949, due to inadequate recruitment and strength in the Reserves, Harry Truman's secretary of defense, Louis Johnson, created the Civilian Components Policy Board, which George Marshall redesignated as the Reserve Forces Policy Board in 1951. By a 1952 act of Congress, it became the principal adviser to the secretary of defense on Reserve matters. Louis Johnson created the board at a time when Reservists were a little-used strategic reserve, not the operational force they have become today. But at the peak of operations in Iraq and Afghanistan, 45 percent of our ground forces there were Guard and Reserve.

Both as a career Reservist and staffer on the Armed Services Committee, I had long observed that even as late as the 1990s little had changed from 1949. The Reserves still did not have adequate equipment or training because the active-duty leadership viewed them as the second string. Luckily, Congress has always been a great supporter and has consistently sought ways to provide them with additional resources. Congress has always added $1 billion more than what the department requested for Reserve and Guard equipment each year.

Unfortunately, over the years, the board had deteriorated and lost its stature within the department. The Committee on the National Guard and the Reserve had recommended dissolving and reconstituting the RFPB as an independent board, reporting directly to the secretary of defense. So I was thrilled when, in 2011, Secretary Leon Panetta asked me to serve as chairman of the newly reorganized board, to which I was subsequently reappointed by Secretaries Hagel and Carter.

One of the first items I directed the board to undertake was a year-long analysis of the fully burdened and life-cycle costs of military personnel. "Fully burdened" is a business term used to describe the labor rate of an employee, accounting for hidden or other costs not included in his or her wages. These may include pensions, taxes, benefits, and supplies.

My purpose was twofold. First, the DOD had never done this analysis. It had no idea how much a service member cost the department over his or her lifetime. This struck me as odd, since the life-cycle costs for a major weapons program were always calculated long in advance for comparison and budgeting. Second, senior active-duty officers such as Gen. Larry Spencer, the vice chief of staff of the Air Force, and even Leon Panetta had asked me why the Guard and Reserves were more expensive than active forces.

Well, as we say down in Georgia, that dog won't hunt. The total costs of our active-duty personnel, including all the nonmonetary benefits and pensions for retirees and the VA system, is more than half of the total defense budget. Though the size of the force has remained much the same, its costs have more than doubled since 2000. Health care expenses have risen more than 170 percent between 2001 and 2012, due mostly to the massive number of retirees. The RFPB study we published in 2013, *Eliminating Major Gaps in DoD Data on the Fully-Burdened and Life-Cycle Cost of Military Personnel*, proved conclusively that the fully burdened costs of the active military was 70 percent *more* than that of the Guard and Reserve on an individual basis. Not only that, it was clear to me that the life-cycle costs—where we pay active personnel for sixty years (twenty years of service and forty years of retirement)—were making it harder for the country to fund the force we need.

Today, defense spends more for weapons that take too long to produce and deliver less-than-superior performance. It pays much more for a force that's smaller than it was twenty years ago. And as the department's budget shrinks, instead of seizing the opportunity to rethink how it does business, the bureaucracy defends the status quo.

One of the initiatives by Gates to reduce overhead took aim at the sixty-plus DOD boards and commissions themselves. He and his senior advisers wanted to eliminate some and reduce the scope of others. They saw many as a nuisance since they didn't always support existing policies. Some were truly moribund and worthy of elimination. I believed that each board should be considered on its individual merits, but even if you added up all their costs, it was still "budget dust" (rounding errors) in a $600 billion defense bill.

The major boards remain, however, and Congress continues to use them today to obtain independent analysis and recommendations on complex and controversial topics. In 2013, Congress created two high-profile commissions, one to examine the military compensation and retirement system and another to review the structure of the Air Force. These temporary, highly focused commissions have a greater ability to effect change because they were established outside the Pentagon to work on problems the DOD could not or would not solve. Having served on both types and using the ability to effect change as a metric, I have to conclude that the outside boards have a much better track record.

While a few boards, commissions, and task forces have had negligible impacts, their overall record is impressive, from the Gates Commission creating the all-volunteer force to the Packard Commission on acquisition reform to the CSIS study on defense reform that provided the underpinning to the Goldwater-Nichols Act. Their influence has run the gamut from revolutionary reforms to more mundane, workaday changes at the margins. Leaders inside and outside the defense establishment have used the results to push the bureaucracy to deliver better results. They are and will continue to be a staple of Washington decision making.

One gray morning in late November 2014 as I was walking into the Pentagon for a murder board for several civilian assistant secretaries, news dropped that shook Washington: Chuck Hagel announced he was resigning as secretary of defense just twenty-one months after being sworn in. Hagel, whose confirmation had been the rockiest for a cabinet-level appointment in decades, had entered office weakened, and it dogged him throughout his tenure.

A couple weeks after Hagel's announcement, President Obama named Dr. Ashton Carter to be the twenty-fifth secretary of defense. Carter's resume and fitness for the job were impeccable. He'd previously served in the Obama administration as the deputy secretary of defense and the undersecretary of defense for acquisition, technology, and logistics. He'd been an excellent assistant secretary in the Clinton administration. He held a PhD in theoretical physics from Oxford and a master's in medieval history from Yale. Without any disrespect to Chuck Hagel, Ash Carter was his antithesis.

Nowhere was this more apparent than in his preparation. Given his résumé and his intellect—he was routinely referred to as the smartest guy in the room—he probably could have prepared adequately simply by reading memos furnished by the DOD to refresh his memory on everything the department had done since he'd left as deputy in December 2013. But people don't rise to Carter's level by doing the bare minimum. He approached his confirmation hearing and subsequent transition with a comprehensive precision that reminded me of Senator Nunn's exhaustive preparation for a Sunday TV show.

The president announced Carter's nomination on December 5, but the holidays and a medical procedure to fix a bad back delayed his confirmation hearing until February 4. Carter appointed his and my good friend Michael Bayer to lead his transition team. Bayer divided the transition into three phases. Originally, I was brought on just to assist with the confirmation phase, but I ended up participating in all aspects of his transition as a full member of a small team, composed mostly of outsiders hand-picked by Ash. The Pentagon had named their own team, which wanted total control, and this was a source of friction and confusion. But Carter was determined not to be run by the Pentagon, and we were able to show we had significant advantages over them, since much of the work they submitted was subpar.

By early January 2015, I was working out of the Pentagon full time in a nondescript office on the E-ring just down the hall from the secretary's office. Determined to maintain his independence, however, Ash worked out of an office in the Eisenhower Executive Office Building near the White House. He began preparation in earnest on December 26, reading dozens of large binders full of memos and information papers from the Pentagon, think tanks, and academia. He met daily with defense officials and outside experts to get a sense of the issues and challenges he was facing. Meanwhile, our team was at work identifying the top forty-five issues that would come up in the hearing. These ran the gamut from Iraq and Syria to weapons cost overruns to sexual assault. For each, we put together a two-page paper that listed the crux of the problem, key facts, current administration policy, and suggested talking points. We spent the entire month editing and refining these papers in concert with Carter, since he was determined to demonstrate he would be a strong, independent voice, beholden to nothing but his own objective analysis.

On January 7, the second phase began when Carter met with John McCain, the new chairman of the Armed Services Committee. Known as a courtesy call, these meetings were invaluable because they let Carter know what issues each senator prioritized and, moreover, whether he was going to have their support. He met with every senator on armed services and the defense appropriations subcommittee before his hearing. But he also went further and met with any senator who requested a meeting.

On the last Sunday in January, Carter's transition team, representatives from the White House and Pentagon legislative affairs offices, and our murder board guys and gals arrived at the Eisenhower Building for the first of two formal sessions. The second occurred a week later on Super Bowl Sunday. We spent a total of six hours questioning him on every possible issue. He was rusty at first, but it didn't take him long to get his sea legs. In addition to the two formal sessions, Ash requested two informal sessions and another two special focus discussion groups, where we gathered to talk through a couple of the thorniest issues, like Ukraine and Syria.

D-day was February 4. That morning, he arrived at the Russell Senate Office Building for his hearing. Everything he'd done—and we'd helped him do—up to that moment was to ensure that the committee, military personnel and their families, and the American people knew that Ash Carter was prepared to take on one of the most difficult jobs in the world. And he proved it beyond a shadow of a doubt. I used to recommend that people follow the Bob Gates model; now I'll recommend they follow the Ash Carter model.

～

I've spent most of my civilian professional career trying to reform the Pentagon. In recent years, I have focused my efforts on trying to get the department's non-war-fighting costs under control, getting more bang for the buck, as I like to say. Serving on boards and commissions and consulting on the confirmation process could mean a salary or stipend. Every time I've been offered one, I have refused on principle. Jim Van Riper, Senator Nunn, and Jim Jones were all exceptional government and military leaders because they led by example. I took this lesson to heart. And it will come as no surprise to many that it's actually quite difficult, in terms of the paperwork involved, to refuse money from the government. Bureaucracy at its finest!

LESSONS LEARNED

The History Channel dubbed 1969, the year I fought in Vietnam, "The Endless War." As I look back over four decades, from bloody firefights in the Que Son Mountains to policy battles in the nation's capital, one lesson should stand out in stark, flaming letters of scorching white phosphorus. Unless we take decisive action now, the threats and challenges facing today's national leaders, both around the world and here at home, will turn into real "endless wars" for our children and grandchildren.

Perhaps some of the lessons I've learned can help us address the most pressing and consequential crises. These lessons have taken me a lifetime—in combat, politics, and business—to accumulate. Now I will try to pull them together into something constructive.

Reinforcing the values of my childhood, in a way, the Marine Corps taught me to judge an individual not by his or her education, finances, title, or rank, but by his or her moral courage and integrity. Those traits lead to physical courage under pressure and doing the right thing regardless of the consequences.

My time in the Senate was particularly useful. I learned how to deal with differing personalities and situations and how to understand and read people. I learned to analyze relationships, an important skill for working in government, which is rife with expansive egos and clashing agendas.

I've had the great fortune to work alongside fantastic leaders. I could not have come across a finer officer than my Vietnam company commander, then Capt. J. K. Van Riper. He epitomized combat leadership. Later in his career, when he was pressured by seniors in the Corps to sign an unqualified recruit because of political ties, he flat-out refused. When, as commanding general of the 4th Marine Division, I met his son Andy, one of my sergeants, I told him his father was one of the finest military officers with whom I'd ever served.

I worked with Sen. Sam Nunn, a man of impeccable integrity and superb moral character, for twenty-four years. He treated everyone with respect but had a backbone of steel on matters of principle. He challenged presidents of both parties when he thought they were wrong, and he supported them when they were right. Nunn was the intellectual force behind most of the improvements in our defense posture during his career. He knew no one party could solve the nation's problems on its own. He always pushed for a bipartisan approach, a rarity today on either side of the aisle.

One key Republican partner for Nunn was Sen. John Warner. A sailor in World War II and a Marine in Korea, this former secretary of the Navy became one of our nation's most respected national security leaders. Working with many others, he and Nunn produced legislation that saved the volunteer force in the 1970s, decreased the risk of hair-trigger nuclear response, protected the career force during the post–Cold War drawdown, and modernized the military.

When I first came into contact with and then entered the American business world, I found that top executives operated very differently from the public sector. In fact, they were more like military officers in battle. Phebe Novakovic of General Dynamics, Ken Dahlberg of SAIC, and David Joyce of GE Aviation made timely, informed decisions. They wasted no time in endless meetings, debating issues to death, nor did they prize consensus (usually the lowest common denominator). In business, time *is* money, and they had an obligation to employees and share-holders to provide return on investment. Since for-profit companies have extensive reporting requirements, everyone's track record is in the spotlight. When I decided to start my own business, I was armed with knowledge imparted by great mentors and examples.

As I said: today our nation faces threats and challenges both around the world and here at home. At the same time, our resources to solve them are increasingly constrained. But these problems aren't insurmountable. We can ensure a positive future for our nation and our families. We need to protect the freedoms and quality of life previous generations bought for us with blood and sacrifice.

During my time in the Senate, we faced the Cold War and the Soviet invasion of Afghanistan, troubled weapons systems, intransigent leaders and intractable conflicts, global economic recessions, meltdowns, and scandals. There were major victories and some disappointing defeats, but usually responsible compromises. The legislative and executive branches worked together to overcome those challenges and reach solutions that offered each side some of what it wanted.

The thread connecting the positive achievements was a willingness of leaders to attack the toughest issues head-on in a bipartisan fashion, to let the facts and the situation on the ground drive decisions, and ensure that the nation attained its objectives—to benefit all the people in some way—even if that meant political risk for an individual, or even a whole party.

The following are the most important lessons I've learned. If today's leaders could find the courage to apply these, they would be well on their way to solving most of today's legislative gridlock, finger pointing, and failure to act on even the most pressing issues.

1. Lead from the front. The motto at Marine Corps OCS is *"Ductus Exemplo—lead by example,"* and that's exactly what leaders need to do. They must base decisions on objective facts and gather all possible intelligence but then be willing to take real risks. This can only be done from up front. I have zero respect for a man or woman who walks away from his or her obligation to lead. If they don't want to serve our country, why are they cashing the paycheck?

True leadership spells the difference between life and death on the battlefield. In the same vein, the decisions made in Washington will affect the lives of millions, both now and in the future. Yet so many of today's political leaders seem to be more comfortable back in the rear echelon, rather than out on point. They've consistently refused to solve or even honestly grapple with our $18 trillion debt. Continued deficit spending puts our long-term economic health at risk. Our country can't build a strong defense with a crumbling infrastructure, a poorly educated work force, and a weak economy. We've neglected the foundations too long.

2. Take the objective. In combat, tactical objectives are tied to a strategic mission. During the Cold War, we had a clearly identified enemy and an unambiguous mission—to contain and eventually defeat totalitarian communism—that our leaders stuck with through easy times and hard. Eventually, the Berlin Wall fell and the Soviet Union collapsed.

But today, our elected leaders lurch from crisis to crisis without any long-term strategy. Both sides defer tough decisions, but in different ways. One side of the aisle avoids making them by endlessly ratcheting up debt ceilings, celebrating kicking the can down the road to later generations. The other registers meaningless protest votes rather than actually attacking the tough issues. In recent years, due to this mutual incompetence and, yes, lack of backbone, they've failed even to produce a long-term budget! This amazing negligence on both sides has resulted in endless recrimination, shutdowns, the sequester, a damaged image for democracy and our country around the world, and an uncertainty about the future that hampers our military and business leaders, who have to make long-term investment decisions. Our elected leaders have failed to clear the battlefield of the real threats: unsustainable domestic and military entitlements, an outmoded tax code, cracks in the Social Security and Medicare structures, atrophying industrial readiness, and shortfalls in our military and productive capabilities vis-à-vis rising challenges from increasingly dangerous competitors and nonstate actors.

3. Maintain unit cohesion. A military unit draws together people of diverse backgrounds, talents, opinions, and abilities, for a common cause. Despite these differences, it's essential to victory and even survival that they develop mutual respect, understanding, and concern for one another. This is absolutely vital in combat. In a cohesive unit, individuals care more about others than themselves. Unit success also requires bold, decisive action.

The body politic is similarly diverse. But even though its members have different opinions, come from different regions, and belong to different parties, they should respect the opinions of others and demonstrate a willingness to work toward the common good. Yet, as illustrated in recent years when certain members refused to pass an appropriations bill leading to a sixteen-day shutdown, there are some in Congress who would rather pursue their own feuds than compromise. And then they celebrated this as a victory! Members must stop working for their individual interests, or even their party interests, and start working for the national interest. Voters should not re-elect candidates who don't take this advice to heart and act on it.

4. Be willing to take a bullet. In combat, every Marine, soldier, sailor, and airman knows there's a chance he or she might not make it out alive. They accept that risk to protect one another and take the objective. Most of today's leaders in Washington wouldn't rate a footnote in John Kennedy's *Profiles in Courage*. They spend more time ducking tough issues than researching, analyzing, and *solving* them, putting their prestige and clout on the line to advance the nation's interests, the way I witnessed the titans doing. Today's so-called "leaders" are fully aware of the problems that need solving. They just don't seem to have the courage to make the hard choices. Not if it means they may lose votes or campaign contributions. I believe it's because most of today's bureaucrats and elected officials have never faced a *real* battle or had to risk their very lives in a shared effort. In 1981, when we could still compromise, 64 percent of the members Congress were veterans. In 2015, only around 18 percent had served.[1] No one could intimidate, coerce, or suborn Normandy paratroopers like Strom Thurmond, or pilots like Barry Goldwater, or enlisted sailors like John Warner, or infantry riflemen like Dan Inouye, or POWs like John McCain. They'd been tested in the fiery crucibles of World War II, Korea, and Vietnam, and their steel was of a very tough alloy indeed. At the same time, they knew when mutual sacrifice was necessary to achieve a common goal.

Today's leaders, both men and women, need to strap on their helmets and flak jackets, grab their rifles, and charge up Capitol Hill. Some will fall. But all that means for them is a return to life outside government . . . exactly what the Founders had in mind. They never wanted us to have a permanent, professional governing class. They thought they'd gotten rid of that, for good, more than two hundred years ago.

5. Follow your moral compass. In combat, a good compass is necessary to keep you going in the right direction. Many Washington politicians lack convictions, drifting aimlessly in the tides of public opinion. We need politicians of sound moral character who know what they stand for and will steer the nation in the right direction. There is no digital app for this. Character must be achieved through self-reliance and by making the best, most honest choices.

6. Pick the best people and hold them accountable. One of the first lessons we learned at TBS was that as Marine officers we would be responsible for everything our units did or failed to do. The key to success in any organization is having the best people at all levels. Leaders should spend much of their time selecting, mentoring, and assessing the personnel below them. An essential element of this must be holding subordinates accountable for their actions. When business leaders fail, they're quickly replaced (at least in well-functioning companies). When people don't meet standards, they need to be removed. When leaders don't lead, they need to step down or be fired.

7. Leave no one behind. Never abandon your wounded or dead; this is a fundamental principle on the battlefield. While our country should not be an entitlement state, we should never leave those behind who, through no fault of their own, cannot help themselves. President Lincoln said in his second inaugural address that it is our duty "to care for him who shall have borne the battle, and for his widow, and his orphan," and we must hold true to this standard. This applies equally to those who have struggled both in combat *and* here at home.

8. The next vote is the most important. Despite the intensity of the close-in battle, there's always another battle over the next hill. It's the same in politics. There's always going to be another vote, another battle. And the most vociferous opponent during one intense policy debate may turn into a fierce ally in the next. Mutual respect, courtesy, and observance of the rules of the game help ensure the probability of a good working relationship in spite of different opinions. Whether in politics, government, or business, there will always be another important debate, meeting, or decision when an old enemy may become, at least temporarily, an ally. The old cliché of not burning bridges holds true. You can shake hands at the end of the day . . . and be ready for the next battle.

9. Don't take things personally. Closely aligned with the previous lesson, don't take opposition or criticism personally. More likely than not, the disagreement is about the issue, not the individual. It is important not to turn a difference, even a major one, about policy into a personal vendetta. Making an enemy over an issue is a sure recipe for a lifelong grudge, and it is entirely counterproductive in terms of actually solving a problem.

10. Take the long view. Without the benefit of modern-day analytical tools, polls, and digital modeling, our Founding Fathers were able to forge a new nation by thinking far in advance, not just about the near term. True, life moved more slowly back then. James Madison had the leisure to ponder in his library just what a durable constitution might look like. He, Alexander Hamilton, and John Jay could carry on long debates in the newspapers about ratification. The point is they understood it was *far more important* to think about the long-term objectives and consequences of a decision than simply calculate the short-term fallout or that day's rewards. That is why our Declaration of Independence, Constitution, and Bill of Rights have proven so resilient. Today's leaders owe it to future generations to break their myopic focus on the short term and the personal.

These are my takeaways and advice from forty years in the trenches of the military, Senate, and business. They may strike some as naïve or simplistic or impossible to apply in today's polarized and purchased Washington. I'm convinced they're not. We still have men and women inside the Beltway who truly have the public interest at heart. We simply need to search out the best in ourselves and call on the better angels of our nature, and we *will* save this great country of ours once again.

⌒

Over the years I've been asked the same questions over and over about my Vietnam service. "Was it worth it, even though we lost the war?" "What do you tell the families of those who didn't return?" My unhesitating answer is that my Marines did everything their country asked of them and more. They answered the call, whether they were drafted or volunteered. They didn't run for cover or cower when the bullets were flying. It doesn't matter whether what they were doing was popular back home, then or now. Hindsight cannot strip them of that honor. Their contribution was just as meaningful as those of the Minutemen of the Revolutionary War, the doughboys of World War I, the GIs of World War II and Korea, and the servicemen and women of today's War on Terror.

The Corps always requires 110 percent under even the worst conditions. Leading a platoon in combat is a life-changing experience. My Marines endured incredible hardships, demonstrated extraordinary bravery, and conducted themselves with the utmost professionalism when the opposite would have been understandable. We never had enough senior noncoms, a full complement of personnel, or adequate supplies—not even dry socks—but we always accomplished the mission. The most ordinary Marine would perform in the most extraordinary manner under fire. I remain humbled at their example, their perseverance, and their undaunted courage. They brought honor to the Eagle, Globe, and Anchor.

I have the keenest sense of obligation to those who served with me, especially to those who made the ultimate sacrifice and never got to experience the life I enjoy today. Here, lyrics from the musical *Les Miserables* vividly express my feelings: "There is grief that can't be spoken, there's a pain goes on and on." Even though I live close to the remarkable Vietnam Veterans Memorial, I'm always overcome with grief before I can get close enough to read the countless names on that black granite wall.

Every day I ask myself: *What have I done, what can I still do, to make myself worthy of their sacrifice?* I admit, sometimes this brings a fiery intensity to my attitude. One has to be willing to push the envelope sometimes, to tilt at windmills, to try to blast away seemingly immovable obstacles.

Semper fidelis—always faithful. It's not just a slogan; it's a way of life. I recall as a young staffer how the government lied, claiming Agent Orange wasn't harmful to our troops. For years, the DOD refused to help veterans who had serious, often fatal health problems because of their exposure to that chemical. Our senators and I pushed back until the department ultimately admitted its mistake. While that doesn't cure the cancers, it made the government provide care to tens of thousands of those veterans. Another problem that we took far too long to acknowledge was mental health, specifically posttraumatic stress. When our Vietnam vets came back, no one bothered to acknowledge or treat their psychological issues. Many wrote them off as weak, lazy malingerers. Our country failed them, but I'm proud to say our efforts in Congress paid off; this mistake was not repeated after the Gulf War and the Iraq and Afghanistan wars. We fought to make sure today's troops receive the support they deserve. And I personally will keep on pushing the system to fulfill our obligations to those who fought our battles for us.

⁓

It's been hard to sum up where I stand today, because I'm still in many ways on the battlefield and just as much in the thick of the fight as ever.

But as I reflect on my childhood, military service, and Senate and business careers, what comes to mind is Lou Gehrig's farewell speech: "I consider myself the luckiest man on the face of the earth." Nothing could sum up my feelings more perfectly.

My success is anchored in family. Jan and I have been married forty-two years and have been blessed with four terrific children and five wonderful grandchildren, all of whom live within fifteen minutes of our home. Our Italian-Irish family has Sunday dinners that are just as much a barely controlled pandemonium as they were in my youth. Kids running around the house, screaming, crying, and laughing; we love every minute of it. After dinner, they take baths, get into pajamas, and head home, but not without their special treats from Granddaddy. I rarely do grocery runs, except on Sunday mornings to pick up sugary goodies for the grandkids.

Some Sundays I do wish Grandmother Punaro—"Top Sergeant"—was still around to keep order. She taught me no sacrifice is too great for your family. Both my grandparents and parents worked hard, and often went without, so their children could have the opportunities they never would. I've striven to meet this same standard for my own life: my father's nonstop drive for excellence and my mother's burning desire to help those in need. Jan is an example of this as well. She left a promising career to begin another: raising our children and running our household. Today, she's the CEO—chief of everything officer—helping in our business, supporting our children and extended family while continuing her volunteer work. I know full well I wouldn't have been able to succeed without her.

I also have the tremendous joy of working alongside both my sons nearly every day, which is a source of great pride. Joe, a serial entrepreneur, is running his third start-up, along with Dan, also a business expert, as partners in IronArch Technology, named after the University of Georgia icon. Both made the decision (on their own, without any pressure from me) to serve in uniform. Joe was a Marine officer in the Iraq War, and Dan is an Airborne-qualified signal officer in the Army National Guard. Meghan, a math whiz, teacher, and coach, is the athletic director at one of the area's top high schools. Julie, after nine years of teaching, coaching, and working with a major consulting firm, decided to stay home with her two young children. She works with Joe's wife Laura, a registered nurse, who started her own business teaching infant CPR. I feel immense pleasure in all their accomplishments, but, more importantly, in the caliber of individuals they've become and the examples they're setting for their own children.

Personally, I intend to continue the Sisyphean ordeal I've spent most of my adult life engaged in: the seemingly eternal effort to reform the Pentagon. At the moment of writing, I chair the secretary of defense's Reserve Forces Policy Board, serve on his Business Board, lead several industry associations, am a visiting scholar with several think tanks, serve on the board of advisers of several universities, and am active in other ways as a concerned individual citizen. And perhaps my service will not end there. We owe it to our war fighters, and to our fellow taxpayers as well, to address the threats we face as Americans, but to do so in the most economical manner. We should never spend a dollar more than we need to; but we should never spend a dollar less than we ought to. Finding that balance, I think, is within the grasp of a rational consensus, if our leaders will only commit to it.

⌒

In closing, let me point to where I think credit for the enormous triumph of this great country, this unprecedented experiment in self-governance by all the people, really lies.

We stand on the shoulders of those who came before us. We are here today, and have the opportunity to succeed on our own merits in a free country, because of the sacrifices of men like Roy Hammonds.

He put me, his fellow Marine, first. He took the bullets an enemy aimed at me.

Every day I pledge to make myself worthy of his sacrifice and to ensure that all the Corporal Hammondses, of the past, present, and future, do not give up their lives in vain. We, the living, are still here, I firmly believe, not just for ourselves, but to carry forward the banner for those who fell before us. So when that Judgment voice asks, "Did you fail? Did you falter? Did you leave anyone behind?"

We should all stand ready to answer, "No. Not on my watch."

＊

Notes

CHAPTER 1. AMBUSH AT HILL 953

1. Unless otherwise noted, facts and occurrences are from dictated material and interviews with Arnold L. Punaro conducted from January through April 2012, as well as his letters from Vietnam to family and friends.
2. Charles F. Widdecke, quoted in Graham Cosmas and Terrence Murray, *U.S. Marines in Vietnam: Vietnamization and Redeployment* (Washington, DC: History and Museums Division, Headquarters, U.S. Marine Corps, 1986), 218.
3. "Fox Company: NVA Unit Deployment in I Corps," http://www.foxco-2ndbn-9thmarines.com/new_page_8.htm, accessed May 8, 2015.
4. U.S. National Archives and Records Administration, "Marine Corps Command Chronologies for the Vietnam War," http://www.archives.gov/research/military/marine-corps/command-chronology.html, accessed May 8, 2015.
5. The jungle camouflage pattern was commonly referred to as the "lowlands" pattern, with its mid-brown and grass green organic shapes with black branches on a light green background. This was well suited to the lush, triple-canopy jungles of Vietnam.
6. "Robert S. McNamara," *The Vietnam Center and Archive: Robert S. McNamara Resources,* Texas Tech University, http://www.vietnam.ttu.edu/resources/mcnamara/, accessed March 5, 2015.
7. C-rations, shorthand for MCI (meal, combat, individual), was a box that included a can for one meat item, one bread item, one cracker item, and one dessert item. Each box had an accessory pack of cigarettes, toilet paper, and gum. It weighed about two pounds and contained about 1,200 calories. Typical resupply was six meals, which added more than twelve pounds of weight to a grunt's pack. Ham and mothers was the nickname for ham and lima beans, one of the most detested of the twelve different meals.
8. Edward F. Murphy, *Semper Fi, Vietnam: From Da Nang to the DMZ: Marine Corps Campaigns, 1965–1975* (New York: Ballantine Books, 1997), 284.
9. Cosmas and Murray, *U.S. Marines in Vietnam*, 230.
10. "Permanent Exhibit—The Things They Carried," *National Veterans Art Museum*, August 17, 2013, http://www.nvam.org/permanent-exhibit-the-things-they-carried/, accessed May 7, 2015.
11. The thick vegetation made radio communications impossible without the full whip antennae displayed.

12. Grim Reaper Six was the radio call sign of the regimental commanding officer, Col. Gildo Codispoti.

13. This is the first line of the Catholic Act of Contrition.

CHAPTER 2. THE EARLY YEARS

1. Lida Mayo, *The Ordnance Department; On Beachhead and Battlefront* (Washington, DC: U.S. Army Center of Military History, 1991), 262–83.

2. "History," *Mount De Sales Academy*, http://www.mountdesales.net/about_us/history.aspx, accessed March 10, 2015.

3. I joined Omicron Sigma, which was celebrating its fiftieth anniversary as a local fraternity. The friendships I developed with the "brothers on the Hill" have lasted more than fifty years. Our group still gets together at least every five years.

4. After Anthony's military service, he suffered from what we now know as post-traumatic stress. As this was not recognized back then, he did not get proper treatment and committed suicide on Veterans Day, November 11, 1970.

CHAPTER 3. UNITED STATES MARINE CORPS

1. "The Battle for Iwo Jima," *The National WWII Museum*, http://www.national ww2museum.org/focus-on/iwo-jima-fact-sheet.pdf, accessed March 6, 2015.

2. The fact that my recruiter misled me was never far from my mind. When I was a Senate staffer I dealt with military recruiting scandals and was always skeptical of the rosy scenarios the military painted about how well they were doing.

3. U.S. Department of the Navy Marine Corps Order 6100.3E, A03C23-bab, May 10, 1968, Physical Fitness and Weight Control. The minimum and maximums for each event were as follows: sit-ups (35 minimum, 82 maximum in two minutes), dead-hang pull ups (6 minimum, 20 max), squat thrusts (26 min, 40 max), broad jump (6' 8" min, 8' 6" max), and a three-mile run in boots with 19 minutes as a perfect score and 26 minutes as failure.

4. Until well after the Vietnam War, some aviators did not attend TBS. Rather, they took the course via correspondence. Today, every officer must attend the six-month course.

5. Charles A. Fleming, Robin Austin, and Charles Braley, *Quantico: Crossroads of the Marine Corps* (Washington, DC: U.S. Marine Corps, History and Museums Division, 1978), 94.

6. Kathleen Johnson, "Summer of Love and Woodstock," *The Cold War Museum*, http://www.coldwar.org/articles/60s/summeroflove.asp, accessed March 6, 2015.

CHAPTER 4. ARRIVAL IN VIETNAM

1. Richard Nixon, "Address Accepting the Presidential Nomination at the Republican National Convention in Miami Beach, Florida," August 8, 1968, online by Gerhard Peters and John T. Woolley, *The American Presidency Project*, http://www.presidency.ucsb.edu/ws/?pid=25968, accessed March 4, 2015.
2. Tim Kane, "Global U.S. Troop Deployment, 1950–2003," *The Heritage Foundation*, October 27, 2004, http://www.heritage.org/research/reports/2004/10/global-us-troop-deployment-1950-2003, accessed March 4, 2015.
3. U.S. National Archives and Records Administration, "Statistical Information about Casualties of the Vietnam War," http://www.archives.gov/research/military/vietnam-war/casualty-statistics.html#date; "Marine Vietnam Casualties," accessed March 4, 2015; http://www.marzone.com/7thMarines/usmc_cas_stats.pdf, accessed March 4, 2015; Bonnie Heater, "Vietnam: You Just Survived," November 30, 2010, http://www.army.mil/article/48776/Vietnam_You_just_survived/, accessed March 4, 2015.
4. "Marine Vietnam Casualties"; "In the Belly of the Dragon: Life and Death in I Corps," *Wisconsin Veterans Museum*, http://www.wisvetsmuseum.com/exhibitions/online/belly_of_dragon/, accessed March 10, 2015.
5. All facts on weapons were verified using *Jane's Infantry Weapons 1991–92*. Ian V. Hogg, *Jane's Infantry Weapons, 1991–92* (Coulsdon, UK: Jane's Information Group, 1991). Additional checks were made with infantry weapons experts who served in Vietnam.
6. According to the MGRS, coordinates on a map are divided into three sections: grid zone designators, grid squares, and location coordinates. Grid zone designators are overlaid on a Mercator projection map and run A–Z latitudinal and 1–60 longitudinal. In central Vietnam, we were in grid zone 49P. Each grid zone designator is roughly six degrees wide and eight degrees tall. The next section of a map coordinate is the 100,000-meter-square identifier. Each grid zone designator is subdivided into 100,000-meter squares labeled A–Z by column and A–Z by row, thus the BT identifier in the text. The final section is the numerical location within a 100,000-meter square. This is read in an n + n format and these can range from two to ten digits. Each successive digit gives greater precision.
7. Years later as a Senate staffer I would learn that war-fighting gear for individuals, including boots, were the product of nameless, faceless bureaucrats at

Natick Labs in Massachusetts. They clearly had no clue about designing and producing a serviceable boot for Vietnam, and during my twenty-four years in the Senate the Army (the lead agency for Natick and boots) would screw up at least a dozen more variants. With aircraft, the Pentagon usually followed a "fly before you buy" model. They should have "worn before they bought" the boots and they might have had more success.

CHAPTER 5. FREE FIRE ZONE

1. Keith Nightingale, "Why Hollywood Can't Do It," *Small Wars Journal,* February 28, 2015, smallwarsjournal.com/blog/why-hollywood-can't-do-it, accessed November 11, 2015.
2. Years later, I was talking with Van Riper about one of the fitness reports he wrote on me. I had received high marks in all areas except one: gear discipline. Van Riper told me he gave me low marks because I lost too many e-tools. He said that even though gear lost during contact with the enemy was understandable, the Marine Corps's reputation for thriftiness knew no bounds.
3. Edward F. Murphy, *Semper Fi—Vietnam: From Da Nang to the DMZ: Marine Corps Campaigns, 1965–1975* (New York: Ballantine Books, 1997), 33.
4. Eric Hammel, "Que Son Valley," in *Vets With A Mission*, 1994, http://www .vwam.com/vets/queson.html, accessed March 5, 2015.
5. Murphy, *Semper Fi*, 33.
6. U.S. Air Force, Air Force Global Strike Command, "ARC LIGHT Marked Beginning of B-52 Involvement in Vietnam," December 4, 2012, http://www .afgsc.af.mil/news/story.asp?id=123328478, accessed March 10, 2015; Byron Simmons, "Battleship USS New Jersey," 1998, http://www.vspa.com/crb-simmons-new-jersey-dreadnought-1968.htm, accessed March 5, 2015.
7. Ronald B. Frankum, *Historical Dictionary of the War in Vietnam* (Lanham, Md.: Scarecrow Press, 2011).
8. Back at Quantico, I was put in High Intensity Language Training–Vietnamese. While my courses in Latin and German must have helped on the test, Vietnamese is a tonal language. The same word can mean six different things depending on how it's pronounced. The test didn't factor in my southern accent, which did not mix at all well with the Vietnamese tones. "Where is the church?" became, in my Georgian-flavored Vietnamese, "Where is the whore house?" At least I amused the instructors. They liked it that I tried, but they concluded early on that I was never going to be a coherent Vietnamese speaker.
9. U.S. Department of Defense, "Armed Forces Day," http://www.defense.gov/ afd/marinecorps.aspx, accessed March 5, 2015.

10. The government sprayed Agent Orange all over Vietnamese jungles as a defoliant. It was an extremely powerful and toxic chemical to which Marines and soldiers were exposed, as well as civilians and the enemy. For years after the war, despite medical evidence to the contrary, the government argued that Agent Orange was not harmful to humans. Years later the government admitted it caused serious health issues, like cancer, heart disease, diabetes, and death. In recent years, I have attended too many funerals of Marines who succumbed to Agent Orange diseases.

CHAPTER 6. HOSPITAL

1. "Medical Units Where Women Served During the Vietnam War," *Illyria*, June 22, 2006, http://www.illyria.com/evacs.html#1st, accessed March 5, 2015.
2. U.S. Marine Corps, History Division, "General Leonard Fielding Chapman, Jr., USMC (Deceased)," http://www.mcu.usmc.mil/historydivision/Pages/ Who's Who/A-C/Chapman_LF.aspx, accessed March 5, 2015.
3. John 15:13, KJV.
4. Actually, we used Eric's dad's connection with General Barrow to get orders to Quantico. Col. Hal Chase had served with Bob Barrow in World War II and as a Reservist on active duty in Vietnam. He would be promoted to major general in the Reserves and serve in the Carter administration as deputy assistant secretary of defense for Reserve affairs. I later worked with him when I was a Senate staffer.

CHAPTER 7. BACK IN THE REAL WORLD

1. U.S. Marine Corps, "Marine Corps Base Quantico," http://www.quantico .marines.mil/, accessed March 16, 2015.
2. U.S. Marine Corps, History Division, "Lieutenant General Lewis 'Chesty' B. Puller, USMC (Deceased)," http://www.mcu.usmc.mil/historydivision/ Pages/Who's Who/P-R/puller_lb.aspx, accessed March 31, 2015.
3. U.S. Marine Corps, "The Basic School," http://www.trngcmd.marines.mil/ Units/Northeast/TheBasicSchool.aspx, accessed March 31, 2015.
4. With Senator Nunn in the late 1970s, we would reform this law that governed officers' careers called the Defense Officers Personnel Management Act (DOPMA). Now, forty years later, it needs fundamental reforms again.
5. U.S. Navy, Naval History and Heritage Command, "Louis H. Wilson," http:// www.history.navy.mil/our-collections/photography/us-people/w/wilson-louis-h.html, accessed March 31, 2015. He would go on to be commandant

and I would meet him again, later, too, when he worked with Senators Nunn and Stennis on the Corps's size and quality.

6. I later named one of my companies IronArch Technology after the famed UGA Arch.

CHAPTER 8. THE ORDER OF BATTLE

1. I would later secure a permanent spot in her family's good graces by procuring several of these tablecloths for Jan and her sisters on my future trips to Hong Kong.

2. Unlike my college classmate Dr. Tom Myers, who served his time in uniform. After medical school, Dr. Myers, a superb doctor, served for two years at Fort Bragg, going in as an Army captain. When I visited him there, it was clear that the Army provided no training on military appearance as he wore his captain's bars on only one collar as opposed to the two required.

3. A rare exception is the budget for personal staff, which is based instead on the population of the state a senator represents.

4. Herman Wouk, *The Caine Mutiny: A Novel* (Garden City, NY: Doubleday, 1951, rprt., Boston: Back Bay Books, 1992), 105.

5. Nadine Cohodas, *Strom Thurmond & the Politics of Southern Change* (Macon, GA: Mercer University Press, 1994); Joseph Crespino, *Strom Thurmond's America* (New York: Hill and Wang, 2012).

CHAPTER 9. THE WASHINGTON BATTLEFIELD

1. In 2009, it was renamed the Kennedy Caucus Room in honor of the three Kennedy brothers and their legacies as senators. Both John and Robert Kennedy (along with several other senators) announced their presidential candidacies from the Caucus Room.

2. Unless otherwise noted, facts and occurrences in the following chapters are from Senator Nunn's private oral histories, which covered all the major issues and activities during Senator Nunn's twenty-four years in the Senate. "Oral History: Senator Sam Nunn," tape transcript, Washington, DC, 1996.

3. We used this same model for his three seminal reports on NATO: *Policy, Troops and the NATO Alliance, NATO and the New Soviet Threat,* and *NATO: Can the Alliance Be Saved?* These reports highlighted the problems with NATO, such as its conventional inferiority to the Warsaw Pact and that member nations weren't spending the mandatory 3 percent of their GDP on defense.

4. Sam Nunn, *Vietnam Aid—The Painful Options*, report prepared for Senate Armed Services Committee, 94th Cong., 2d sess., 1975, S202-2, 20.

5. John Jorgenson, "Duty, Honor, Country and Too Many Lawyers," *American Bar Association Journal*, April 1977 (63 ABAJ 564-S67).

6. Even aside from this scandal, the two of them had their hands full; that was the first year women were admitted into this previously all-male institution. The year 1976 marked a low in West Point's history, though at the same time it was graduating a striking number of recent top officers. Army Chief of Staff Gen. Ray Odierno, Gen. Stanley McChrystal, and Lt. Gen. Dave Barno were all in the class of '76, to name a few. Of the 855 graduates, an unprecedented 33 are now active or retired generals. None of them were involved in the cheating.

7. Yochi Dreazen, "A Class of Generals," *Wall Street Journal*, July 25, 2009, http://www.wsj.com/articles/SB10001424052970204886304574308221927291 030, accessed April 2, 2015.

8. David Stout, "Andrew J. Goodpaster, 90, Soldier and Scholar, Dies," *New York Times,* May 17, 2005, http://www.nytimes.com/2005/05/17/national/17good-paster.html?_r=0, accessed April 2, 2015.

9. While Senator Nunn did not support Warnke for either job, Nunn became the chief advocate for Carter's nomination of Bert Lance for director of the Office of Management and Budget. Lance was a banker from Calhoun, Georgia, and had been state highway director when Carter was governor. He was dogged by allegations of mismanagement of bank funds, obtaining loans at favorable rates, and using a company plane to fly to UGA football games. Nunn defended him during the confirmation process and also when the committee went after him a year after he became director. Years later, Lance was found not guilty on all charges but was barred from the banking industry. I did not do staff work for Senator Nunn on this issue, but he was never one to make snap judgments based on press reports or speculation.

10. U.S. Department of State, *Treaty Between the United States of America and the Union of Soviet Socialist Republics on the Limitation of Strategic Offensive Arms* (Washington, DC: Department of State, 1979).

11. Richard Burt, "Senate Panel Votes Antitreaty Report," *New York Times*, May 4, 1979; Richard Burt, "Limited Ceiling: Treaties That Slow the Arms Race Usually Speed It Up," *New York Times*, December 24, 1978; U.S. Department of State, Office of the Historian, "'Buried in the Sands of the Ogaden': The Horn of Africa and SALT II, 1977–1979," October 31, 2013, https://history .state.gov/milestones/1977-1980/horn-of-africa, accessed March 26, 2015.

12. I was taking a real chance by calling Thurman, but the seeds had been sown by the Army's chief Senate liaison, Col. John Campbell. Campbell and I

had developed a good working relationship, especially after Nunn and I took on Army leaders like Alexander on some of those untouchable issues that professionals like Campbell really appreciated. He said Max Thurman was the best and would get us what we needed. I would work with General Thurman throughout his career as head of Army recruiting, commander of the U.S. Southern Command, and vice chief of staff of the Army.

13. Frank Jones, A "Hollow Army" Reappraised: President Carter, Defense Budgets, and the Politics of Military Readiness (Carlisle Barracks, PA: U.S. Army War College, Strategic Studies Institute, 2012), http://www.strategicstudies institute.army.mil/pdffiles/PUB1125.pdf.

14. John Finney, "Rickover, Father of Nuclear Navy, Dies at 86," New York Times, July 8, 1986, http://www.nytimes.com/1986/07/09/obituaries/rickover-father-of-nuclear-navy-dies-at-86.html, accessed April 3, 2015.

15. Sam Nunn, "Nunn Proposes Reductions in Generals, Admirals," press release, March 22, 1977.

16. We revisited this at the end of the Cold War when the active-duty forces were reduced from 2.4 million to 1.4 million but the number of admirals and generals remained the same. I directed our Manpower Subcommittee lead Fred Pang to make cuts commensurate with the drawdown. Fred asked me how many we should cut. I replied, "The Pentagon will fight this to the death so let's cut 25 percent over five years and maybe we'll get 5 percent." To our surprise, Gen. Colin Powell, chairman of the Joint Chiefs of Staff, agreed to the cuts, except for the Marines. General Mundy, the commandant of the Marine Corps, came to see Senator Nunn to make the case that the USMC had far fewer generals per thousand Marines than any other service. Senator Nunn agreed and told General Mundy, "Don't make any cuts, keep quiet and we'll fix it down the road." Five years later we put a "technical correction" in the bill that eliminated the reduction requirement for the USMC.

17. Nor had he lived in Panama for the required seventeen years to even become a citizen.

18. The Neutrality Treaty was ratified on March 16, 1978, and the Panama Canal Treaty was ratified on April 18, 1978, both by a 68–32 margin. The implementation legislation was signed by President Carter on September 27, 1978.

19. "Panama Canal Treaties: Major Carter Victory," CQ Almanac 1978, 34th ed. (Washington, DC: Congressional Quarterly, 1979), 379–97, http://library .cqpress.com/cqalmanac/cqal78–1238869.

20. Mark Bowden, "The Desert One Debacle," The Atlantic, May 2006, http://www.theatlantic.com/magazine/archive/2006/05/the-desert-one-debacle/304803/, accessed November 5, 2015.

21. RAND Corporation, "Research Brief: Evolution of the All-Volunteer Force," 2006, http://www.rand.org/pubs/research_briefs/RB9195/index1.html, accessed April 3, 2015.

22. Jones, *A "Hollow Army" Reappraised.*

23. Bernard Rostker, "I Want You: The Evolution of the All-Volunteer Force," *RAND Corporation*, 2006, http://www.rand.org/content/dam/rand/pubs/monographs/2007/RAND_MG265.pdf, accessed April 3, 2015.

24. White and Danzig would later serve with distinction as deputy secretary of defense and secretary of the Navy, respectively, and today remain highly respected and influential in national security matters.

25. Edward F. Bruner, *Military Forces: What Is the Appropriate Size for the United States?*, U.S. Library of Congress, Congressional Research Service, RS21754 (2005).

26. U.S. Department of Defense, Reserve Forces Policy Board, *Eliminating Major Gaps in DoD Data on the Fully-Burdened and Life-Cycle Cost of Military Personnel: Cost Elements Should be Mandated by Policy* (Washington, DC, 2013), http://www.ngaus.org/sites/default/files/RFPB_Cost_Methodology_Final_Report_7Jan13.pdf, accessed April 27, 2015.

27. U.S. Marine Corps, "Making Marines: Part I: Recruiting, Core Values, and the Perpetuation of Our Ethos, January 1973–May 2014," https://www.mca-marines.org/sites/default/files/BowersAllVolunteer1wmissinggraph.pdf, accessed May 11, 2015.

28. Stanley Karnow, "East Asia in 1978: The Great Transformation," *Foreign Affairs*, http://www.foreignaffairs.com/articles/31968/stanley-karnow/east-asia-in-1978-the-great-transformation, accessed April 21, 2015.

29. "War & Cambodia," *PBS*, http://www.pbs.org/independentlens/refugee/war_cambodia.html, accessed November 5, 2015.

30. Michael Peel, "Thailand Stifles Memories of Past Conflicts," *Financial Times*, October 3, 2014, http://www.ft.com/cms/s/0/8df58de2–4ac7–11e4–839a-00144feab7de.html#axzz3YXM3GcYz, accessed April 27, 2015.

31. President Carter may not have been one of our strongest presidents, but there is a general agreement that he is one of our best former presidents, based on his incredible record of accomplishments since 1980. He and Senator Nunn have worked together on many important projects since, such as the time they helped prevent an invasion of Haiti in the 1990s. Both Senator Nunn and I hold him in the highest regard.

CHAPTER 10. IN THE BELLY OF THE BEAST

1. Leslie Gelb, "Reagan May Turn to MX Missile Plan Based on Carter's," *New York Times*, August 22, 1981, http://www.nytimes.com/1981/08/23/us/reagan-may-turn-to-mx-missile-plan-based-on-carter-s.html, accessed April 24, 2015.

2. Richard Halloran, "Reagan Proposes 'Dense Pack' of 100 MX Missiles in Wyoming; Seeks Arms Pacts with Soviet," *New York Times*, November 22, 1982, http://www.nytimes.com/1982/11/23/world/reagan-proposes-dense-pack-100-mx-missiles-wyoming-seeks-arms-pacts-with-soviet-051579.html, accessed April 24, 2015.

3. At the time, there were five members of the Joint Staff: the four service chiefs and the chairman. Today, there are seven: the four service chiefs and the chairman, plus the vice chairman and the chief of the National Guard Bureau.

4. A good example of this SASC requirement occurred when Adm. Frank Kelso was appearing before Chairman Nunn to be chief of naval operations. Senator Nunn asked, "Will you give your personal views when asked, even if they differ from the administration in power?" Admiral Kelso hesitated and finally said, "I would have to check with the secretary of defense." Nunn snapped back, "Admiral Kelso, the answer is either yes or no and you can pick either. I will say that if your answer is no, you will not be confirmed." Admiral Kelso immediately replied, "Yes."

5. Amy Woolf, *U.S. Strategic Nuclear Forces: Background, Developments, and Issues*, RL33640 (U.S. Library of Congress, Congressional Research Service, 2015), https://fas.org/sgp/crs/nuke/RL33640.pdf.

6. U.S. Department of State, *Treaty Between the United States of America and the Union of Soviet Socialist Republics on the Elimination of Their Intermediate-Range and Shorter-Range Missiles* (Washington, DC: Department of State, 1987).

7. Peter Tarpgard, *Building a 600-Ship Navy: Costs, Timing, and Alternative Approaches* (Washington, DC: Congressional Budget Office, 1982), 146.

8. "Defense Bill Cuts 7 Percent, Removing Funding for the MX Missile Program," *CQ Almanac 1982*, 38th ed. (Washington, DC: *Congressional Quarterly*, 1983), 277–92, http://library.cqpress.com/cqalmanac/cqal82–1164292.

9. U.S. National Archives and Records Administration, "The Senate Committee on Armed Services, 1947–1996," http://www.archives.gov/legislative/finding-aids/reference/senate/armed-services/, accessed May 15, 2015.

10. Jackson's death was a shock to the Senate and the committee. He and Nunn had had a close relationship, working together on a number of key pieces of legislation, including the 1973 Jackson-Nunn amendment, which required a

proportional U.S. troop withdrawal from NATO if our allies did not offset some of the costs of keeping them in Europe.

11. "Senate Supports Reagan on AWACS Sale," *CQ Almanac 1981*, 37th ed. (Washington, DC: *Congressional Quarterly*, 1982), 129–40, http://library .cqpress.com/cqalmanac/cqal81-1171966.

12. "C-5 Galaxy: Heavy Lifting," Lockheed Martin, http://www.lockheed martin.com/us/100years/stories/c5.html, accessed October 26, 2015.

13. "Strategic Arms Top List of Defense Cuts," *CQ Almanac 1982*, 38th ed. (Washington, DC: *Congressional Quarterly*, 1983), 77–101, http://library.cqpress .com/cqalmanac/cqal82-1163645.

14. U.S. Department of State, Office of the Historian, "China Policy," October 31, 2013, https://history.state.gov/milestones/1977–1980/china-policy, accessed May 14, 2015.

15. Robert McFarlane, interview by PBS Frontline, *PBS*, http://www.pbs.org/wgbh/ pages/frontline/shows/target/interviews/mcfarlane.html, accessed April 24, 2015.

16. Robert Oakley, interview by PBS Frontline, *PBS*, http://www.pbs.org/wgbh/ pages/frontline/shows/target/interviews/oakley.html, accessed April 24, 2015.

17. Nunn moved from Russell to Dirksen for more space and for a Capitol view as he gained seniority.

18. These views were outlined in three reports published by the Government Printing Office titled *Policy, Troops and the NATO Alliance* (April 1974), *NATO and the New Soviet Threat* (January 1977), and *NATO—Can the Alliance Be Saved?* (May 1982).

CHAPTER 11. THE BATTLE CONTINUES

1. A full, definitive account of the passage of the Goldwater-Nichols Act, from the painstaking analysis of the problems to the development of solutions to the passage of the legislation to the enactment and subsequent implementation, is found in James R. Locher, *Victory on the Potomac: The Goldwater-Nichols Act Unifies the Pentagon* (College Station: Texas A&M University Press, 2002). Locher was the principal staffer for the SASC for Goldwater and Nunn during this period.

2. "Major Pentagon Reorganization Bill Approved," *CQ Almanac 1986*, 42nd ed. (Washington, DC: *Congressional Quarterly*, 1987), 455–59, http://library .cqpress.com/cqalmanac/cqal86-1149236.

3. Locher, *Victory on the Potomac*, 524.

4. Jack Smith, "$37 Screws, a $7,622 Coffee Maker, $640 Toilet Seats; Suppliers to Our Military Just Won't Be Oversold," *Los Angeles Times,* July 30, 1986,

http://articles.latimes.com/1986–07–30/news/vw-18804_1_nut, accessed June 4, 2015.

5. David Packard et al., *A Quest for Excellence: Final Report to the President* (Washington, DC: President's Blue Ribbon Commission on Defense Management, 1986).

6. David Christensen, David Searle, and Caisse Vickery, "The Impact of the Packard Commission's Recommendations on Reducing Cost Overruns on Defense Acquisition Contracts," *Acquisition Review Quarterly* (Summer 1999): 251–62, http://www.dau.mil/AckerLibrary/AckerLibraryDocs/searle.pdf.

7. "Reagan Vetoes Defense Bill, Protests Return to 'Weakness': Says He's Losing Patience with Military Erosion," *Los Angeles Times*, August 3, 1988, http://articles.latimes.com/1988–08–03/news/mn-6858_1_defense-veto, accessed October 12, 2015.

8. Mehtab Ali Shah, *The Foreign Policy of Pakistan: Ethnic Impacts on Diplomacy, 1971–1994* (London: I. B. Tauris, 1997), 30.

9. U.S. Department of State, Office of the Historian, "U.S.-Soviet Relations, 1981–1991," October 31, 2013, https://history.state.gov/milestones/1981–1988/u.s.-soviet-relations, accessed May 22, 2015.

10. Things like this were normally considered deception operations and were tightly controlled by the CIA, but this was entirely of our own doing.

11. We were so impressed with Dick Combs that when he retired from the State Department, I hired him on to the Armed Services Committee staff and he was an integral part of passing the Nunn-Lugar amendment to dismantle nuclear weapons in Ukraine, Belarus, and Kazakhstan after the dissolution of the Soviet Union, the groundwork for the Cooperative Threat Reduction Program. Senator Nunn and Sen. Richard Lugar, a Republican from Indiana, created the program in 1991, and since then it has successfully deactivated more than 7,600 nuclear warheads, destroyed more than 2,300 missiles and 33 nuclear-capable submarines, and secured 24 nuclear weapons storage sites.

12. "Special Report: The Iran-Contra Affair." *CQ Almanac 1986*, 42nd ed. (Washington, DC: *Congressional Quarterly*, 1987), 415–47, http://library.cqpress.com/cqalmanac/cqal86-1149164.

13. On a personal basis, it was easy to like Ollie North. When Ollie visited the troops in the early stages of the 2003 Iraq War, he came across my son Joe, then a Marine platoon commander, and Ollie's personal visit with Joe and his men was a highlight. I am a fan of his History Channel show, *War Stories with Oliver North*.

14. Thomas Ricks, "Annals of Wars We Don't Know About: The South African Border War of 1966–1989," *Foreign Policy*, March 12, 2015, http://foreignpolicy .com/2015/03/12/annals-of-wars-we-dont-know-about-the-south-african-border-war-of-1966-1989, accessed June 18, 2015.

15. "Hill Overrides Veto of South Africa Sanctions," *CQ Almanac 1986*, 42nd ed. (Washington, DC: *Congressional Quarterly*, 1987), 259–373, http://library .cqpress.com/cqalmanac/cqal86–1149011.

16. "South Africa Sanctions Bill Stalled," *CQ Almanac 1988*, 44th ed. (Washington, DC: *Congressional Quarterly*, 1989), 525–38, http://library.cqpress.com/ cqalmanac/cqal88–1142457.

17. Howard French, "Anatomy of an Autocracy: Mobutu's 32-Year Reign," *New York Times*, May 17, 1997, http://partners.nytimes.com/library/world/ africa/051797zaire-mobutu.html, accessed June 18, 2015.

CHAPTER 12. BATTLES LOST AND WON

1. U.S. Air Force, Air Force Space Command, "Factsheets: Milstar Satellite Communications System," March 25, 2015, http://www.afspc.af.mil/library/ factsheets/factsheet.asp?id=4857, accessed June 18, 2015.

2. R. Jeffrey Smith, "$40 Billion Satellite Project Symbolizes Hill Split Over Defense Needs," *Washington Post*, August 2, 1990, http://www. washingtonpost.com/archive/politics/1990/08/02/40-billion-satellite-project-symbolizes-hill-split-over-defense-needs/8dffe361-d0a1–4489-b030–3224960b5ecd/, accessed June 19, 2015.

3. Federation of American Scientists, "BB-61 IOWA-class," October 21, 2000, http://fas.org/man/dod-101/sys/ship/bb-61.htm, accessed August 18, 2015.

4. Bernard Trainor, "Explosion and Fire Kill at Least 47 on Navy Warship," *New York Times*, April 19, 1989, http://www.nytimes.com/1989/04/20/us/ explosion-and-fire-kill-at-least-47-on-navy-warship.html, accessed August 5, 2015.

5. The name was changed to the NCIS, Naval Criminal Investigative Service, in 1992.

6. Bernard Trainor, "Iowa Blast Inquiry Turns to Possibility of Foul Play," *New York Times*, May 24, 1989, http://www.nytimes.com/1989/05/25/us/iowa-blast-inquiry-turns-to-possibility-of-foul-play.html, accessed August 5, 2015.

7. U.S. General Accounting Office, *Issues Arising from the Explosion aboard the USS Iowa*, NSIAD-91-4 (Washington, DC: GAO, 1991).

8. U.S. Department of State, Office of the Historian, "The Gulf War, 1991," October 31, 2013, https://history.state.gov/milestones/1989–1992/gulf-war, accessed September 22, 2015.

9. Stephen Walt, "WikiLeaks, April Glaspie, and Saddam Hussein," *Foreign Policy*, January 9, 2011, http://foreignpolicy.com/2011/01/09/wikileaks-april-glaspie-and-saddam-hussein/, accessed September 22, 2015.

10. U.S. Congress, Senate Armed Services Committee, *Crisis in the Persian Gulf Region: U.S. Policy Options and Implication*, 101st Cong., 2d sess., 1990, S. HRG. 101-1071.

11. My relationship with General Gray went all the way back to when I was a captain and first met him on a training exercise in Norway when I was on his staff and he was the One Star Expeditionary Force commander. He developed a close working relationship with the SASC as the head of the research command at Quantico when he pioneered the light armored vehicle that the SASC added into the budget over the objection of the Pentagon and even some in the USMC. When he became commandant, his senior military aide was then Col. Jim Jones, and we worked closely with both of them.

12. "Gulf Crisis Grows into War with Iraq," *CQ Almanac 1990*, 46th ed. (Washington, DC: *Congressional Quarterly*, 1991), 717–56, http://library.cqpress.com/cqalmanac/cqal90-1118567.

13. Nolan Walters, "Nunn Looks Back on the Persian Gulf War—and Forward to Life in the Private Sector," *Macon Telegraph*, December 30, 1996.

14. U.S. Department of State, "The Gulf War, 1991."

15. "Tailhook: Scandal Time," *Newsweek*, July 5, 1992, http://www.newsweek.com/tailhook-scandal-time-200362, accessed August 6, 2015.

16. Rowan Scarborough, "Tailhook 'Injustice' Righted," *Washington Times*, July 31, 2002, http://www.northofseveycorners.com/write/thook.htm, accessed August 18, 2015.

17. Protect Our Defenders, "Military Sexual Assault Fact Sheet," 2014, http://www.protectourdefenders.com/factsheet/, accessed August 24, 2015.

18. John Cushman, "Adm. Frank B. Kelso Dies at 79; Tied to Tailhook Scandal," *New York Times*, June 28, 2013, http://www.nytimes.com/2013/06/29/us/adm-frank-b-kelso-dies-at-79-tied-to-tailhook-scandal.html, accessed August 6, 2015.

19. "Congress Challenges, Confirms Clinton's Military Promotions," *CQ Almanac 1994*, 50th ed. (Washington, DC: *Congressional Quarterly*, 1995), 439–41, http://library.cqpress.com/cqalmanac/cqal94-1103890.

20. Former commandant of the Marine Corps Al Gray had impressed me on an operation in Norway, when Gray was the only one who didn't wear cold-weather garb.

21. Philip Shenon, "Admiral, in Suicide Note, Apologized to 'My Sailors'" *New York Times*, May 17, 1996, http://www.nytimes.com/1996/05/18/us/admiral-

in-suicide-note-apologized-to-my-sailors.html?pagewanted=1, accessed August 6, 2015.

22. Thirty years after Goldwater-Nichols, I recommend we go back to the four-year tour to preserve the independent professional military advice the act originally aimed to produce.

23. "Women in the Civil War," *History.com,* 2010, http://www.history.com/topics/american-civil-war/women-in-the-civil-war, accessed August 27, 2015; "A Brief History of Women in Combat," *NPR,* January 25, 2013, http://www.npr.org/sections/pictureshow/2013/01/25/170177873/a-brief-history-of-women-in-combat, accessed August 5, 2015.

24. De Anne Blanton and Lauren Cook, *They Fought Like Demons: Women Soldiers in the Civil War* (New York: Vintage Books, 2002), 7.

25. "Way Is Cleared for Women to Fly Combat Missions," *CQ Almanac 1991,* 47th ed. (Washington, DC: *Congressional Quarterly,* 1992), 414, http://library.cqpress.com/cqalmanac/cqal91–1110981.

26. "Combat Roles for Women a Step Closer," *CQ Almanac 1993,* 49th ed. (Washington, DC: *Congressional Quarterly,* 1994), 463–64, http://library.cqpress.com/cqalmanac/cqal93–1106255.

27. U.S. Naval Institute, "Key Dates in US Policy on Gay Men and Women in Military Service," http://www.usni.org/news-and-features/dont-ask-dont-tell/timeline, accessed August 5, 2015.

28. Pamela Harriman, the doyenne of Democratic fundraisers for Clinton, used her Georgetown home for gathering powerful people. She would later serve as Clinton's ambassador to France.

CHAPTER 13. THE CORPORATIONS

1. It would soon become the Defense Threat Reduction Agency, based on a recommendation from the Defense Reform Task Force, which I chaired for Secretary of Defense Bill Cohen.

2. Years later, I would be involved in another IPO for a cybersecurity company called SourceFire as a member of its board. We ultimately sold the company to Cisco for $2.7 billion.

3. When I was staff director, this was one of those special access classified programs that only a handful of people worked on. Because of this, it hadn't received much oversight or scrutiny from the committee. Both Presidents Reagan and Bush emphasized the importance of this program, especially Bush when he was Reagan's vice president. The only reason it came up on my radar is because I was alerted by a "closet patriot" to misbehavior by a senior Army general, who was cooking the books on some of the contracts.

The more I looked into the program, the more wrongdoing I found. When I brought this up with Nunn, he was willing to make significant cuts but was unaware of the support for it in the White House. We were summoned to a meeting at the White House with Vice President Dan Quayle and the leaders of the House Armed Services Committee and the House and Senate Defense Appropriations Subcommittees. But, ultimately, Nunn was successful in convincing his congressional colleagues that the program needed oversight and significant cuts.

4. When the company split in 2013 into SAIC and Leidos, Leidos retained the intelligence functions of the original company. At that point, I'd already left SAIC, but I was asked to chair the Special Projects Committee for Leidos, and I still do to this day. The SPC reviews highly sensitive activities that Leidos supports for government customers.

CHAPTER 14. CITIZEN MARINE

1. Andy Effron was the best Title 10 lawyer I'd worked with. He went on to be the Chief Judge of the Court of Appeals for the Armed Forces and after retirement led a review for the Pentagon of the Uniform Code of Military Justice. When teamed with the minority counsel Pat Tucker—an expert on Senate procedures and Title 10—our committee was unbeatable.

2. Lawrence Kapp and Barbara Salazar Torreon, *Reserve Component Personnel Issues: Questions and Answers*, RL30802 (U.S. Library of Congress, Congressional Research Service, 2014).

CHAPTER 15. THE OUTSIDE INFLUENCERS

1. These institutions have some of the leading thinkers on complex policy issues, like Michèle Flournoy at CNAS, John Hamre at CSIS, Mackenzie Eaglen and Thomas Donnelly at AEI, and Rudy deLeon at CAP.

2. Gary Hart et al., *Road Map for National Security: Imperative for Change, Phase III Report* (Washington, DC: The United States Commission on National Security/21st Century, 2001), http://govinfo.library.unt.edu/nssg/PhaseIIIFR .pdf.

3. Another outside group I belong to meets every other Wednesday to discuss national security matters. We call ourselves the "Green Frogs." We all used to be high-level government or military officials, so our motto is "We used to be princes, now we're frogs."

4. Arnold Punaro et al., *Transforming the National Guard and Reserves into a 21st-Century Operational Force* (Washington, DC: U.S. Department of

Defense, Commission on the National Guard and Reserves, 2008), https://www.loc.gov/rr/frd/pdf-files/CNGR_final-report.pdf.

5. Senator Warner, speaking on the Commission on the National Guard and Reserve, 110th Cong., 2d sess., *Congressional Record* 154, No. 70 (April 30, 2008): S 3589.

6. An oversight hearing is typically one in which a congressional committee calls witnesses from the executive branch to receive updates about ongoing military operations or plans.

7. Arnold Punaro, personal letter to Senator Chuck Hagel, January 12, 2013.

8. U.S. Department of Defense, Defense Business Board, *Linking and Streamlining the Defense Requirements, Acquisition, and Budget Processes* (Washington, DC: DOD Defense Business Board, 2012), http://dbb.defense.gov/Portals/35/Documents/Reports/2012/FY12-2_Linking_And_Streamlining_The_Defense_Requirements_Acquisition_Budget_Processes_2012-4.pdf.

CHAPTER 16. LESSONS LEARNED

1. "Who Will Fight the Next War?" *The Economist*, October 24, 2015, 25.

~

Bibliography

Adams, Gordon, and Cindy Williams. *Buying National Security: How America Plans and Pays for its Global Role and Safety at Home.* New York: Routledge, 2010.

Augustine, Norman R. *Augustine's Laws: An Irreverent Guide to Traps, Puzzles and Quandaries of the Defense Business and Other Complex Undertakings.* New York: American Institute of Aeronautics and Astronautics, 1983.

Berens, Charlyne. *Chuck Hagel: Moving Forward.* Lincoln: University of Nebraska Press, 2006.

Binnendijk, Hans. *Transforming America's Military.* Washington, DC: National Defense University Press, 2002.

Blanton, De Anne, and Lauren Cook. *They Fought Like Demons: Women Soldiers in the Civil War.* New York: Vintage Books, 2002.

Bowman, William, Roger Little, and G. Thomas Sicilia. *The All-Volunteer Force after a Decade: Retrospect and Prospect.* Washington, DC: Pergamon-Brassey's International Defense Publishers, 1986.

Brown, Harold. *Thinking about National Security: Defense and Foreign Policy in a Dangerous World.* Boulder, CO: Westview Press, 1983.

Cohodas, Nadine. *Strom Thurmond & the Politics of Southern Change.* Macon, GA: Mercer University Press, 1994.

Cosmas, Graham, and Terrence Murray. *U.S. Marines in Vietnam: Vietnamization and Redeployment.* Washington, DC: History and Museums Division, Headquarters, U.S. Marine Corps, 1986.

Crespino, Joseph. *Strom Thurmond's America.* New York: Hill and Wang, 2012.

Eisenhower, Dwight D. *Mandate for Change.* Garden City, NY: Doubleday & Company, Inc., 1963.

Fleming, Charles A., Robin Austin, and Charles Braley. *Quantico: Crossroads of the Marine Corps.* Washington, DC: U.S. Marine Corps, History and Museums Division, 1978.

Fosdick, Dorothy. *Staying the Course: Henry M. Jackson and National Security.* Seattle: University of Washington Press, 1987.

Frankum, Ronald B. *Historical Dictionary of the War in Vietnam.* Lanham, MD: Scarecrow Press, 2011.

Gansler, Jacques S. *Affording Defense.* Cambridge, MA: MIT Press, 1989.

Gates, Robert M. *Duty: Memoirs of a Secretary at War.* New York: Alfred A. Knopf, 2014.

Goldwater, Barry M., and Jack Casserly. *Goldwater.* New York: Doubleday, 1988.

Hart, Gary. *The Minuteman: Restoring an Army of the People.* New York: The Free Press, 1998.

Heinemann, Larry, *Close Quarters.* New York: Vintage Books, 1974.

Hogg, Ian V. *Jane's Infantry Weapons, 1991–92.* Coulsdon, UK: Jane's Information Group, 1991.

Kelley, Michael P. *Where We Were in Vietnam.* Central Point, OR: Hellgate Press, 2002.

Locher, James, *Victory on the Potomac: The Goldwater–Nichols Act Unifies the Pentagon.* College Station: Texas A&M University Press, 2002.

MacDonald, Stephen G. *War Stories: An Enlisted Marine in Vietnam.* CreateSpace Independent Publishing Platform, 2011.

Mackenzie, G. Calvin. *Innocent Until Nominated: The Breakdown of the Presidential Appointments Process.* Washington, DC: Brookings Institution Press, 2001.

Marr, David G. *Vietnam 1945: The Quest for Power.* Berkeley: University of California Press, 1995.

Mayo, Lida. *The Ordnance Department; On Beachhead and Battlefront.* Washington, DC: U.S. Army Center of Military History, 1991.

McCain, John, and Mark Salter. *Why Courage Matters: The Way to a Braver Life.* New York: Random House, Inc., 2004.

———. *Worth the Fighting For: The Education of an American Maverick, and the Heroes Who Inspired Him.* New York: Random House Trade Paperbacks, 2002.

Murphy, Edward F. *Semper Fi Vietnam: From Da Nang to the DMZ: Marine Corps Campaigns, 1965–1975.* New York: Ballantine Books, 1997.

Nagl, John A. *Knife Fights: A Memoir of Modern War in Theory and Practice.* New York: Penguin Press, 2014.

"Oral History: Senator Sam Nunn." Tape Transcript, Washington, DC, 1996.

Panetta, Leon, and Jim Newton. *Worthy Fights.* New York: Penguin Press, 2014.

Powell, Colin, and Joseph E. Persico. *My American Journey.* New York: Random House, 1995.

Reed, Thomas C. *At the Abyss: An Insider's History of the Cold War.* New York: Ballantine Books, 2004.

Rumsfeld, Donald. *Rumsfeld's Rules: Leadership Lessons in Business, Politics, War, and Life.* New York: Broadside Books, 2013.

Rush, Kenneth, Brent Scowcroft, and Joseph J. Wolf. *Strengthening Deterrence: NATO and the Credibility of Western Defense in the 1980s.* Cambridge, MA: Ballinger Publishing Company, 1982.

Shah, Mehtab Ali. *The Foreign Policy of Pakistan: Ethnic Impacts on Diplomacy, 1971–1994*. London: I. B. Tauris, 1997.

Smith, Hedrick. *The Power Game: How Washington Works*. New York: Ballantine Books, 1988.

Stevenson, Charles A. *Congress at War: The Politics of Conflict Since 1789*. Washington, DC: National Defense University Press and Potomac Books, Inc., 2007.

——. *SecDef: The Nearly Impossible Job of Secretary of Defense*. Washington, DC: Potomac Books, Inc., 2007.

Stoessinger, John G. *Why Nations Go to War: Second Edition*. New York: St. Martin's Press, 1978.

Tenet, George, and Bill Harlow. *At the Center of the Storm: My Years at the CIA*. New York: HarperCollins Publishers, 2007.

Timberg, Robert. *John McCain: An American Odyssey*. New York: Free Press, 1995.

Williams, Cindy. *Filling the Ranks: Transforming the U.S. Military Personnel System*. Cambridge, MA: MIT Press, 2004.

Woodward, Bob. *The Commanders*. New York: Simon & Schuster, 1991.

Wouk, Herman. *The Caine Mutiny: A Novel*. Garden City, NY: Doubleday, 1951. Reprint, Boston: Back Bay Books, 1992.

Zakheim, Dov S. *A Vulcan's Tale: How the Bush Administration Mismanaged the Reconstruction of Afghanistan*. Washington, DC: Brookings Institution Press, 2011.

Index

ABOUT THE AUTHOR

Maj. Gen. Arnold L. Punaro, USMCR (Ret.), served thirty-five years in uniform, both active and reserve. He spent twenty-four years in the U.S. Senate, becoming staff director of the Senate Armed Services Committee. Currently CEO of a small business, he was a top industry executive and continues to serve on numerous boards and commissions on national security.